Understanding Macroeconomics

David Gowland

Director of In-Service Courses
Department of Economics and Related Studies
University of York

Edward Elgar

Published by
Edward Elgar Publishing Limited
Gower House
Croft Road
Aldershot
Hants GU11 3HR
England

Edward Elgar Publishing Company
Old Post Road
Brookfield
Vermont 05036
USA

British Library Cataloguing in Publication Data

Gowland, David
  Understanding macroeconomics: an introduction to economic
  policy in the 1990's.
  1. Great Britain. Macroeconomic policies
  I. Title
  339. 0941

Library of Congress Cataloguing in Publication Data

Gowland, David.
    Understanding macroeconomics / David Gowland.
        p.   cm.
    Includes bibliographical references and index.
        1. Monetary policy.   2. Economic policy   3. Economic
    stabilization.   4. Macroeconomics.   I. Title.
    HG230. 3. G68 1990   90–40316
    339–dc20   CIP
ISBN 1 85278 326 5 (cased) 1 85278 327 3 (paperback)
Printed in Great Britain by
Billing & Sons Ltd, Worcester

Contents

Figures

Tables

Preface

The moving finger writes; and, having writ moves on: nor all thy piety nor wit shall have it back to cancel half a line nor all thy tears wash out a word of it.

Omar Khayyam's adage seems all too true to most authors as soon as their book is published: 'If only, I'd...' Sometimes, however, authors do have a chance to rewrite a book as they now wish they had written it. This is one such opportunity.

This book is a successor to two books I edited (and wrote most of) some years ago, *Modern Economic Analysis* and *Modern Economic Analysis 2* (Butterworths, 1979 and 1983 respectively). With the passage of time parts have become outdated and discussions with those who use the books have suggested various structural alterations. As Butterworths no longer publish economics books the new volume has a new publisher. Butterworths have nevertheless given me permission to incorporate (revised) versions of some material in this volume.

Modern Economic Analysis was extensively used in universities and polytechnics as a supplementary text. It seemed to fulfil two functions. It was very useful as a revision aide. One of the minor pleasures of authorship is meeting satisfied readers. In this context a surprisingly large number of figures now prominent in the City have informed me that they passed schools at Oxford largely thanks to *Modern Economic Analysis*. Its appeal to lecturers was as a suitable bridge between the inevitably limited text book analysis and the complexities of journals.

The major change is that instead of two volumes each covering both macroeconomics and microeconomics these will merge into one book covering each topic, *Understanding Macroeconomics* and *Understanding Microeconomics* respectively. This will enable the book to fit better into most courses even though a major theme of this volume is that macroeconomics is largely the application of microeconomic techniqes to macroeconomic problems.

No one writes a book without acquiring many debts to those who help in countless ways. In this case I am especially indebted to those who read and commented on drafts of the book: Pauline Lightfoot, Brian Parkinson, Stephen James, Chris Lawson, Michael Green, Fran Mitchell, Anne Usher and Ros Hayes. Margaret Johnson and Kim Knight typed the bulk of the manuscript with assistance from Ann Hillier. Anyone who has read my handwriting will realise both the magnitude of this task and therefore the extent of my gratitude.

1. Macroeconomic Policy and Theory

D.H. Gowland

1.1 BASIC CONCEPTS

Macroeconomic policy describes the actions of governments when they seek to manipulate the economy so as to influence the level of inflation and unemployment. Macroeconomic policy is often used to try to stimulate the level of economic activity so as to increase the level of output and employment and thereby reduce unemployment. These policies are referred to as *expansionary*, or *reflationary*. Critics of such policies point out that they sometimes lead to inflation and so term them inflationary policies. On other occasions governments seek to reduce the level of economic activity in an attempt to reduce inflation. These policies are referred to as *deflationary* or occasionally *disinflationary*. In the UK the government first started to pursue active macroeconomic policies in 1941 when Kingsley Wood introduced a famous Budget, acting on the advice of Keynes (p. 48). As the date suggests this was one of the reforms introduced or planned during the Second World War so as to create a better and more just society. In addition it was hoped that economic management would help to win the Second World War in the most efficient and equitable manner. For most of the period since 1941 governments have frequently referred to macroeconomic policy as *stabilization* policy. This presumed that the level of economic activity was otherwise likely to fluctuate. Hence the role of macroeconomic policy would be to minimize the fluctuations of output around its long-run trend level. Logically, the term macroeconomic policy could be used to refer either to policies which sought to influence aggregate supply or to policies which sought to influence aggregate demand. In practice, however, the term macroeconomic policy is normally used to refer only to demand management policies. The phrase *'supply-side'* policies is used to describe policies designed to influence aggregate supply (see Chapter 5, p. 113).

The underlying objective of governments in formulating economic policy is to achieve the best available (that is the optimal) combination of output, inflation, employment and other desiderata such as the distribution of income (or more generally equity). These are usually called the *goals* or *final targets* of economic policy. None of the available combinations is likely to seem ideal either to the government or to its citizens. Hence the government is likely to have to trade off one objective against another, that is to choose whether, for example, to give priority to reducing unemployment in the short term or to fighting inflation. Different governments, and even the same government at different times, are likely to have different preferences. The (West) German government, for example, has always given absolute priority to avoiding inflation whereas French governments usually give a higher priority to keeping unemployment low. Mrs Thatcher's Conservative government gives greater weight to efficiency objectives and less to equity (distributional) ones than its Labour predecessors. Economists call these preferences an *objective function* – a statement of a government's goals and its trade-offs between them.

In the UK it is generally agreed that the government's macroeconomic objective function should include:

a.   the level and growth of output
b.   the level of employment (or unemployment)
c.   the rate of inflation
d.   the variability of these three; it is usually thought preferable to have a stable than a fluctuating level of output, see above for stabilization policy
e.   the balance of payments. This has traditionally been listed as an objective (see, for example, Lipton, 1968). It needs to be stressed that any balance of payments objective is really a target for the composition of the balance of payments since the balance of payments is an accounting identity which must therefore balance. For example, a target for a current account surplus of £1 billion implies that some other part of the account (probably the capital account) should be in deficit by £1 billion (see Chapter 8). Mr Lawson when Chancellor argued that the balance of payments need not be a target at all; his policies had caused a current account deficit of £15 billion 1988 and £20 billion in 1989 so he had an interest in the matter. His argument was that private sector transactions need not concern the authorities. If I borrow from a Welshman to buy a new home it is no concern of the government's, so why should it be worried if I borrow from a German? Mr Lawson's argument is not generally accepted. However, it is possible that the balance of payments is a constraint (see below).

To achieve its policy a government has a number of *instruments*, such as the basic rate of income tax or the intervention rate in short-term money markets; the rates of interest at which the government is prepared to buy or sell, for example, Treasury bills. These devices are called instruments because the government can directly control them and so can fix their value at whatever level it believes is necessary to *maximize its objective function*, that is to achieve the best available combination of its goal variables. The phrase 'best available combination' is used because the government cannot achieve everything it wants. It has to recognize that it is restricted by, for example, the resources and technology available in the country and by the behaviour of other countries. These restrictions are called *constraints*. It is possible to reinterpret some objectives as constraints. For example, it has been argued that the balance of payments is a constraint: the constraint is that the deficit cannot exceed the amount other countries will lend to the UK (see Lipton, 1968, pp. 59–64 and Gowland,1989, pp. 12–16).

Tinbergen's Law states that a government can achieve as many goals as it has independent instruments. So, for example, with five instruments a government can achieve five goals but no more.[1] In practice, because of uncertainty, it is much harder to make economic policy than Tinbergen's law suggests. Attempts to modify this approach to incorporate uncertainty and other real world complexities are called *optimal control*. A number of economists (including a Labour party spokesman, Jeremy Bray) have worked on this for 20 years but with little result so far.

1.2   TYPES OF ECONOMIC POLICY

As there are various ways in which instruments can influence targets, it is useful to group these into three forms of economic policy:

a.   direct controls
b.   'Keynesian' policy (fiscal policy is the best known form of this)
c.   financial policy (monetary policy is one form of financial policy).[2]

Direct or one-stage controls are so named because they operate directly on the goal variable. For example a government seeking to control inflation might issue an ordinance setting out maximum prices and draconian penalties for charging in excess of them (the penalty in Stalin's Russia was death). Such policies are easy to understand because it is clear to the general public how they are intended to work. However, economists believe they are generally ineffective because of the problem of *black markets*; the control creates an incentive to set up an unofficial market in which mutually beneficial exchanges can be made in violation of the control.

Nevertheless, direct controls are extensively used in the third world. Traditionally they have been an important form of policy in France, Italy and Spain but these devices are being dismantled – very slowly – as the European Community moves towards a 'single market'. In France, for example, 18 000 inspectors were employed in Paris alone in the 1950s to inspect shops to see if they were charging prices in excess of those laid down by government edict. Direct controls were used in the UK between 1939 and 1954 but now the only widely advocated ones are some form of incomes policy, that is direct controls on wages, or direct controls on credit (see p. 55). The general form of an incomes policy consisted of a direct attempt by the government to reduce the level of wage settlements either by law or through 'voluntary' agreements. It hoped to reduce not only the level of wages but thereby the level of prices and to increase the level of output. Mrs Thatcher's Government immediately abandoned incomes policy when it came into power in 1979 at least in the sense in which it is normally understood. However, critics of Thatcherite policy still feel that this was a mistake, and the issue of incomes policy still forms one of the principal issues dividing Thatcherite opinion from that of its opponents.

Keynesian policy consists of using instruments in the goods market. The government operates so as, it hopes, to change either supply or (more usually) demand in the goods market. Thus Keynesian policy involves two stages: the instrument is used so as to influence the goods market which in turn influences the goal variable. For example, if the government sought to reduce inflation it would use its instruments to reduce demand in the goods market (the 'real sector') and would hope that lower demand would reduce the price level (below the level at which it would otherwise have been). For example a government faced with inflation might choose to reduce its spending on goods and services. Alternatively, it might increase income tax in the hope that this would lead to a fall in consumers' expenditure.

Keynesian policy can fail if either[3]

a. the government's instruments do not influence demand in the predicted fashion, or
b. the reduction in demand does not influence price (or output) as intended. This may occur, for example, because (aggregate) supply shifts.

Financial policy is the most indirect of the three forms of economic policy, and involves three stages; hence Friedman's famous aphorism that monetary policy would operate only with a long and variable lag (see Friedman, 1970). It is important to distinguish financial policy in general from monetary policy. Narrowly used, the phrase monetary policy refers to control of the money supply. Financial policy encompasses not only monetary policy but also credit policy, interest rate policy and exchange rate policy. The latter two terms are quite straightforward. Interest rate policy is mainly concerned with influencing the level and structure of interest rates, and thereby influencing the rate of interest which firms and persons pay when they borrow to finance expenditure. Credit policy is discussed below (p. 14ff). Exchange rate policy describes government actions designed to influence the exchange rate, that is the price of the pound sterling in terms of foreign currency. Such policies include maintaining the rate at (or close to) a particular level called a *parity*. This policy has both micro- and macroeconomic aspects, certain of which are analysed in Chapter 8.

The three stages of financial policy are:

a. The monetary authorities – an umbrella term to describe all branches of the government including the central bank (Bank of England in the UK) – do something. This disturbs the financial system in a way that can be analysed using supply and demand analysis. This disturbance is often called a shock, because it disturbs equilibrium. More formally this stage (a) is called the use of an *instrument* of policy (see above). In the case of monetary policy narrowly defined this is called a *technique of monetary control*.

b. The objective of stage (a) is to change either a price or quantity in financial markets. The quantity might be the quantity of money or of credit (see below). The price might be the price of borrowing (the rate of interest) or the price of foreign currency (the exchange rate). This variable is called the *intermediate target*. Chapter 2 examines the arguments for the money supply being the intermediate target in comparison with the alternatives. Table 2.3 gives a complete list of alternative intermediate targets.

c. The objective of stage (b) is to influence the real sector, that is the goods or labour market. In this way the government hopes to achieve its final target, or *goal variable*.

Because three stages are involved the possibility of error is much greater than with direct or Keynesian policy. This does not mean that financial policy is less effective or less important – perhaps the contrary. It does, however, mean that greater care is essential in its use. Friedman concludes that the problems of using monetary policy are too great for any activist policy to be successful. Hence he argues for a passive policy; letting the money supply grow at a constant rate. His ally, Laidler (1982) elaborates this by stating 'the bottom line of monetarism is ignorance', that is the case for Friedman's policy is that no-one knows enough in a complex world to do any better than by following this passive approach. Ironically, Friedman's arch opponents – the post-Keynesians – accept the argument but not the definition of passivity. Post-Keynesians such as Sheila Dow Davidson and Minsky argue that financial factors can have a very large impact on the economy especially through speculative booms and crashes in financial markets such as the stock exchange. To offset the impact of these and changes in confidence the government should vary the money supply, see Gowland (1985) pp. 165–6.

1.3 TRANSMISSION MECHANISMS

The crucial debate about the analysis of financial policy is concerning the means by which changes in financial markets influence developments in the real sector; how stage (b) above leads on to stage (c). This is usually called the *transmission mechanism* of monetary policy – the means by which developments in financial markets are passed on to (or transmitted to) the real sector.

There are two views of the transmission mechanism of money to income. Keynesians argue that it is *indirect;* monetarists *direct.* An indirect transmission mechanism means that money influences an intermediate variable. This intermediate variable in turn influences income. Hence money does influence income but only through its effect on the intermediate variable – usually the exchange rate or the rate of interest (see Table 2.3 for a full list).

Indirect mechanism

An indirect transmission mechanism works as follows. The rate of interest adjusts to ensure equilibrium in the money market, that is that supply is equal to demand. The government is assumed to be able to determine the money supply so the supply curve is inelastic at the level determined by the authorities. When the government changes the money supply the interest rate adjusts to equate the demand for money with the government-determined supply of it. This is illustrated in Figure 1.1, where the effect of an increase in the money supply from S_1 to S_2 is illustrated. In Figure 1.1(a) and 1.1(b) the rate of interest falls from R_1 to R_2. It can be seen that the magnitude of the change is much greater in 1.1 where the demand curve for money is steeper, that is, it is less interest-elastic. In the extreme case (Figure 1.1(c)) the demand curve is horizontal (infinitely elastic) so the interest rate does not alter. This – the 'liquidity trap' – is of historical interest only since it has been shown to be both theoretically impossible and empirically non-existent. The impact of money on interest rates does, however, depend on the interest elasticity of demand for it. When the interest elasticity of the demand for money is high, a change in the money supply has only a small effect on the rate of interest.

The change in interest rates should then change aggregate demand, depending on how responsive expenditure is to a change in interest rates. Hence the impact of monetary policy will be greatest when the interest elasticity of the demand for money is low and that of expenditure is high. Similarly, the Keynesian case, of ineffective monetary policy occurs when the demand for money is very interest-elastic and/or the demand for goods very interest-inelastic.

Modern Keynesians usually prefer to regard the exchange rate as the transmission mechanism, rather than the interest rate. Figure 1.1 is still relevant except that the demand for money now includes the demand by overseas residents so it is usually renamed the demand for sterling curve. An increase in the quantity of money represents an increase in the quantity of pounds sterling relative to other currencies. This causes disequilibrium in the foreign exchange market which can only be removed by a fall in the exchange rate and *vice versa.* Thus the price which adjusts to equilibrate the market is now the exchange rate, not the rate of interest. Hence expansionary monetary policy still shifts the supply curve in

Figure 1.1 An indirect transmission mechanism: money to interest rates

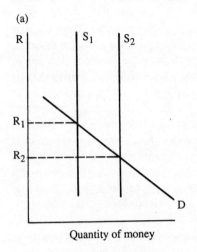

(a)

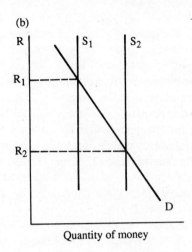

(b)

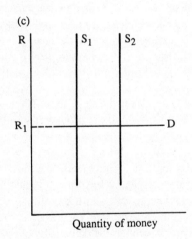

(c)

Figure 1.1 from S_1 to S_2 but 'R' is now the exchange rate. The 'liquidity trap' case would be equivalent to perfect (infinitely elastic) capital mobility with fixed exchange rates (Mundell, 1968, chapter 12).

The effect of a variation in the exchange rate is illustrated in Figure 1.2. The underlying idea behind this analysis is that most UK firms are price takers in markets (both in the UK and abroad) in which the price at which they sell is determined by the world price and the exchange rate. (The world market may be competitive or the UK producers may be relatively small firms in a market in which a foreign price leader or cartel determines the price.[4]) Figure 1.2 illustrates this for a representative UK producer – and thus for the entire UK economy. The diagram shows the marginal cost and revenue curves for a producer of a representative good, 'leets'. 'Leets' have a world price of $1. Originally the exchange rate is $2=£1, so the world price expressed in pounds is 50p, the world price divided by the exchange rate.[5] The UK producer faces a perfectly elastic demand and marginal revenue curve at this price. Hence his output of leets is q_1 at a price of P_1 (50p).

The exchange rate then falls to $1=£1. The world price expressed in sterling is now £1. Hence the fall in the exchange rate causes the MR curve to shift upwards to MR=£1. Output of leets rises to q_2 and price to P_2 (£1). This can be generalized:

a fall (rise) in the exchange rate will lead domestic producers to increase (decrease) their output and prices. Hence a fall in the exchange rate increases output (and so reduces unemployment) but at the cost of higher prices (more inflation); a rise in the exchange rate will reduce inflation but at the price of more unemployment.

However, this result only applies in the short term. The lower exchange rate causes a rise in prices. This means domestic producers will face a rise in costs because:

a.   costs of raw materials and inputs have risen and, much more importantly
b.   real wages are lower and marginal value product higher.[6] Hence, whatever model of the labour market is used, wages will rise.

The rise in marginal cost is shown in Figure 1.2(b). The MC curve shifts upwards from MC_1 and ultimately reaches MC_2, where output has fallen back to Q_1 – that is the economy moves from 1 to 2 to 3. This diagram can be reversed to show the effect of an appreciation. This is one way to illustrate the UK economy in the 1980s, Figure 1.3. The appreciation in sterling from 1979–81 caused a fall in output and price, hence the economy reached the point marked '1982' in that year. Thereafter the supply curve shifted rightwards as marginal

Figure 1.2   The effect of the exchange rate on the economy

(a) Short term

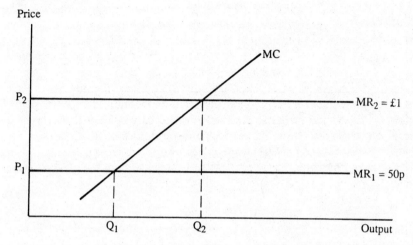

(b) Long term

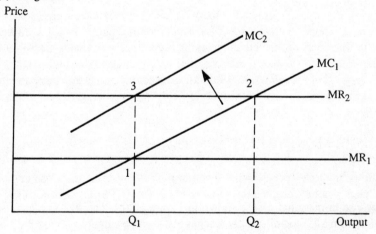

Figure 1.3   The UK economy in the 1980s

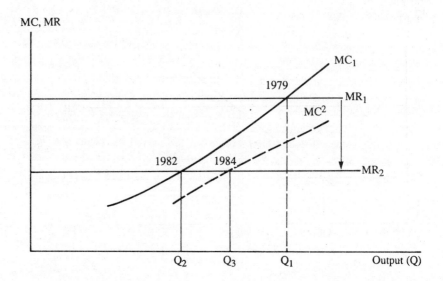

cost was below the level it would otherwise have been and output rose steadily until the inflationary effects of Mr Lawson's policy changes in 1985 worked through. The spirit of this model has influenced UK governments since 1974. Whenever they have wanted to reduce inflation they have sought a high exchange rate (1974–5, 1977–8, 1979–80, 1988–9). On other occasions they have sought a lower rate to reduce unemployment (1976, 1985).

1.4   THE MONETARIST APPROACH

In contrast to these Keynesian indirect transmission mechanisms of the impact of monetary policy on income, monetarists believe in a *direct transmission mechanism*. The simplest and best known is Friedman's reformulated quantity theory. This is an example of a portfolio model of stock adjustment. Equilibrium is expressed in terms of stocks, such as wealth, not as in Keynesian model flows, such as income.[7] In a stock model, expenditure and so income are determined as a by-product of stock adjustment. The following story illustrates the effect of a fall in the money supply, but the example can be reversed.

a. Individuals always want to hold money balances equal to about x weeks' income (or alternatively to x weeks expenditure; given the national income convention, the two are identical. In the USA x might be 6 if the definition of money were M_{1c}). In economic jargon there is a stable demand for money.
b. The government reduces the money supply.
c. It is assumed that the money market was previously in equilibrium, so that economic agents held the quantity of money they desired. In consequence of the reduction in the money supply individuals no longer hold as much money as they did before. So individuals no longer hold as much money as they wish to. In other words the money market is in disequilibrium because demand is greater than supply.
d. Individuals, therefore, seek to rebuild their money balances. They can do this either by spending less on the goods they normally buy, or by buying fewer assets, or by selling assets they already own.[8]
e. As a consequence of d. there is excess supply in both goods and assets markets. This may have arisen because of reduced demand or because of increased supply, that is people may have bought less or sold some of their existing holdings.
f. Hence the excess demand for money caused by monetary policy has been transmitted to goods and asset markets as excess supply.
g. Excess supply means that either prices will fall or output will fall or both depending on the elasticity of supply. As a macroeconomic level this means that a fall in the money supply will lead to a fall in either prices, output or both.

1.5   THE EFFECTS OF MONETARY GROWTH

Different monetarists have different opinions about which of price or output changes in response to a change in the money supply. Classical monetarists believe that it is always price which changes, whereas French monetarists tend to emphasize that it is output which changes. Friedman believes that output changes in the short term and prices in the longer term. It is also possible that the extra demand will lead to a change in neither price nor output. This occurs when the demand is satisfied from foreign sources at previously prevailing prices (or where excess supply is absorbed by the world market). This is true by definition for a small economy (see note 4). In this case variations in monetary policy lead only to a balance of payments surplus or deficit: *the monetary theory of the balance of payments* or international monetarism. However, the exchange rate may also adjust, in which case the international monetarist model becomes indistinguishable from the Keynesian model discussed above. Hence the hybrid is the basis of much advanced macroeconomic theory and modelling, for example the Bank of England model in the UK.

The key features of this analysis are:

a. A change in the money supply causes disequilibrium in the money market which is directly transmitted to the goods market.
b. Adjustment occurs via the asset market.

The latter is common to all modern models of monetary policy, whether Keynesian or monetarist. For most consumers, two assets predominate: houses and consumer durables – washing machines, cars etc. The main asset for companies is stocks of raw materials and finished goods; most of the latter are consumer durables. Hence monetary policy is likely to have a disproportionate effect on the housing market, the market for consumer durables and (to some extent) that for raw materials. Hence expansionary monetary policy will lead to a rise in the demand for houses and consumer durables. *House prices* In consequence *house prices* will rise – expansionary monetary policy led to explosions in house prices in 1972–3, 1978–9 and 1985–8. Builders respond to higher house prices by building more houses (Table 1.1).

Undoubtedly, the monetary expansion in the UK after 1984 caused the explosion in house prices. This generated a rise in housebuilding but it also caused serious social problems as well as impeding labour mobility. More generally unbalanced demand management (fiscal tightness and monetary laxity) led to the concentration of growth in a few sectors of the economy and a few

Table 1.1   Money supply and housebuilding

	Money supply (per cent)	Housing starts one year later (000)
1979	13	88
1980	19	112
1981	13	138
1982	9	170
1983	11	160
1984	10	168
1985	14	168
1986	18	194
1987	23	211
1988	21	233

regions, notably the South East. Monetary policy was not the only factor leading to the North–South divide but it was probably the most important.

Extra demand for consumer durables will largely be met from foreign sources, especially in the UK with imports from Germany and Japan. Hence expansionary monetary policy will lead to a large balance of payments deficit as in 1973–4 and 1988, when the current account deficit was 15 billion; in 1989 it was £20 billion.

1.6 TARGETS, INDICATORS AND CREDIT

Keynesian and monetarist analyses of the transmission mechanism agree that a rise in the money supply will cause a rise in output and inflation but disagree about how it will do this. In consequence they will differ about how policy should be formulated. For example, in 1985–7, some Keynesians argued that it was not necessary to worry about monetary growth of 20 per cent per annum because the exchange rate was not falling; monetarists believe that such rapid growth must lead to disaster. Another way of looking at this aspect of the monetarist–Keynesian debate is to distinguish between (proximate) targets and indicators.

Monetarists believe that money should be a *target* whereas Keynesians believe that it should be regarded only as an *indicator*. The formal distinction is that the causal chain runs through the target but not the indicator, which merely reflects developments, whereas changing a target is both sufficient and necessary to change income. The distinction between proximate targets and indicators can be elucidated with the aid of an analogy. Thermostats and thermometers frequently look alike but are crucially different within a heating system. A thermometer is a good indicator of temperature, but the heat of a room cannot be altered by direct manipulation of the thermometer (for example by plunging it into ice or by heating the bulb with a lighter). Such, Keynesians believe, is the relationship between money and income. A thermostat, on the other hand, is a proximate target since manipulation of its dial is both necessary and sufficient to change the room temperature. So monetarists believe money is akin to a thermostat in its relationship to income.

A number of important points are true both in the analogy and the real world.

a. The response of the room temperature to manipulation of the thermostat may not be fixed and may vary from day to day. It may depend on whether a door is open or closed. Similarly, the impact of monetary policy will only be felt after a 'long and variable lag', to quote the most famous of all monetarists, Friedman (1970).
b. Moreover, the thermometer is more closely related to the room temperature than the thermostat. Similarly, Keynesian theory actually implies a closer relationship of money to income than monetarism. An attempt to use an

indicator as if it were a proximate target not merely fails to change the goal variable but renders it useless as an indicator; putting a thermometer in ice not only leaves the room temperature unchanged but also means that the thermometer ceases to register it accurately. The economic equivalent is often referred to as 'Goodhart's Law': to try to control a definition of money will distort its relationship to income (Goodhart, 1984).

A good example of the Keynesian view of money as indicator can be found in the analyses of Ben Friedman, probably the leading American younger Keynesian. Following a long Keynesian tradition he puts emphasis on the role of *credit* rather than money. The distinction has been regarded as vital by both sides in the monetarist–Keynesian debate, since the 1950s when Johnson (for example 1972) stressed its importance. Money is an asset, that is what a person owns. Credit is what a person owes; his debts and the opportunity to extend his borrowing. Monetarists argue that a person's expenditure is influenced by his assets – in the simplest form, that 'money burns a hole in his pocket'. Keynesians believe that consumers' expenditure is very likely to be influenced by the cost and availability of credit to the personal sector. If the cost of borrowing falls then Keynesians expect expenditure to rise. Moreover, if individuals are allowed to borrow more, then their expenditure will rise. This is called *credit availability*. Keynesians stress the importance of credit availability, known in the USA and continental Europe as the availability doctrine. Such a general increase in borrowing possibilities occurred in the UK in the 1980s due to financial innovation. Keynesians believe that credit availability is critically important in economic analysis because they believe that individuals are rarely able to borrow as much as they would wish to. Consequently, any relaxation in credit limits is likely to lead to increased spending.

Keynesians believe that measures of credit are important but a good measure of credit may be money, because 'every loan creates a deposit': lending by banks creates money so the money supply measures credit expansion. Hence while Ben Friedman's position is Keynesian on conceptual issues – money is unimportant in itself – it is policy-equivalent to a monetarist's in that it implies UK policy was far too expansionary in the period 1984–8 (if anything credit grew faster than money).

The purpose of this chapter has been to introduce some basic concepts and to show how with their aid the monetarist–Keynesian debate can be more clearly understood. Moreover, even such basic analysis throws considerable light upon UK economic policy. This analysis is extended in later chapters.

GUIDE TO FURTHER READING

Gowland (1989) provides a more extensive introduction to the material covered in this chapter and to macroeconomics generally.

NOTES

1. Tinbergen's Law is equivalent to the mathematical proposition that in general n independent (simultaneous) equations are necessary to find unique solutions for n variables.
2. Stephen James has drawn my attention to variations in the use of this term by different authors. The meaning in the text is the most usual as well as the most useful.
3. See Gowland (1989) for an extensive discussion of these possibilities.
4. This is equivalent to the small country assumption in the theory of international trade.
5. Or multiplied depending on how exchange rates are measured (p. 167).
6. In labour market analysis, the demand for labour is equal to the marginal value product: the value the employer places on the output of the marginal worker. If the output is sold, this is equal to the marginal revenue product.
7. A Keynesian stock model is possible – such as Tobin's (1969) model discussed in Gowland (1979), pp. 104–7.
8. Other possible responses also exert deflationary pressure – for example an increase in labour supply if individuals try to obtain money by selling labour.
9. World commodity prices seem to be determined by the world money supply which in turn is heavily influenced by US monetary policy. A tightening of US monetary policy usually leads to a fall in commodity prices.

REFERENCES

Friedman, M. (1970), *The Counter Revolution in Monetary Theory,* 1st Wincott Memorial Lecture, reprinted as Occasional Paper 33, Institute of Economic Affairs, London.

Goodhart, C.A.E. (1984), *Monetary Theory and Practice,* Macmillan, London.

Gowland, D.H. (1979), *Modern Economic Analysis,* Butterworths, Sevenoaks.

Gowland, D.H. (1985), *Money, Inflation and Unemployment,* Wheatsheaf, Brighton.

Gowland, D.H. (1989), *Whatever Happened to Demand Management?,* RJA (Books), Bedford.

Johnson, H. G. (1972), *Further Essays in Monetary Economics,* George Allen and Unwin, London.

Laidler, D.E.W. (1982), *Monetarist Perspectives,* Harvard University Press, Cambridge, Mass.

Lipton, M. (1968), *Assessing Economic Performance,* Staples Press, London.

Mundell, R. (1968), *International Economics,* Macmillan, London.

2.   Monetary Policy

D.H. Gowland

2.1.   INTRODUCTION

The object of this chapter is to assess the proper role of monetary policy especially in the context of the UK. Monetary policy is one of the means by which governments can seek to manipulate the economy so as to influence inflation and unemployment (p. 100). In 1960 it was unfashionable in the UK and regarded as of little importance. Thereafter, its importance grew steadily until 1981, especially after the adoption of *monetary targets* in June 1976. A monetary target has two aspects: one formal and one substantive. The formal is a stated official objective, that the money supply should grow by x per cent over a specified period, for example the first published money supply target in the UK was announced in July 1976: 12 per cent growth in M_3 'over the year (1976–7) as a whole'. The substantive one is that the authorities should be prepared to sacrifice other objectives, that is alternative intermediate targets, to achieve the target. The second part of the target is the more important, a willingness to forgo other desiderata such as interest rates, exchange rates etc. so as to try to achieve the target. There are numerous examples of such sacrifices during the period of monetary targets in the UK.[1] Moreover it is not necessary to adopt a black and white position on the issue; one can be a moderate. For example one can be a 'pragmatic monetarist', that is willing to sacrifice most but not all other targets as Paul Volcker described himself during the period when he ran US monetary policy (1979–87). Since 1981, the Conservative government has de-emphasized the role of monetary policy particularly after Mr Lawson became Chancellor of the Exchequer. In 1985 monetary targets were abandoned in the UK.[2] Table 2.1 shows the somewhat mixed record of the pursuit over the period 1975–85. Between 1975 and 1980 21 industrialized countries adopted monetary targets (Foot, in Griffiths and Wood,1981). This was a common response to the monetarist resurgence. (Indeed, belief in a monetary target is the best definition of a monetarist.) Several other countries have, like the UK, abandoned targets. However, the extent of controversy has been much greater in the UK.

Some critics believe that the government was wrong to abandon monetary targets in 1985. In their view the price for this mistake could be seen in 1988 with rising inflation, soaring house prices and an enormous and growing balance of

16

Table 2.1   Monetary targets and outcomes

Annual percentage rates of growth				
Date target set	Period of target	Target aggregate	Target range	Out-turn
June 1976	12 mths to Apr. 77	£M$_3$	12	–
Dec. 1976	12 mths to Apr. 77	£M$_3$	9–13	7.2
Mar. 1977	12 mths to Apr. 78	£M$_3$	9–13	16.4
Apr. 1978	12 mths to Oct. 79	£M$_3$	8–12	11.3
Nov. 1978	12 mths to Oct. 79	£M$_3$	8–12	13.4
Jun. 1979	10 mths to Apr. 80	£M$_3$	7–11	10.0
Nov. 1979	16 mths to Oct. 80	£M$_3$	7–11	17.5
Mar. 1980	14 mths to Apr. 81	£M$_3$	7–11	19.1
Mar. 1981	14 mths to Apr. 83	£M$_3$	6–10	12.9
Mar. 1982	14 mths to Apr. 83	£M$_3$	8–12	11.1
		PSL2	8–12	10.8
		M$_1$	8–12	12.1
Mar. 1983	14 mths to Apr. 84	£M$_3$	7–11	9.5
		PSL$_2$	7–11	12.2
		M$_1$	7–11	13.5
Mar. 1984	14 mths to Apr. 85	£M$_3$	6–10	11.9
		M$_0$	4–8	5.6
Mar. 1985	14 mths to Apr. 86	£M$_3$	5–9	–
		M$_0$	3–7	–

Notes:
1.   The June 1976 target was dropped at the request of the IMF
2.   No out-turns are shown for abandoned targets
3.   £M$_3$ is now called M$_3$, M$_3$ is now called M$_3$c and PSL$_2$ M$_5$.
4.   The definition of £M$_3$ was altered on various occasions.

Source: Peter Browning, *The Treasury & Economic Policy, 1964–1985*

payments deficit. Their view was put eloquently by Sir Alan Walters, a close associate of Mrs Thatcher.[3] In this view the need to increase interest rates nine times, by 5 per cent in all, in the second half of 1988 was a belated attempt to correct for the error but probably too late. At the very least the need for such strong medicine showed to monetarists the extent of the error in abandoning their prescription.

Other critics of the government argued that the government had been wrong to put as much emphasis on money as it had. Instead it should have sought to manage and indeed stabilize the exchange rate. Many such critics believed that the attempt to control the money supply in 1978–81 had led to an excessively high exchange rate and so to deindustrialization. Some argued that membership of the European monetary system, EMS, was the best form of exchange rate policy – keen supporters of the Common Market believed that it was inevitable anyway and the sooner the UK joined the better (see Section 2.7 and Chapter 9).

2.2 A FRAMEWORK OF ANALYSIS

The same macroeconomic instrument may have both a direct (Keynesian) impact on the goods market, and also an indirect one through its effect on financial markets. For example, an increase of £100 million in government expenditure on currently produced goods and services can be regarded as a Keynesian policy designed to raise the level of planned injections (exports plus investment plus government spending) at each level of income, and so to raise the equilibrium level of income. However, *ceteris paribus*, such a policy also increases the money supply permanently by £100 million, that is by the exact amount of the spending, and is therefore also an instrument of monetary policy. In whichever way the instrument is regarded, its effect is nevertheless to raise income. However, the amount and duration of this change in income may depend crucially on how it is viewed. Thus the interdependence of policy instruments, as it is usually called, is essential to understanding macroeconomic policy in practice. It is the source of both theoretical and practical controversies in economics, because it means that it is usually impossible for a government to achieve all of its intermediate targets simultaneously. If one target variable is too high, for example, the money supply, and one too low, for example a measure of fiscal policy, then the use of an instrument which will bring the first back on course (lower government spending) will tend to depress the other (fiscal) target still more and so cause it to move even further away from its desired value.

It is therefore necessary to have some sort of conceptual framework both in order to elucidate this interrelationship between variables and also to analyse their impact. The most useful such framework is the flow-of-funds or supply-side counterpart equation. This uses the orthodox definition of the money supply:

Money supply =   Currency held by the non-bank private sector
                 + bank deposits

This is a very general definition of money. In practice, a number of definitions of money are consistent with it; UK policy makers use eight, their US opposite numbers over 40. The UK definitions are M_0, non-interest bearing M_1, M_1, M_2, M_3, M_{3c}, M_4 and M_5,[4] (see Table 2.2). (In 1989, the authorities ceased to publish M_3 and M_{3c} after the Abbey National acquired PLC status.) The reason for this

Table 2.2 Relationships among the monetary aggregates and their components[1]

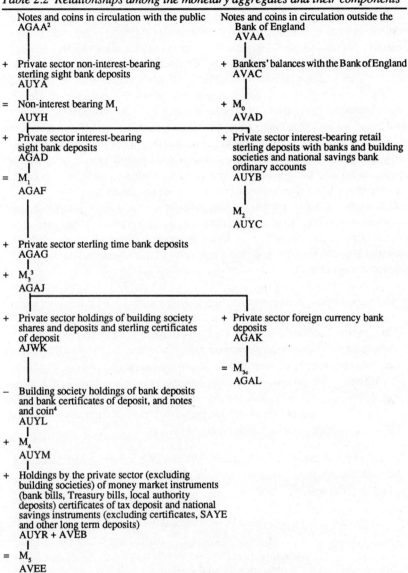

Notes and coins in circulation with the public
AGAA[2]

+ Private sector non-interest-bearing
sterling sight bank deposits
AUYA

= Non-interest bearing M_1
AUYH

+ Private sector interest-bearing
sight bank deposits
AGAD

= M_1
AGAF

+ Private sector sterling time bank deposits
AGAG

+ M_3[3]
AGAJ

+ Private sector holdings of building society
shares and deposits and sterling certificates
of deposit
AJWK

− Building society holdings of bank deposits
and bank certificates of deposit, and notes
and coin[4]
AUYL

+ M_4
AUYM

+ Holdings by the private sector (excluding
building societies) of money market instruments
(bank bills, Treasury bills, local authority
deposits) certificates of tax deposit and national
savings instruments (excluding certificates, SAYE
and other long term deposits)
AUYR + AVEB

= M_5
AVEE

Notes and coins in circulation outside the
Bank of England
AVAA

+ Bankers' balances with the Bank of England
AVAC

+ M_0
AVAD

+ Private sector interest-bearing retail
sterling deposits with banks and building
societies and national savings bank
ordinary accounts
AUYB

M_2
AUYC

+ Private sector foreign currency bank
deposits
AGAK

= M_{3c}
AGAL

Notes:
1. M0 is actually published as the average amount outstanding for all the Wednesdays in the month.
2. AGAA etc. now appear with official data as identification codes for Information Technology
purposes such as SWURC.
3. M_3 is no longer published but its definition is included because of its relevance to the 1970s and
1980s.
4. In the published tables, this series is included with the sign increase −.

multiplicity of definitions is that it is not clear in practice which institutions are banks. Given that a building society is similar, but not identical, to a clearing bank, it was treated as a bank for some definitions (M_5) but not for others (M_3). Similarly, it is unclear what a deposit is – conceptually it is an 'almost perfectly liquid' claim on a bank. However, is a seven-day account 'almost perfectly liquid'? Is an account almost perfectly liquid if the funds can be obtained instantly, but only subject to the payment of a penalty? Is an account almost perfectly liquid if the funds can only be obtained by queueing rather than by using a cash machine (ATM)? Different answers to these questions lead to different definitions of money. It is preferable to examine a range of definitions, rather than to risk being misled by a single one, just as someone booking a holiday might consider a range of indicators of a resort's sunbathing potential – average temperature, minimum temperature, average hours of sunshine.

This basic definition of money (deposits plus currency) is often used by economists to analyse financial developments, and is referred to as demand-side analysis. However, supply-side analysis is more common. The supply-side counterpart equation is derived in the appendix to this chapter by making two substitutions into the definition of money, namely;

a.   the bank balance sheet equation: bank assets are equal to liabilities so loans (assets) can be substituted for deposits (liabilities);
b.   the government finance equation: bank loans to the government are replaced by a rearrangement of the government finance equation. PSBR is the public sector borrowing requirement, a definition of the budget deficit.

$$PSBR = \Delta \text{ bank loans to the government} +$$
$$\Delta \text{ non-bank private sector loans to the government} +$$
$$\Delta \text{ non-bank private sector holdings of currency}$$
where Δ means 'change in'.

These substitutions are merely rearrangements of accounting identities, that is they are always true. The purpose is to derive a useful and economically meaningful relationship:

$$\Delta \text{ money supply} = \text{public sector borrowing requirement} +$$
$$\Delta \text{ bank loans to the non-bank private sector} -$$
$$\Delta \text{ non-bank private sector loans to the public sector (gov-}$$
$$\text{ernment}) + \text{Overseas effect}$$
where Δ means change in.

The full derivation of this equation is given in the appendix to this chapter. The resulting flow-of-funds or supply-side counterpart equation is the key to the analysis of monetary policy in the UK, and will be used extensively in this and the next chapter.

2.3   POSSIBLE TARGETS

The purpose of this chapter is to analyse the desirability of monetary targets in the UK. This involves a consideration of alternatives – see Table 2.3 for a complete list. The first group of alternatives are Keynesian measures of the impact of financial policy. They are usually based on some sort of indirect transmission mechanism, see Chapter 1, whereby money matters, if at all, only through its impact upon some other variable. Three have been implicitly suggested already:

a.   The exchange rate. This is the preferred policy of young Keynesian econo-
      mists like Buiter as well as international monetarists, like Ball. A particular
      form of exchange rate target is membership of the exchange rate mechanism
      of the European monetary system.
b.   The level of credit. This is the preferred target of Ben Friedman (p. 14).
c.   The interest rate. This was the preferred target of old Keynesians, such as
      Harrod.

A particular variant of the rate of interest was suggested by Tobin:

d.   The level of share prices. The rate of interest is usually defined as the rate
      of return on long-term financial assets in the form of bonds. Instead Tobin
      suggested looking at the rate of return on equities (ordinary shares) or its
      inverse, the level of share prices. The policy implications of this are usually
      followed, for example, the need for expansionary monetary policy in the
      period *immediately* after the Stock Market crash of 19 October 1987.[5]

Nigel Lawson, the Chancellor of the Exchequer until October 1989, argued that instead of either monetarist or Keynesian targets there should be no target at all or only a budgetary one. The argument for no targets was originally put by Waud (1973). This is that the introduction of an intermediate target introduces an extra source of error into the system – from instrument to intermediate target and from intermediate target to goal (or final target). It would normally be more effective in this view to concentrate only on the final target and adjust the instruments accordingly. In its simplest form the argument is if the final target (inflation for Mr. Lawson) is at an acceptable level what does it matter about an intermediate target? The answer is that the intermediate target is likely to be a good predictor of what the final target will do in the future, see below.

Mr. Lawson has had a variety of budgetary targets – usually for the Public Sector Borrowing Requirement, PSBR, a definition of the budget deficit (being equal to government spending less asset sales, less taxation plus public sector lending).[6] From 1985–8 his target was for a PSBR of 1 per cent of GDP, thereafter for a surplus. Buchanan has been the principal economist in favour of budgetary targets, largely on discipline grounds, see below; for Buchanan's views see Brennan and Buchanan (1981).

The PSBR is an indicator of fiscal policy but not the only one. For example, the level of government spending and taxation could be calculated by assuming a given level of unemployment and a *high employment budget deficit* thereby calculated.[7] Keynesian measures of fiscal policy could be weighted averages of the first, second and fourth of these. For example *'fiscal leverage'* might be government spending – 0.7 taxation + 0.5 public sector loans (Musgrave's values, 1968). Moreover, Keynesians might disaggregate some components

Table 2.3 *Possible intermediate targets*

	Monetarism	
Money supply	Quantity	Milton Friedman
	Non-monetarist targets	
Exchange rate	Price	Young Keynesians–Buiter European monetary system
Credit	Quantity	Ben Friedman
Interest rate	Price	Old Keynesians – Harrod
Share prices/rates of return on shares	Either	Tobin
Nothing		Lawson, Waud
PSBR	Quantity	Lawson
High employment budget deficit	Keynesian artefact	Ward and Neild (1978)
Fiscal leverage	Keynesian artefact	Musgrave (1968)
Domestic credit expansion (DCE)	Quantity	IMF
Nominal income	Quantity	Meade
Money base	Quantity	Minford (instrument)

further – government spending might be divided into expenditure on goods and services and on transfers, with a higher weight given to the former.

There is a large number of other candidate targets of which the most important is domestic credit expansion, DCE see Table 2.3. This is the domestic component of the supply-side counterpart to the money supply, that is that part of monetary expansion that can be attributed to domestic causes. The meaning of this concept can best be seen in the context of the flow-of-funds equation; DCE is approximately the first three items of this relationship, that is the change in the money supply (M) less the overseas influence (0).

The IMF, and now it seems the European Commission, favour this because it produces an automatic adjustment to balance of payments surpluses and deficits, rather like the gold standard. The money supply grows by DCE plus the overseas component, approximately the overall balance of payments surplus. Hence if a nation has a balance of payments surplus money grows faster than DCE. So the economy expands and the surplus is reduced. With a deficit money grows less rapidly than DCE so economic policy is deflationary, and the deficit shrinks. None of the other targets are any longer serious candidates for use in the UK. Many of the rival candidates for the role of intermediate targets can be identified from the flow of funds equation and their interrelationship thereby elucidated. They are:

a   Money supply: this, the preferred target of monetarists such as Milton Friedman, is the sum of the four supply-side counterparts.

b.   Domestic credit expansion (DCE): this is the domestic component of money creation, that is the first three of the supply-side counterparts.

c.   Public Sector Borrowing Requirement: the first component.

d.   Credit. This, the preferred target of Ben Friedman and other Keynesians, is measured by the second supply-side counterpart: bank lending to the non-bank private sector.

e.   Interest rates: the level of interest rates influences both bank lending and non-bank private sector purchases of public sector securities (National Savings and gilt-edged). Higher rates reduce the demand for bank loans and increase the demand for public sector debt. Hence the level and structure of interest rates are critical determinants of these supply-side counterparts.

f.   Exchange rate: the overseas influence on the money supply, the fourth of the supply-side counterparts, is closely related to the balance of payments surplus – hence exchange rate policy will be reflected in monetary developments and *vice versa*.

2.4   MONETARY POLICY IN THE UK

In the 1960s the UK monetary authorities sought to control money and credit by means of quantity ceilings on bank lending and some other forms of credit. The authorities, however, decided in 1971 that these should be abandoned, because of the problems caused by the growth of various 'parallel markets', that is black markets in economists' jargon. This meant that the direct controls on credit were neither effective nor efficient. The authorities were determined not to introduce a textbook reserve ratio/reserve base system (Chapter 3) so they had few options open to them. They therefore introduced the 'new approach' to 'competition and credit control' – the control of money via the effects of interest rates on the demand for bank lending. The results determined not only economic policy but British politics for twenty years.

The new approach proved a fiasco; the money supply grew 60 per cent in 27 months and the new approach was abandoned in December 1973. The causes of the disaster are various: technical failings in the scheme, and incompetence and lack of political will by the Prime Minister (Mr Heath) and his Chancellor Mr Barber).[8] The consequences were clear. Mr Heath lost both the Premiership (February 1974) and the leadership of the Conservative Party (December 1974), Mrs Thatcher replacing him. As far as the economy was concerned the effects were equally dramatic: 25 per cent inflation, a massive balance of payments deficit and a 100 per cent increase in house prices.

To economists and politicians alike the lesson of the 1971–3 period then seemed clear: it was necessary to control the money supply. In 1976 the Labour government introduced monetary targets, for a broad definition of money (M_3). Control of money was sought via ceilings on bank deposits (often called the 'corset'), manipulation of the PSBR and an aggressive policy of selling public sector debt to the non-bank private sector. The authorities missed the first two targets, for 1976–7 and 1977–8 and in 1978 the money supply was expanding rapidly. The authorities responded by raising interest rates, letting the exchange rate rise and generally tightening up on monetary growth. They succeeded in meeting their target for 1978–9.

However, the effects of the 1977–8 monetary expansion seem to have produced a repeat of 1971–3 on a smaller scale:

a.   there was a house price boom; house prices rose over 50 per cent in 1978;
b.   much of the monetary expansion finished up in the coffers of companies (that is there was an increase in corporate liquidity) who paid some of it out as large pay increases – in breach of an incomes policy. Private sector pay rose faster than earnings in the public sector. Public sector workers initiated strikes – the 'winter of discontent'. As a partial consequence, the Labour

government lost the 1979 election and Mrs Thatcher became Prime Minister.

c. inflation accelerated to 20 per cent in late 1980, from 10 per cent in May 1979. However, as well as monetary expansion, the increase in VAT in June 1979 may have contributed, through its effect on inflationary expectations.

Conservative monetary policy can be simply summarized. They had monetary targets until October 1985, which they successively missed until they hit one in 1983–84 and narrowly missed one (1984–85). In October 1985, monetary targets and so monetarism were abandoned. In fact pure monetarism was practised only until around October 1981. From 1981–2 monetary policy was to be guided by a number of 'considerations' (a list of nearly all possible indicators and targets). These were listed in the Chancellor's Mansion House speech in November 1981. A further break occurred in 1983 when the Chancellor of the Exchequer changed, Mr Lawson replacing Sir Geoffrey Howe. Table 2.4 shows

Table 2.4   Financial indicators

	Exchange Rate[1] (1975=100)	PSBR (£m)	Base Rate (per cent)	Money supply[2]
1980	117.7	11786	16.32	14.1
1981	119.0	10507	13.26	19.6
1982	113.7	4480	11.93	12.7
1983	105.3	11605	9.82	10.8
1984	100.6	10281	9.68	9.7
1985	100.0	7476	12.25	13.4
1986	91.5	2418	10.90	18.2
1987	90.1	1455	9.74	22.9
1988	95.5	−11627	10.09	20.4
1989	95.9	−9324	13.85	–

Notes:
1. When the Conservatives were elected the value was 85.1
2. M_3 (Annual percentage change)

Sources: Financial Statistics, Bank of England Quarterly Bulletin.

the movements of three indicators of monetary policy, M_3, interest rates and the exchange rate as well as PBR. It can be seen that they present conflicting views of the tightness of financial policy. Moreover, fiscal and monetary policy suggested different policy stances. This sharpened the debate about the desirability of monetary targets; the effect of a choice between money and alternatives was much greater. Until 1980 it was easy to measure the stance of macroeconomic policy with some exceptions such as 1977 when DCE grew slowly but money rapidly. Governments normally used monetary and fiscal policy together. For example during the Barber (1971–3) expansion, the money supply grew rapidly *and* there was a record budget deficit. During the Jenkins squeeze (1968–9) both monetary and fiscal indicators measured the tightness of policy (the first budget surplus for 50 years, the smallest monetary growth for 15 years). On occasions governments used one instrument earlier than another – monetary policy was tightened in 1974, fiscal policy in 1975 or eased one without adjusting the other as when monetary policy was eased in 1977–8. Nevertheless the three tools were always in approximate balance. Since 1980, however, government policy has been unbalanced.

Hence, it is necessary to examine the impact of an unbalanced policy: easy money, tight fiscal. (At the same time the USA under President Reagan pursued an equally unbalanced policy the other way round.) The effects of this lack of balance mean that one of the basic assumptions of macroeconomics must be relaxed – the economy can no longer be treated as if it were producing a single good. Instead it is both necessary and possible to examine the form and direction that the stimulus to demand takes.

Monetary policy operates through changing the demand for assets, so for an expansionary policy:

a.   an increase in the money supply creates an excess of supply over demand in the money market;
b.   some of the excess demand is switched to those assets which are substitutes for money (say, houses, antiques and holiday villas);
c.   this extra demand means that there is excess demand for these assets, hence either their price rises (antiques), or their quantity (holiday villas), depending on the elasticity of supply. The two cited examples are unusual examples of (almost) perfectly inelastic and elastic supply respectively and more often both price and output rise (houses).

Hence to examine the effects of the imbalance one must examine the assets that private sector economic agents, companies and persons, wish to purchase with their excess money holdings:

a.   Foreign assets – factories, shares, property; from 1980–87 these totalled over £100 billion.
b.   Consumer durables - cars and electrical goods in particular. Most of these came from abroad so there was little effect on prices but an enormous balance of payments deficit was created (£15 billion in 1988).
c.   Shares and financial assets - hence one reason why in the boom prior to October 1979, share prices rose faster in the UK than elsewhere,
d.   Houses.

Undoubtedly, the monetary expansion caused the explosion in house prices (over 200 per cent 1983–8). This generated a rise in house building – from 117 000 in 1981 to 213 000 in 1988 (see Table 1.1).

2.5 THE CASE FOR TARGETS

In this section the arguments for targets in general and monetary ones in particular are assessed.

The most basic case for targets is that they give information about the future behaviour of goal variables. In the UK monetary developments in 1986–7 suggested that inflation would accelerate – eventually. It did in late 1988. Advance knowledge should make it possible to take corrective action, and such action should be less than if action is delayed ('A stitch in time saves nine'). The dramatic 5 per cent rise in UK interest rates in May–October 1988 and the further rises thereafter would not have been necessary if the authorities had raised rates earlier – perhaps a 1 per cent increase in 1986 or 2 per cent in 1987 would have sufficed. The best target is therefore the one which gives the most reliable and earliest warnings.

In addition, three arguments have been put in favour of targets. The first is an argument that a money-supply target acts as an automatic stabilizer; that is, it will reduce the deviation of output from its trend level. The stabilizing nature of monetary targets is most easily demonstrated by reference to the flow-of-funds equation (see above):

Δ money = public sector borrowing requirement +
$\qquad\qquad \Delta$ bank loans to the non-bank private sector –
$\qquad\qquad \Delta$ non-bank private sector loans to the public sector (government)+
$\qquad\qquad$ overseas effect
$\quad$ where Δ means 'change in'.

The shock analysed is a fall in exports caused, for example, by a world recession. This will reduce the overseas impact to a level below that which it would otherwise be. In this case it is necessary to influence one of the other items so that it is larger (or less negative) than it otherwise would be and thus offset the monetary effects of the fall in exports. Any action that would do this would be expansionary in any model – whether lower interest rates, higher public spending or a relaxation of credit ceilings. Consequently, the reduction in output and employment caused by a fall in exports would be offset.

It is universally accepted that observance of a monetary target will be stabilizing. However, whereas Brunner and Friedman argue that this is the maximum attainable degree of stability, Keynesian writers would either rely on discretionary action or on automatic stabilizers of a fiscal kind. The monetarist argument is that by setting the economy on an automatic pilot in this way, better results will ensue than if the authorities use their judgement about how to respond to the shock.

The simplest argument concerning monetary targets is beguilingly attractive. The private sector needs information about the public sector's behaviour if it is to plan its activities optimally. Information about government monetary policy is the most useful information that private sector agents could have, so a government should commit itself to a specific path of monetary growth. This proposition is very similar to the arguments put forward for indicative planning in the 1960s – for example, at the time of George Brown's ill-starred national plan of 1965. The counter-arguments of opponents of monetary targets are that more useful information could be given (for example a commitment to price stability or full employment) or that the benefits of more information are less than the costs imposed by monetary targets.

However, much more attention has been given in the UK, at least, to the more sophisticated argument of the role of the money supply in the formation of inflationary expectations. This argument can range from a purely economic argument to one incorporating a large element of politics. Minford (in Griffiths and Wood, 1981), for example, argued that the function of monetary targets was to show that the government meant 'business about inflation'. (He went on to add: 'It is this that the UK authorities should build up. They still have a long way to go'.) Ten years later this may still be true.

The third argument for targets, is that they are necessary to constrain or discipline governments. Buchanan has been a frequent proponent of this view (see Brennan and Buchanan, 1981) but it is even more closely associated with Friedman, for example (1970). This view can be put in a rather illiberal, un-democratic fashion: governments, left to themselves, will pursue policies that cause inflation, perhaps to buy votes, so it is necessary to find devices which will constrain them. In the 1920s Lord Bradbury used this as an argument for the gold standard: it is 'knave-proof' (Clarke, 1988). This method of presentation is, however, unfair to its proponents who, to use Buchanan's terminology, want to see the introduction of an 'economic constitution'. Governments have enormous potential political power but accept constraints upon it, either through a written constitution as in the USA, or tacitly as in the UK. Such constraints involve both an acceptance of 'rules of the game' (the opposition is not kept out of power by force) and of rights such as freedom of the press, as well as procedural safeguards such as trial by jury. Buchanan and Friedman would argue that it is equally necessary to constrain the economic power of government by analagous devices. Against this one may argue that the majority's right to use economic power is sufficiently circumscribed by a political constitution.

To summarize, monetarists believe that governments should accept a commitment to a monetary target and should be prepared to make sacrifices to achieve the target. This is justified because of the impact of monetary targets on expectations and because their adoption constrains governments and tends to stabilize output. None of these is without foundation. The 'automatic stabilizer' proposition is incontestably valid; the dispute is whether discretion or an alternative rule could do better. Monetary targets do convey information and influence expectations but it is as easy to overstate as to ignore this case for their introduction. Nevertheless, a missing link in this case is 'why money?' Similar arguments could be constructed for interest rate targets; for other quantity targets, for exchange rate targets or for more complex rules. This is seen most clearly in the discipline case. Buchanan acknowledges that a balanced budget rule (or a maximum tax to GDP ratio) or fixed exchange rates (especially the gold standard) may be better constraints on governments. Similarly membership of the exchange rate mechanism (ERM) of the EMS might increase the credibility of anti-inflation policy (p. 30).

In the rest of this section a number of arguments concerning the desirability of monetary targets as opposed to other targets are examined.

2.5.1 Price and quantity targets

Since Wicksell, in the 1880s, economists have argued that some quantity target, such as money, is necessary as well as a price target, usually the rate of interest but more topically the exchange rate. Otherwise, the price level is indeterminate in theory and hyperinflation is possible in practice. For example if the government maintains a fixed rate of interest and inflationary expectations rise in response to some shock then inflation and inflationary expectations both rise in a vicious cycle until prices reach infinite levels or the economic system collapses. However while the system requires some 'anchor' (Minford in Griffiths and Wood,1981) to avoid this, the institutional structure of the UK provides this without any target. Hence whilst this argument is both reasonable and theoretically important it has little practical relevance.

2.5.2 Uncertainty in goods markets

It has been demonstrated (see the survey in Gowland,1985, Chapter 12) that a money target is desirable if the economy is subject to shocks in domestic goods markets and an interest rate target if it is subject to monetary shocks. Similarly a monetary target is preferable if shocks come from foreign sources and an exchange rate target if they come from domestic sources. The predominant nature of uncertainty in the UK in the 1980s was probably from the foreign and goods rather than domestic and monetary sectors.

2.5.3 Definitions of money

There are eight definitions of money used in the UK and over 40 in the USA. Some critics argue that surely it is impossible to target a variable which is so hard to measure. This is specious. There are over 50 definitions of unemployment (see Chapter 6) and money is less hard to measure than most variables. What is relevant is whether alternative measures tell different stories. Except in the very short term, they do. It is necessary to adjust for income elasticities. Thus 6 per cent M_0 growth may imply the same as 15 per cent growth in figures; the implication of each series is the same. For example money grew too fast from 1984–8. In general, except in the very short term, alternative monetary data do tell the same story, whether one's interest is in annual changes or in longer-run changes.

2.5.4 Money and financial innovation

One argument is that financial innovation has so changed the nature of financial assets and the reasons for holding them that a consistent measure of money is impossible; Mr Lawson frequently cited this proposition, as in his 1987 Budget speech. This is true but irrelevant. Financial innovation has made all assets more liquid (see chapter 4). Hence some assets which were not previously money have now become money. Thus the bias due to financial innovation is that all measures of money understate its true growth, so the UK money supply in 1980 should have excluded building society deposits; it should now include them. So true UK money has grown faster than either M_3 (which excluded building society deposits) or M_4 (which includes them). Hence the official response to innovation should be a *slower* growth rate of the money supply.

2.5.5 Narrow effects of money

In 1984–8 Mr Lawson tried to expand the economy by using monetary policy. This concentrated growth in a few sectors and regions (consumer durables, housing and the South East). The alternative of fiscal expansion and tight money (to control inflation) should produce a more balanced growth of output. This result is exemplified by US experience under President Reagan, 1981–8.

2.5.6 Post-Keynesian argument

The most interesting argument against monetary targets is the post-Keynesian critique: money is so powerful in its effects that control of the money supply is likely to have dramatic and unpredictable effects. It is better to let money adjust to shocks, especially to changes in speculative sentiment, than to seek to control it. Money is the best buffer. Milton Friedman argues on similar lines that the best buffer is no change in money. In other words post-Keynesians accept Friedman's argument for a neutral financial policy but disagree about the meaning of neutrality. In the UK context, the argument is that devastating as have been the effects of no control, the effects of trying to control money would be still more destabilizing.

2.5.7 Friedman in retrospect

Some economists have postulated a choice between low monetary growth and low interest rates. In contrast Friedman has always argued that excess money growth causes high and variable (nominal) interest rates. Monetary growth raises inflation and inflationary expectations. Both cause interest rates to rise and the monetary authorities moreover have to increase rates still further to reduce inflation. Friedman could argue that 1984–8 in the UK proves his point.

2.5.8 Money and the EMS

In recent years arguments in favour of variable exchange rates (and so opposition to the EMS) are based on domestic macroeconomic grounds. In its negative form, exchange rate constraints may inhibit freedom to exercise domestic instruments to combat inflation and unemployment. The German authorities have found that trying to stabilize the mark tends to lead to excess monetary growth because such intervention leads to a positive overseas impact on the money supply. In the UK the argument is usually more forcefully put: higher exchange rates reduce inflation, lower ones reduce unemployment (see Chapter 1). Hence a government needs the freedom to adjust exchange rates for domestic reasons – as in late 1988 the UK authorities welcomed a higher exchange rate for anti-inflationary reasons. Mrs Thatcher gave this as her reason for dissent from the Delors report after the Madrid summit in June 1989. However it may not be necessary to choose between money and exchange rate targets. Indeed the EMS may necessitate a monetary target. In the UK money growth tends to be the best predictor of the exchange rate; monetary expansion leads to exchange rate depreciation and *vice versa*. Hence, exchange rate stability can probably be best achieved by monetary stability.

Moreover, all European advocates of the EMS argue that it necessitates macroeconomic policy coordination. That is if the EMS is to survive there must be coordinated monetary policies – probably a common DCE target. Otherwise, differential macroeconomic policies will produce differential inflation and so mean that EMS rates cease to be equilibria. Given that the UK's trade pattern is different from the rest of the European Community then it would be harder to maintain EMS membership than for existing members. Hence the need for macro-coordination is greater. Indeed for good or ill, EMS membership probably implies not only a monetary target but a common one with Germany.

2.6   THE ROLE OF MONETARY POLICY

Despite all the controversy which surrounds the topic, it is surprisingly easy to draw at least some conclusions about its appropriate use. Monetary policy has been used as an expansionary instrument on three occasions: 1971–3, 1985–8 and, to a lesser extent 1977–8. On each occasion the results were very unfortunate, as outlined above. The effect of monetary policy on the economy is through its impact on asset markets: property and consumer durables. Whilst house price explosions do stimulate house building a much smaller rate of price increase would almost certainly be as effective. Moreover, not only is the impact of monetary policy on demand concentrated on a narrow range of products but many of these are imported. Tax reductions or government spending must be preferable to credit booms when governments seek to stimulate the economy. For example, fiscal expansion and higher interest rates would almost certainly have been desirable in 1986, or indeed at most times in the 1980s.

The argument against rapid monetary expansion is reinforced by the problems discussed further in the next chapter –those of reining back growth in the money supply when it is judged to be excessive. In 1972–3, 1979–80 and 1988–9 the authorities sought to restrict monetary growth but found it virtually impossible even when they belatedly allowed the nominal interest rate to rocket. Friedman's view that high money growth is the cause of, not the alternative to, high nominal interest rates, certainly seems valid in the UK. Only in 1978 was monetary policy restored with some ease but the authorities (for the last time?) had a viable direct control to reinforce changes in interest rates.

Hence the negative part of Friedman's case can be established and would be generally accepted: it is unwise to expand monetary growth. The positive aspect is more controversial. Is it necessary to seek to offset any acceleration in the money supply which may occur for reasons other than government policy? If it is, the case for a monetary target has been established. Any interpretation of the case for a broad monetary target has to bear in mind that monetary growth should influence *all* prices, not just those of final goods, roughly the retail price index or GDP deflator. Moreover, a lot of the effects of monetary expansion will be aborted by the deterioration of the balance of payments. On three occasions in 20 years, moreover, monetary acceleration has correctly predicted an acceleration in inflation. Thus far the monetarist can claim to be like Cassandra: always right and always ignored.

The argument against monetarism is based on the events of 1979–82. In essence the argument is that monetary data then gave a false signal which, like the thirteenth stroke of a clock, casts doubt on the value of the indicator. The proposition is that the monetary aggregates understated financial pressure on the economy and led the government to pursue an excessively tough deflationary policy. Other variables, especially the exchange rate which appreciated rapidly, gave a more accurate picture. The consensus view is that the costs of Thatcherism were greater and its benefits longer-delayed than its proponents had hoped; the question of whether the benefits exceeded the costs can be left aside here (see Gowland,1989, for an appraisal). Many commentators ascribe much of the reason for this to the mistake generated by misleading monetary statistics in 1981.

In these circumstances it is worth examining the mistake in detail to examine its nature and if it was really a mistake. The money supply grew rapidly in 1980; by 19 per cent in 1980–81. At the same time inflation was rising and output falling. Any Chancellor would have been faced with an agonizing dilemma in these circumstances: monetary data perhaps exaggerated inflationary tendencies but may not have given a misleading signal.

Sir Geoffrey Howe responded on monetarist lines by tightening macroeconomic policy, especially with the real tax increases of the 1981 budget. It has been argued that the monetary data gave a further misleading signal by suggesting that further deflation was needed in late 1981 or early 1982. This is untrue. Monetary growth was erratic but the trend was downwards after the 1981 Budget; in 1981–2 M_3 grew by less than 13 per cent. With considerable justice, uncritical proponents of Thatcherism as well as more neutral commentators regard this budget as the turning point of her administration. Sir Alan Walters who is neither neutral nor unsympathetic calls it a 'clear and resolute decision to restore financial integrity' (Walters 1986, p. 86). Despite the criticism of 364 economists in a famous letter to the *Times* (31 March,1981), it is not difficult to justify this Budget. Almost certainly once the government had commenced on the Thatcher experiment it was right to carry on to the end. Hence the 'mistake' may not have been a mistake. Given the 'Thatcher experiment', monetary data did not give a misleading signal. The experiment may or may not have been a mistake but that is irrelevant to the case for monetary targets. The accuracy or otherwise of a speedometer is not affected by an argument that the driver is on the wrong road!

2.7 THE UK AND THE EMS

The main alternative to a monetary target in the UK is usually held to be membership of the exchange rate mechanism (ERM) of the European Monetary System (EMS). This would mean that the UK would commit itself to keeping the exchange rate within a narrow presented range around a temporarily fixed but adjustable parity, see Chapter 9. This would mean that the UK was subject to an external discipline (a fixed exchange rate) instead of an internal one, such as a money supply target. In practice, the two might not be alternatives. Lord Rees-Mogg, for example, has argued that they are complementary (*Independent,* Monday 23 October 1989). As argued above, membership of the ERM may necessitate common targets for financial policy – probably for DCE. All this said, the decision about whether or not the UK should join the ERM is a crucial one; probably the most important macroeconomic policy choice since Mr Lawson abandoned monetarism in 1985. Whether the UK joins or not it will remain a critical issue and a staple of debate about UK macroeconomic policy for many years (and a new chestnut for exam setters!) Its importance is not restricted to economic policy. Arguments about the issue led to considerable division within the Conservative party and cabinet in 1988–9. This culminated in the resignation of Mr Lawson as Chancellor of the Exchequer on 26 October 1989 in protest at Sir Alan Walters's vocal opposition to the ERM. Sir Alan, Mrs Thatcher's economic adviser, resigned the same day. No other economic policy issue has led to such a political cause celèbre. Analysis of different facets of the issue can be found in Chapters 1, 3, 8 and 9. Hence it seems useful to bring these strands together in this section, and to provide a critique of the main arguments for and against (which are italicised) as well as to provide cross-references to the other chapters.

Membership of an exchange-rate fixing agreement involves a commitment to support one's currency. Say the parity is fixed at £1 equals 3DM, then every time anyone presents the Bank of England with £1, they must exchange it for 3DM (or 10 French francs, etc. for all the currencies in the ERM). This means that the UK would need sufficient foreign exchange to meet all such demands; the ERM puts the responsibility on a country to maintain the value of its currency, not to stop it rising too fast – if the pound rose in value against the DM it is Germany's problem not the UK's. Usually there is little problem in keeping a currency within its limits but sometimes most people believe that it is over-valued and seek to sell it. This is called a crisis of confidence.

This is an especial problem for the UK given that the pound is held internationally on a far wider scale than continental European currencies. This is why the UK government argues that a necessary condition for UK membership is that our inflation rate be equal to Germany's. In this case it is reasonable to expect the pound to maintain its value against the DM so there is little incentive to convert pounds into DM. Otherwise, the UK has argued, membership would involve excessive heavy expenditure (buying DM for pounds) that will not be successful (pp. 52, 169, 200ff).

If a country does not have enough reserves on such occasions it has three options – to leave the ERM, to impose direct exchange controls or to change its economic policy in such a way that it convinces people that the currency is worth holding. This leads to three arguments against membership of the ERM.

1. British membership of the ERM could prove an expensive fiasco.
The UK joined the previous version of the ERM in 1972 and had to leave after a few weeks because it did not have enough revenue. The effect was not only to humiliate the UK but also to set back the cause of European economic integration.

2. Membership may involve actions that impede European economic integration.
To ease the problem described above, most of the members of the European Community have used exchange control, that is regulations which forbid some or all transactions in a foreign currency. An Italian, for example, could not have a UK or German bank account, nor any other sterling or DM asset without government permission until 1990. Hence he could not convert lire into DM so it is much easier to support the lire's value against the DM. These restrictions impede the European Community's goal of a single market. Hence the UK's requirement that the remaining members of the EEC abandon their exchange control before the UK joins the ERM. They promised to do this at Hanover in June 1988 (with a waiver for Italy until 1992 and Portugal, Spain and Greece until 1995). Following further British pressure at the Madrid summit in 1989, France and Italy abandoned their exchange control in the first half of 1990. It remains to be seen how the ERM functions without it (pp. 52 and 200 ff).

3. A country may be forced to change its macroeconomic policy so as to remain a member of the ERM. For example the French government in 1983 had to abandon a Keynesian policy of reflation adopted after the election of President Mitterand. Usually this is regarded as a consequence of a wider proposition.

4. If the UK is a member of the ERM, it loses autonomy of domestic policy.
The exchange rate is linked to the money supply (and other domestic targets such as interest rates). Hence if one fixes the exchange rate, it is impossible to retain complete control over the other variables, just as a monetary target involves sacrifice of other objectives. Hence the UK government would not be able to manage the UK economy. However, some may think this a good thing – argument 5).

5. The Bundesbank will manage the UK economy better than UK politicians.
Many economists and people in the City welcome the loss of autonomy. They argue that if membership of the ERM involves management of the UK economy by the Bundesbank (the German equivalent of the Bank of England), the sooner

the UK joins the ERM, the better. This is the same economic argument as 4 with a different interpretation.

6. If the UK is a member of the ERM, it cannot use the exchange rate as a weapon of domestic policy
UK government have used a high exchange rate to reduce unemployment and a low one to reduce inflation. Obviously if the exchange rate is fixed, it cannot be varied in this way, nor to achieve any other objective, p. 9.

7. Joining the ERM will lead to a lower level of inflation.
It was argued above that under some circumstances the UK price level is determined by the exchange rate and world prices. If the exchange rate is fixed the UK's prices would be determined only by world prices – in practice within the EMS, Germany's prices – and Germany has a low inflation rate.

8. Membership of the ERM would increase the credibility of UK anti-inflation policy.
Given the importance of expectations in determining inflation, it is desirable if people expect a low rate of inflation. This means that inflation policy will work only if people have confidence in it. This is called credibility. Membership of the ERM has increased the credibility of anti-inflation policy in France, p. 201.

9. Membership of the ERM would facilitate trade with Europe and European integration generally (see pp. 169 and 200–204.)
On the whole many of the problems stem from lack of confidence that the UK will stay in and many of the benefits from confidence that it will! For example lack of confidence could lead to very high interest rates (argument 3) whilst a credible anti-inflation policy could lead to lower ones (argument 8). As often in economics a policy will work if, but only if, people believe in it – a point first made by Keynes (1930, p.239).

GUIDE TO FURTHER READING

Gowland (1990) presents the argument from this chapter in more detail. Goodhart (1984) is exceptionally useful. Walters (1988), Minford (1987), Congdon (1982) and Artis and Lewis (1981) present contrasting analyses. The issues of the most appropriate target and indicators of economic policy are analysed in Gramlich (1990) and in Artis and Miller (eds) (1981); Goodhart's sceptical essay is of especial value. Bank (1990) is the definitive work on measuring money in the UK.

NOTES

1. For example, the reduction in public spending in July 1983, the increases in interest rates in the summer of 1984 and the fall in the exchange rate in the autumn of 1984.
2. The situation is slightly more complex than stated in the text in that M_o targets were later restored but with a stated total unwillingness to sacrifice anything to achieve them.
3. For Sir Alan's views and associated press speculation on a Thatcher/Lawson split see the quality press in June–July 1988. Sir Alan's own views were set out in an article in the *Independent* on 18 July. Walters (1986) is also relevant. The controversy continued *sub rosa* and re-emerged in October 1989 when it led to Mr Lawson's resignation, in response to publicity given to an article written by Sir Alan in 1987, reproduced in the *Independent*, 26 October 1989.
4. The authorities have decided to cease to collect M_1, M_3 data. Various of the definitions have been amended over the years. Various other definitions have been used at various times.
5. See for example Gowland (1988).
6. Nationalized industry losses appear here, as lending by the National Loans Fund to for example British Coal. Profits appear as a repayment of such loans. When the PSBR is negative it is sometimes referred to as PSDR (public sector debt repayment).
7. See Ward and Nield (1978).
8. See Gowland (1982, 1984) pp. 104–43 for an analysis of the 'new approach'.

REFERENCES

Artis, M.J. and Lewis, M.K. (1981), *Monetary Control in the United Kingdom*, Philip Allan, Oxford.

Artis, M.J. and Miller, M. (eds) (1981), *Essays in Fiscal and Monetary Policy*, Oxford University Press, Oxford.

Bank (1990), 'Monetary Aggregates in a Changing Environment', *Bank of England Discussion Paper* no. 47, London.

Browning, P. (1985), *The Treasury and Economic Policy*, Longman, London.

Buchanan, J.M. and Brennan, H.G. (1981), 'Monopoly in Money and Inflation', *Hobart Paper* no. 88, Institute of Economic Affairs, London.

Caves, R.E. (1968), *Britain's Economic Prospects*, Allen and Unwin, London.

Clarke, P. (1988), *The Keynesian Revolution in the Making 1924–36*, Oxford University Press, Oxford.

Congdon, T. (1982), *Monetary Control in Britain*, Macmillan.

Friedman, M. (1970), *The Counter Revolution in Monetary Theory*, 1st Wincott Memorial lecture; reprinted as Occasional Paper 33, Institute of Economic Affairs, London.

Goodhart, C.A.E. (1984), *Monetary Theory and Practice*, Macmillan, London.

Gowland, D.H. (1982, 1984), *Controlling the Money Supply* (2nd edition, 1984), Croom Helm, Beckenham.

Gowland, D.H. (1985), *Money, Inflation and Unemployment*, Wheatsheaf, Brighton.

Gowland, D.H. (1988), 'Il Processo Di Deregolamentazione Finanziara Alla Luce Della Recente Crisi dei Mercati Borsistici Mondiali' *Economia Italiana*, no. 3, pp. 389–410, Banco di Roma, Rome.

Gowland, D.H. (1989), *Whatever Happened to Demand Management?*, RJA (Books), Bedford.

Gowland, D.H. (1990), *Monetary Control in Theory and Practice*, Routledge, London.

Gramlich, E.M. (1990), *Fiscal Indicators*, OECD Working Paper No. 80, OECD, Paris.

Griffiths, B. and Wood, G.E. (eds) (1981), *Monetary Targets*, Macmillan, London.

Keynes, J.M. (1930), *The General Theory of Employment, Interest and Money*, Macmillan, also in vol. VII of his collected works (Keynes 1971).

Keynes, J.M. (1971), *The Collected Writings of John Maynard Keynes*, Macmillan for the Royal Economic Society.

Minford, P.L. (ed.) (1981), *Monetarism and Macroeconomics*, Institute of Economic Affairs, London.

Musgrave, R.A. and Musgrave, P.B. (1968), 'Fiscal Policy' in Caves (1968).

Walters, A.A. (1986), *Britain's Economic Renaissance*, Oxford University Press, New York.

Ward, T.S. and Neild, R.R. (1978), *The Measurement and Reform of Budgetary Policy*, Heinemann (for the Institute of Fiscal Studies), London.

Waud, R.N. (1973) Proximate Targets and Monetary Policy, *Economic Journal*, vol. 83 I (March) PI.

APPENDIX: THE DERIVATION OF THE FLOW-OF-FUNDS EQUATION

Money   = Deposits held by the non-bank private sector (D) + currency held by the non-bank private sector (C).   (2.1)

This is the definition of a monetary aggregate such as M_4 in the UK.

Bank deposits are bank liabilities and for simplicity other liabilities are ignored (see Gowland, 1990, for a relaxation of this).

D   = bank liabilities   (2.2)

Bank liabilities = bank assets   (2.3)

by combining (2.2) and (2.3)

D   = bank assets   (2.4)

Over 95 per cent of bank assets are bank loans so the other assets are ignored. (If other assets besides loans and liabilities besides deposits are incorporated an extra term in 'net non-deposit liabilities' appears as in the Bank *Bulletin*, Table 12.3.)

Bank assets   = bank loans   (2.5)

Combining (2.4) and (2.5)

D   = bank loans   (2.6)

Bank loans can be made to the public sector, or the non-bank private sector, so

D = bank loans = + bank loans to the public sector
                        + bank loans to the (non-bank)
                        private sector   (2.7)

So, substituting (2.7) into (2.1)

Money = C + bank loans to the public sector
                 + bank loans to the private sector   (2.8)

It is convenient to rewrite this equation as a flow, i.e. in changes, using the symbol Δ to indicate 'change in'.

Δ money = ΔC + Δ bank loans to the public sector + Δ bank loans to the private sector (2.9)

By definition,

Δ bank loans to $\quad$ Δ total loans to the public sector -
the public sector = Δ non-bank loans to the public sector (2.10)

Δ total loans to the public sector is equal to the public sector borrowing requirement (PSBR) since lending to anyone must equal their borrowing, so

$\quad$ PSBR = ΔC + Δ bank loans to the public sector (2.11)
$\quad\quad\quad$ + Δ non-bank private sector loans to the public
$\quad\quad\quad\quad$ sector

or

Δ bank loans to $\quad\quad$ PSBR - (Δ C Δ non-bank private
the public sector = $\quad$ sector loans to the public sector (2.12)

All of this is a rearrangement of the government finance equation. Currency is a form of non-interest-bearing loan to the public sector.

Equation (2.12) can be substituted into equation (2.9) in which case ΔC appears once as a positive and once as a negative term and thus cancels out, giving

ΔM = PSBR
$\quad$ + Δ bank loans to non-bank private sector
$\quad$ – Δ non-bank private sector loans to public sector. (2.13)

This is the closed economy version of the flow-of-funds equation. In an open economy it is necessary to add

1. deposits held by non-residents (F)
2. bank loans to non-residents (N)
3. government acquisition of foreign currency (A)
   (this is negative if the government sells foreign currency).

(2.2) now becomes D+F = bank liabilities (2.2a)

and (2.7) bank loans = N + F + P (2.7a)

(2.9) becomes Δ money = ΔN + ΔG + ΔP – ΔF
(ΔN-ΔF) is the increase in bank claims on non residents. 'A' should be added to the PSBR but is not (see p. 52).
Hence A + (ΔN–ΔF) is the overseas influence on the money supply.

3.   Monetary Control

D. H. Gowland

3.1 INTRODUCTION

There has probably been more controversy in the UK about *how* to control
financial variables than about *which* financial variable to control or in more
formal language, about which instrument to use rather than about which
intermediate target. This became evident once more in the second half of 1988.
It was generally agreed by Mr Lawson's critics and supporters alike that some
contractionary financial measures were necessary in view of the rapid deterioration of the balance of payments, accelerating inflation, and explosive growth
of credit and money. However, Mr Lawson chose to rely on a single instrument,
interest rates, and in fact on a single *modus operandi*: the negative effect of interest rates on the demand for bank lending. His critics compared this to 'one-
club golf' and argued that extra instruments were necessary. The European
Commission repeated this point in a particularly searing attack on UK economic
policy in October 1989. Direct controls on credit were the most frequently
advocated but both an aggressive debt management policy and a reserve base
system are alternatives which do not lack advocates, such as Gordon Pepper in
the 1990 Mais lecture. Moreover, the *modus operandi* of UK monetary control
have had about the same degree of permanence as Italian premiers with major
reappraisals of choice of technique in 1971, 1974 and 1979–80. Accordingly, it
is all the more necessary to emphasize the basic theory of monetary control (see
Section 3.2). Within this context the kaleidoscopic pattern of UK monetary
control can be analysed. The alternative instruments could be and indeed have
been used to control other variables besides money such as credit, domestic
credit expansion (DCE) or various price variables, notably the exchange rate.
Nevertheless, it is best to analyse them in the framework of monetary control
because this best shows the full range of alternatives and their interrelationship.
This is reflected in the enduring nature of exam questions such as 'How might
the Bank of England control the money supply? What problems arise with the
various alternatives?' The four major problems of monetary control are naturally
revealed by this approach together with some policy issues. Following the

41

analytical approach of section 3.2, a synoptic approach is adapted in Tables 3.1, 3.2 and 3.3 where the techniques, problems and issues are reproduced in summary. The major choice in monetary control is between price methods, such as interest rates, and direct or quantity controls such as credit ceilings. In view of the importance of this issue, both in theory and in the UK today, it is reviewed in Section 3.3. The other main alternative, the reserve base system, is considered in Section 3.4. The problems of short-term management of financial markets is studied in Section 3.5 followed by some conclusions.

3.2   INSTRUMENTS OF FINANCIAL POLICY

By definition the money supply is equal to bank deposits plus currency held by the non-bank private currency, so long as the terms are appropriately defined (p. 30). This gives the *demand-side* approach to monetary control:

$$\Delta \text{ money} = \Delta \text{ currency}_p + \Delta \text{ bank deposits}$$

where Δ means 'change in' and the subscript p held by the non-bank private sector. In addition it is necessary to have an analysis of the creation of money, the *supply-side* approach. This is the flow-of-funds equation (see p. 18ff). The equation is derived in the appendix to Chapter 2.

Money =   PSBR
          $+ \Delta$ bank loans to the non-bank private sector
          $- \Delta$ non-bank private sector loans to the public sector (government)
          $+$ overseas effect (0)

where Δ means 'change in'.

Within this framework it is possible to analyse the control of money in exactly the same way as any other good. This equation is also the money creation equation. The money supply will change if and only if one of these variables changes. These four variables are known as the supply-side counterparts to money creation. In recent years the PSBR has been in surplus and the surplus known as the PSDR (public sector debt repayment). A PSDR of £10 billion could instead be entered as a PSBR of (–£10 billion). Alternatively, the 'PSBR' could be replaced in the above equation with –PSDR. Either way the PSDR has a negative impact on money creation, reducing it below what it would otherwise have been, in exactly the same way as the PSBR has a positive impact.

In principle, it is possible to restrict the output or consumption of any good by three methods:

Table 3.1   Monetary control

1952–71   The old approach

The technique used was ceilings on bank-lending to the non-bank private sector and other forms of credit. It was often called *moralsuasion* as its legal basis was unclear.

1971–73   The new approach

Interest rate effect on bank lending to non-bank private sector.

1974–79   New new approach

Interest rate effect on non-bank private sector lending to public sector (Duke of York)
Quantity ceiling on deposits (IBELS ceiling or corset)
Public sector borrowing requirement

The new policy 1979– PSBR especially by asset sales

Interest rate effect on bank lending to non-bank private sector

Interest rate effect on non-bank sector lending to public sector; indexation and national savings

Exchange rate

Abolition of exchange control

Table 3.2   Problems of monetary control

1. The authorities control the level of interest rates whereas behaviour of the private sector depends on relative rates
2. Black markets
3. Offset problem
4. Endogeneity (income-dependence) of PSBR

Table 3.3 Issues in monetary policy

1. National savings
2. Exact funding
3. Crowding out
4. Exchange rate and deindustrialization: a connection?
5. Exchange control

1. *by price*, for example a higher price to reduce consumption;
2. *by quantity control*, usually some form of rationing;
3. *by interference with methods of production*, usually by a device designed to make the industry less efficient, for example restricting the number of vines per acre to reduce (French) wine output.

These can be applied to either the supply side or the demand side, producing in principle a vast number of means of monetary control of which ten are important. In the case of money, 3 above is the reserve base system, which is designed to reduce the output of either bank deposits or loans below the industry's unconstrained equilibrium level. Such a system is or has been used in the USA, the Federal Republic of Germany, Australia, New Zealand, South Africa, Venezuela and Mexico, but not in the UK (see below). Both the system and the arguments for and against its use are considered in Section 3.5.

The first equation above represents the liabilities (or demand) approach, the second the assets approach. Before examining the techniques in detail, two points must be made. The first is that, because assets equal liabilities, to alter one necessarily involves changing the other. The distinction is between seeking direct manipulation of bank liabilities (deposits) and accepting, as a consequence, a change in bank assets and, on the other hand, causing a change in bank assets so as to effect the desired change in bank liabilities, and so the money supply. The second preliminary remark is that in the equation the right-hand side variables are not necessarily independent of each other. For example, a bond-financed increase in public spending has no effect on the money supply because the increase in the PSBR is offset by the (negative) impact of the larger private loans item. Similarly there is no point in direct manipulation of currency because deposits are likely to respond in order to offset the initial effect.

3.2.1 Price effects on bank deposits (Method 1)

The rationale for this method is to raise the rate of return on alternative assets relative to that on bank deposits in order to induce a shift out of bank deposits.

The rate of return on a bank deposit may include cash cards, cheque book facilities, free or subsidized use of money transmission facilities, free overdrafts and various free gifts. Nevertheless *at the margin* variations in interest rates are the key factor and so this method means either reducing interest rates paid on bank deposits *or* increasing those on the alternatives. In practice this method cannot be used because bank interest rates are far less sticky than those on some of the alternatives. Thus the authorities could raise the rate of return on some of the alternatives to bank deposits such as savings certificates. The banks would follow suit but the rate of return on alternatives (unit trusts, insurance, property, illiquid or capital-certain deposits) would remain unchanged. Hence, bank deposits would attract money and the effect on the money supply would be perverse.

This illustrates the following problem.

Problem A   The authorities can control absolute level of interest rates but behaviour depends on relative rates (structure of rates)

A decision about whether to put money in a bank or building society or into national savings normally depends on the difference between the rate of return they offer, not on the absolute level of interest rates paid by one or the other. One does not say 'I will put money into the Abbey National because it pays 9 per cent' if either Midland or the Halifax are offering 10 per cent. Instead the investor considers the difference between the rates offered relative to the other attractions of a particular investment; location of an institution, free gifts, period of notice, availability of cheque facilities and cash cards etc. The decision rule may be simple; put the money in X unless Z offers 2 per cent more. Alternatively, the proportion put into each alternative may vary with changes in the relative rate of return. In any case private sector behaviour depends on relative rates of return, that is upon the entire structure of rates: public compared to private, long compared to short etc. The authorities, however, can control the level of interest rates, albeit at a price, but have relatively little influence on the structure of rates.

3.2.2   Quantity controls on bank deposits (Method 2)

Rationing of bank deposits is one – if a crude – method of controlling the money supply. The main example occurred in the UK where the authorities imposed ceilings on IBELs (interest-bearing eligible liabilities, that is deposits) from 1974 to 1980. The rationing was applied at the level of the bank, not the customer. Each bank had a permitted quota of deposits that it could take. Similarly in the same period petrol rationing was effected by giving quotas to filling stations. If a bank exceeded its quota it paid a penalty: a *supplementary special deposit* had to be lodged interest-free with the Bank of England. The third name of the scheme was the corset, a somewhat mixed metaphor as a name for a ceiling. If price controls do not work the obvious alternative is rationing. Hence the general arguments for quantity controls discussed in Section 3.4 are relevant. A major problem is evasion, which arose originally through the 'bill leak'. This is merely an example of the general microeconomic proposition: rationing leads to black markets. A bank can perform the normal banking function by introducing a borrower to a lender and guaranteeing the loan rather than accepting and on-lending a deposit. In this case, the transaction does not appear in the bank's balance sheet even though the investor holds an indirect claim on the banking system, off-balance sheet lending (see p. 81). If a bank lends by discounting and accepting a bill of exchange, and sells this to a potential depositor, as happened in the 1970s, this is called a 'bill leak'. Thus, the form of the control is satisfied but the authorities' intention is evaded. All the key features of intermediation are unchanged: A's funds go to B because A trusts the bank and because of the bank's specialist skills. This was sometimes also called the 'letter of acceptance' leak, from the name of a particular type of bill. After the abolition of exchange control in late1979 evasion involved 'booking' deposits abroad. In the simplest case instead of A holding a bank deposit with, say, Midland's York branch which grants B a loan, A holds the deposit with Midland's Paris branch and B's loan is similarly granted by this overseas branch. Unless exchange control is reintroduced, such evasion is a danger with any direct control on either bank liabilities or assets, that is credit, leading to the following problem.

Problem B Black markets
Just as A is the fundamental problem with *all* interest rate controls so the fundamental danger of rationing devices is a black market.

The remaining eight methods of monetary control all use the supply-side, flow-of-funds, approach.

3.2.3   The PSBR (Method 3)

The public sector borrowing requirement (PSBR) is one of the many alternative definitions of the budget deficit. Alternative definitions are not restricted to financial variables – there are over 40 measures of unemployment in the UK while some variables have proved even more mercurial, notably inequality and the Keynesian concept of autonomous expenditure. However, given the importance attached to the PSBR by Mr Lawson and its role in monetary management, its arbitrary nature is worth noting. If an alternative definition of the PSBR were employed the analysis of money creation and control would be unchanged but a corresponding variation in the definition of another of the four counterparts would be necessary. This can be seen by examination of the PSBR's components:

Central and local government expenditure on goods, services, transfers and assets (other than foreign currency)

– taxation

– asset sales

+ central and local government loans to other domestic sectors

The last term includes the National Loans Fund loans to nationalized industries to cover their losses and the notional repayments made out of their profits (see p. 37). If say the loans item were excluded from the PSBR the impact of this item on the money supply could be captured by a corresponding adjustment to the non-bank private sector loans to the public sector item. Similarly, it would not affect monetary growth if asset sales were treated as loans by the non-bank private sector instead of reductions in the PSBR.

The crucial feature of the PSBR, like the other three supply-side counterparts, is that a change in one of them has exactly the same impact on the money supply. A PSBR of £1 billion causes the money supply, *ceteris paribus*, to rise by precisely £1 billion, no more, no less. This, the first round or *primary, money creation*, is the key not only to the theory of banking but also to understanding UK monetary control. As an example, the payment of £1000 to a teacher in the UK state sector will be analysed. The government in practice makes such payments through local education authorities but for analytical purposes all of the public sector has been consolidated into one. The paying agency could make the payment in only two ways. It could send the teacher £1000 in currency, say 50 £20 notes. In this case the teacher would hold £1000 in cash – non-bank private sector holdings of currency. This would be the increase in the money supply. Although it is common to talk about 'printing money', strictly what is relevant is putting currency into circulation. However many bank notes are printed at Debden the money supply is unchanged until they are put into circulation, for example by government spending. It is one of the merits of flow-of-funds analysis that it lists all the ways of putting currency into circulation.

Alternatively, the government could send the teacher a cheque for £1000. He/she would then pay this into a bank account. The bank's balance sheet then shows a simultaneous increase in liabilities of £1000 (the teacher's deposit) *and* in assets (the cheque which is a claim on the public sector). The increase in deposits represents the change in the money supply. The increase in bank assets represents *bank lending to the public sector (government)*. This process is sometimes called *residual finance*. The bank is in practice likely to pay it into its account with the Bank of England and later use it to buy Treasury bills or gilt-edged securities. However, these all represent only transformations of the form of bank claims on (loans to) the government not changes in its total. Bank loans to the government are created or destroyed only by transactions between the government and the non-bank private (or overseas) sectors. Their total cannot be altered by transactions between the government and the banks. Finally it is worth noting that the change in the money supply generated by the public spending (PSBR) is independent of whether currency or the banking sector is used to finance it.

This is the primary, or direct, impact of government spending and must be distinguished from any subsequent transactions. The bank may convert the cheque into some other asset; it may increase or reduce its lending to other borrowers because of the increase in its assets. If it does, some of these might be a secondary, or induced effect on the money supply; in a reserve base system they will be. However, it is crucial to distinguish direct or primary effects from secondary ones. Moreover, it is vital to emphasize that the impact of the PSBR on the money supply is independent of any induced or secondary effects.

Any act of government spending and taxation, or any purchase or sale of an asset, will necessarily affect the money supply, although two transactions may cancel each other out as in the case of bond-financed expenditure. Thus, it is not surprising that, from 1975–86 the authorities in the UK regarded the monetary effects of public sector actions as the most important factor in determining the appropriate level of the PSBR and thus, of spending and taxation. This revolution in official attitudes was as significant as the famous Kingsley Wood budget of 1941, which inaugurated Keynesian 'demand management' (Sayers, 1983).

The PSBR can be influenced in many ways. Expenditure and tax policy can be altered: thus, for example, the *increase* in petrol tax in the 1981 budget 'to *reduce* inflation'. Nationalized industries can be made more profitable or their losses can be cut. Hence 'the increase in gas prices is an essential part of our anti-inflation strategy' to quote a Cabinet Minister in 1980. A Keynesian could offer an alternative explanation of why these policies could reduce inflation, but he could not explain why the sale of BP shares or the Gleneagles Hotel are thought by the government to reduce inflation. However, in the flow-of-funds framework the explanation is obvious; higher profits by a nationalized industry or asset sales reduce the PSBR as much as tax increases and have identical monetary effects. In fact, one of the major merits of flow-of-funds analysis is that it is the only way in which it is possible to explain or understand the rationale of the policy of the Conservative government elected in 1979 and so to criticize (or defend) it. Many of its key policies were first adopted as means of monetary control, notably privatization and the abolition of exchange control. The government came to realize the other virtues later, especially after 1983, see for example Kay and Bishop (1988).

Asset sales, however, are not a particularly good method of trying to control the money supply. One of the problems with any technique is that it may be offset by a change in another financial aggregate. However, this is probably most serious with asset sales. For example, when the government sells BP shares in order to reduce the money supply, any of the following could have occurred:

a. They may be bought by foreigners (as with the Kuwaiti Investment Office and BP shares in 1987) in which case there is a counterbalancing change in the overseas impact (that is the domestic borrowing requirement is unchanged).
b. They may be bought with a loan from the public sector – as with many sales of council houses.
c. They may be bought instead of public sector debt, for example gilt-edged or national savings.
d. They may be bought by a bank.
e. They may be bought with finance provided by a bank.

In all these cases, there is no effect on the money supply.

The above illustrates two further problems, as follows.

Problem C. The offset problem: items of the flow-of-funds equation are not independent of each other

Problem D The endogeneity problem

Taxation and the level of government spending cannot be determined exactly by the government. This is because they depend not only on policy decisions (such as tax *rates*) but also on income (income tax), expenditure (VAT) or other income-related variables such as the number of unemployed eligible for benefit. When the government adjusts the policy variable, income changes in the opposite direction so as to limit the effect on the PSBR. It has been calculated that about 40 per cent of the apparent effect is offset in this way; a reduction in expenditure of £100 million reduces the PSBR by only £60 million.

3.2.4   Price effects on non-bank private sector loans to the public sector (Method 4)

Any financial transaction between the public and non-bank private sector has the same impact on the money supply irrespective of the cause of the transaction. If I write a cheque for £1000 payable to Her Majesty's Government the money supply will fall by £1000 whether it is to pay my income tax bill, to buy British Steel shares (both of which count as reductions in the PSBR) or to buy savings certificates, the item under consideration here. Private sector loans to the public sector comprise:

a   gilt-edged to the non-bank private sector (gilts)
b   national savings
c   local authority debt
d   other public sector debt sales (such as certificates of tax deposit).

This device seeks to make public sector debt more attractive. This induces greater purchases by the non-bank private sector. They pay for the securities by writing cheques, or using currency, and so both bank liabilities and assets (loans to the public sector) fall. Usually a higher interest rate is used to make government securities more attractive. However, this technique must not be confused with others, such as Method 1 (3.2.1) or Method 8 (3.2.8), that also involve higher interest rates, because different interest rates are in question. In fact, increasing an interest rate for one purpose can make another technique work less well. For example, if bank loan rates go up, so do bank deposit rates and so the attractiveness of government debt, falls relative to that of bank deposits. Hence, it has been argued that relative interest rates are more important for monetary policy than absolute levels (see problem A in 3.2.1). The UK government has manipulated relative interest rates so as to sell public sector debt – the famous 'Duke of York' strategy (Gowland,1990).

Other ways of making government securities more attractive have been used in the UK. Extensive advertising of national savings has been important. Indeed an evening watching television commercials or a visit to the local post office can be as revealing about techniques of monetary control as an analysis of the Bank *Bulletin*. Similarly, a number of marketing devices have been used to make gilts more attractive (see Gowland,1990). The most important device, however, has been indexation: the linking of both interest and capital repayments of some public sector securities to the retail price index. This has been used for both gilts and national savings. Its importance extends outside monetary control since it allows the personal sector to plan consumption over time without worrying about inflation (see p. 226). Friedman regards this as one of the key props of the Thatcher revolution(see p. 160). Indexation as a technique of control is analysed in Gowland (1990).

3.2.5   Quantity controls on non-bank purchases of public sector debt (Method 5)

If the authorities compel individual companies or institutions to purchase public sector debt, the money supply will be reduced in exactly the same way as if they had purchased it voluntarily. This monetary effect of a forced loan seems to have been the main reason why Keynes invented post-war credits. Otherwise, forced loans have had a bad press in the Anglo-Saxon world, being one of the ultimate 'bad things' in the words of *1066 and all that*. Richard II, Richard III, and Charles I all lost their thrones (and lives) partly because of imposing them. They are unconstitutional in the USA. Nevertheless, the Jenkins squeeze in the UK in 1968–1969 seems to have been in large part effective because of the forced loan effect of import deposits. Import deposits required those importing goods to deposit an amount equal to 50 per cent of their value (interest-free) for six months with the Bank of England. They are the only form of import control that is allowed by the Treaty of Rome and other EEC treaties. More generally, the technique of forced loans is used by the German and Belgian authorities, so perhaps the Anglo-Saxon prejudice is unjustified, although the author does not think so. In any case, all the problems of direct controls apply (see Section 3.4).

Debt management has raised three policy issues (Table 3.3): the first is the use of *national savings* as an instrument of economic policy. In the early 1970s national savings were trivial in size and, as the Page Report (1973) put it, regarded as a social service not an instrument of economic policy. Ironically it was only in the late 1970s that, for the first time for a generation, national savings did fulfil their social function of enabling small savers to transfer resources from one period of their life to another. Official attitudes first started to change in 1977. Mr Healey revived national savings as a tool of economic policy in that he sought to maximize their sales. This, however, was a blunt instrument in that the authorities felt that they had little control over the size or timing of sales. From 1980, however, the authorities started to 'fine tune' sales of national savings. They pursued a more vigorous marketing policy from September 1980 and started to offer an ever wider range of new types of security – both index-linked and orthodox, such as the income bond in 1982. The National Savings Bank started to offer competitive rates. The authorities felt that national savings could be used flexibly, by the timing of innovations and by varying NSB and national savings certificate terms. Indeed from 1980–1 onwards precise targets were set, although not revealed until the 1981 Budget when a 1981–2 target of £3 billion was announced. As the target was later raised to £3.5 billion the authorities apparently felt confident of their ability to fine-tune the level of sales, or perhaps that their real objective was still to maximize sales – certainly this is consistent with the out-turn of £4.2 billion. Targets of £3 billion were set for 1982–3 (and achieved, the out-turn was £2958m) and 1983–4. The only return to old habits was shown in late 1982 when national savings terms were altered with the blatant objective of influencing mortgage rates in the run-up to a general election rather than to achieve any level of debt sales. The use of national savings as a tool of monetary policy replete with explicit targets was important. As savings collapsed in the late 1980s national savings ceased to be of such relevance to monetary policy. The authorities sought to revive this technique in 1988–9, for example introducing the capital bond. In 1988–9 the authorities sought to maximize sales of national savings subject to the limits set by their second and somewhat strange policy: *exact funding*. This was a decision to restrict sales of gilt-edged to the non-bank private sector necessary to make the public sector's contribution to monetary growth equal to zero, that is PSBR plus net official intervention in the foreign exchange market. The deliberate forswearing of the use of an instrument of official policy was hard to justify.

There were two reasons: a device to avoid the commercial bill mountain (see below) and to avoid *crowding out*. Crowding out occurs when public sector (government) spending or borrowing leads to an unintended fall in private sector spending or borrowing. The authorities believed, however, not in the usual short-term crowding out but in a structural variant. The argument was that the corporate bond market had disappeared because of the widespread availability of gilts. The alternative explanation was that inflation was the reason. The issue is discussed at length in Gowland (1990) but Mr Lawson's views seem hard to justify.

3.2.6. Price effects on overseas impact (Method 6)

The overseas impact or influence on the money supply stems from two accounting anomalies. The first is that government (exchange equalization account) purchases and sales of foreign currency do not appear in the PSBR even though their monetary impact is the same. It is easy to see that if the government were to sell 12 000 francs to Barbara Jones to finance a skiing holiday in France the money supply would fall because of her payment of £1000 to the government just as if she had bought savings certificates. It is less easy to see that this is what is in effect happening when she buys the francs from her bank and the government intervenes in the foreign exchange market to sell francs to the bank. The overseas impact can also work through the banking system, a loan to a non-resident can create a deposit just as a loan to a resident can. If an American tourist borrowed from a UK bank to pay a hotel bill in York it is easy to see that the money supply may rise (Midland Bank York shows an extra (liability) deposit in the name of Crest Hotels and an extra asset, the tourist's indebtedness). In effect, the finance of international trade can produce the same result. In general a surplus on the balance of payments increases the money supply and *vice versa* (as with the gold standard: money flows in). To reduce the money supply by price means involves a higher exchange rate. This device seeks to induce a deterioration of the balance of payments (appropriately defined) in order to reduce the money supply so the intuitive idea is clear as in the analogous gold standard mechanism. Normally this technique means varying the exchange rate. Hence, Mr Healey let the exchange rate rise in November 1977 and his successor sought the rise in the exchange rate in 1979–80 as it would help control the money supply. This is highly controversial because of its alleged role in causing *deindustrialization*.

3.2.7 Quantity effects on the overseas impact (Method 7)

This technique uses exchange control or other quantity methods to improve the balance of payments and cause monetary expansion or to worsen it and facilitate contraction. Hence, the German and Swiss authorities have imposed inward exchange control to prevent capital flows that would lead to monetary expansion using devices like the Bardepot.[1] The House of Commons Treasury Committee recommended a similar scheme in the UK (Third Report, 1981). The UK government adopted the variant of removing outward exchange control in November 1979 to encourage capital outflows so as to influence money and, hence, inflation. From 1979–86, £100 billion of long-term capital outflows occurred; thereafter net outflows were small. This has also been controversial; for example it was a key Labour plank to partially reverse the policy in the 1987 election. It argued that the capital outflow had been at the expense of UK investment and so employment. Defenders of the policy point to its profitability and claim that, say, a factory in Korea is a complement to one in Llanelli (as with Amstrad), not a substitute. Can anyone, they further argue, really regard a villa in Spain as a replacement for one in Scarborough rather than for holidays abroad? 250 000 domestic properties abroad were purchased 1979–86, presumably some by the elderly (who *might* otherwise have moved to Scarborough?) Sometimes foreign investment does supplant expenditure in the UK and sometimes it increases it but the evidence is unclear.

3.2.8. Price effects on bank loans to the non-bank private sector (Method 8)

Bank loans create deposits. The only confusion is that it is a loan which creates money not any expenditure made with it – indeed the loan may be retained as a deposit as with a compensating balance.[2] With a personal loan or in the USA the loan is made by making an addition to the borrower's bank balance as with TSB's ubiquitous (1989) advert. With an overdraft the deposit is added to a third party's account at the borrower's request. Either way the result is the same: *every loan creates a deposit*. The interesting questions in banking theory concern why money creation does *not* take place, especially the new view versus old (reserve base) debate. The old view is that bank lending is constrained by a lack of reserves. The new view is that bank lending is determined by normal theory of the firm considerations – profit, market share etc. (see below).

There are three ways of controlling bank lending shown in Figure 3.1. In each case the market outcome moves from 1 to 2 and quantity from Q_1 to Q_2. The first method (3.2.8) is to increase the cost of bank loans from r_1 to r_2 and so reduce the demand for bank loans. The second method (3.2.9) is to override demand by rationing. Finally the reserve base system can be used to shift the supply curve (3.2.10).

The aim of this method is to reduce the level of the demand for bank credit below that at which it would otherwise have been by forcing up the rate of interest on borrowing from banks. This reduction in bank assets necessarily means that their liabilities are lower. This policy was, or was intended to be, the centrepiece

Figure 3.1 The control of bank credit

(a) Method 8

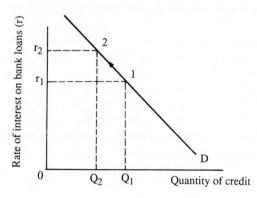

(b) Method 9

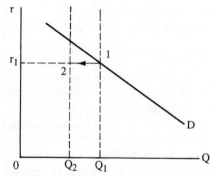

(c) Method 10

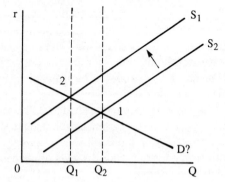

of the 'new approach' to *Competition and Credit Control* (Bank 1971) in the UK in 1971–1973. It has also been a key element of the Conservative government's policy from 1979.

In addition to the general problems with the use of price effects (see Section 3.3), there are a number of problems which apply peculiarly to using interest rates to control bank lending. The first is that there is no clear evidence that bank borrowing is interest-sensitive. Indeed a Bank of England research study suggested that it was not (Moore and Threadgold,1980). The next is that even if it is, the authorities have to react quickly to changing circumstances. Otherwise inflationary expectations can accelerate, thus lowering the real rate of interest and increasing the demand for credit. If the authorities then raise (nominal) rates, the increase is too late to do more than partially offset the fall in real rates. A vicious cycle can develop in which rising nominal rates fail to catch up with accelerating inflationary expectations. This problem occurred in 1973, 1979–80 and at the time of writing (September 1989) seems to be a problem again. Finally, the authorities' attempts to move along a demand curve may be offset by shifts of the curve. For example, in 1979–80 the authorities found that the demand for credit accelerated because the depression shifted the demand for credit function by more than enough to offset any interest rate effect.

3.2.9   Quantity controls on bank lending (Method 9)

Credit ceilings in various forms work in the same way as interest rates, it does not matter why bank lending changes; the monetary consequences are identical. They were widely used in the UK from 1952 to 1971 and have been endemic in France. They are subject to all the problems of direct controls discussed below – evasion, inefficiency, ineffectiveness, distortion of statistics, etc. The black markets that arose in the 1960s are discussed at length in Gowland (1979) pp.8–10.

3.2.10   The reserve base system (Method 10)

This is discussed in Section 3.4.

3.3   DIRECT CONTROLS IN MONETARY POLICY

In 1988 with inflation accelerating and a £15 billion balance of payments deficit, it was clear that either money or credit, or both, needed to be controlled. Moreover, since the PSBR was already in surplus and the government had ruled out the use of debt sales as an instrument of monetary policy, it followed that to control money it was necessary to control bank lending. Thus Keynesian and monetarists were agreed about *what* was necessary, but not about *why*. Many critics suggested that it would be either necessary or desirable to use quantity ceilings or other direct controls on credit but the Chancellor opted for the alternative of a rise in interest rates. This revived an old debate in UK monetary policy which raged throughout 1990. This section reviews the arguments for and against direct controls relative to interest rates.

3.3.1 Arguments against direct controls

1. Direct controls are ineffective
This argument follows directly from the standard proposition that rationing creates an incentive to evade the control (profitably!), that is a black market may emerge. Such evasion will frustrate the authorities' objectives. The most obvious relevant examples are the evasion of the ceilings on bank lending which led to the 'new approach' in 1971, and the erosion of the IBELS ceiling in 1978– 80 prior to its abandonment, see above. The simplest form of evasion involves the use of the overseas sector, and involves a loan (or credit card) from, say, Midland of Paris rather than Midland of York. Evasion is a serious problem with direct controls but with personal sector credit they could probably be effective *for a time*. Indeed this is at the heart of the debate. One group regards evasion as impossible; it is indeed hard to see the UK personal sector using such foreign-based banks, as distinct from their UK branches. However intermediaries or retailers might use foreign banks and on-lend the funds. Moreover, some of those borrowing for house purchase might borrow abroad and the 'anti' group would regard the impossibility of segregating mortgage and non-mortgage credit as critical. Mortgages are a political sacred cow and much personal credit used for other purposes is in practice disguised as a mortgage for tax purposes. Thus to ration credit to the personal sector effectively it is necessary to ration mortgages. In the past regulated building societies did this for the government, in 1974–5, for example. After the financial revolution the government would itself have to ration mortgages – a political non-starter.

2. Direct controls are inefficient
By definition, direct controls override allocation by the price mechanism. Any system of allocation other than by price leads to a (Pareto) inefficient allocation of resources, at least on certain assumptions.

3. Direct controls are inequitable
Since direct controls impede different groups in different ways, they are likely to be unfair. For example, in the UK in the 1960s established banks lost out to new institutions because the controls gave an unfair advantage to them. At the least, those who observe the regulations lose business to those who evade its

spirit. Moreover, UK institutions would tend to lose out to foreign ones: not the authorities' aim.

4. *Direct controls distort statistics*

This is probably the strongest argument against direct controls. No one will make a point of informing the authorities of a successful method of evading controls. Hence, the authorities will be unaware of the volume of black market transactions. Thus, they lack the information necessary for policy making. If the distorted money supply statistics show a level of £60 000 million and the optimal level is £65 000 million it is not clear whether policy is too slack or too tight because one does not know if the volume of black market transactions is more or less than £5 000 million. Moreover, direct controls in themselves cause structural changes which distort statistics (see p. 80). The last days of the IBELs ceiling in the UK in 1980 illustrate the problem vividly. The money supply grew 5 per cent in one month after the ceiling was removed. How much was genuine and how much cosmetic, the result of black market transactions merely re-entering official statistics? No one knows, yet the answer is vital to any assessment of monetary policy in 1979–80 or to the case for reintroducing controls in 1990. Even with hindsight, no one knows precisely what was happening. Distorted statistics make policy making much more difficult.

3.3.2 Arguments in favour of direct controls

1. *Direct controls enable the money supply to be controlled with lower interest rates*

If direct controls work, this is self-evident (see Figure 3.1) The objective may be sought for political or distributional reasons but there is also an economic case for it.

2. *Direct controls permit more stable interest rates*

This is also self-evident. The motive may be political but it can be justified on economic grounds. Stability is normally desirable in itself to facilitate better private sector decision making. However, greater certainty about the rate of interest may be offset, or more than offset, by less certainty about the availability of credit.

3. *Direct controls facilitate planning*

This argument is based largely on French experience; the authorities have used credit controls as an inducement to industry to conform to the targets set by indicative plans.

4. *Direct controls are biased towards investment*

If the debatable proposition that more investment is desirable is accepted, this is an argument for direct controls. The argument is often based on (sometimes casual) empiricism; consumer loan demand is less interest-sensitive than industrial demand. However, there is a sound theoretical case as well. The effect of higher interest rates on investment is clearly negative; the effect on consumption is ambiguous (see p. 226). It is, however, worth pointing out that it may be stock investment rather than fixed investment which is favoured.

5. *Interest rate changes are unfair to the building industry*

Most buildings are erected by builders who depend upon bank credit to finance their operations. Most buildings are purchased with the aid of loans (lovers of atrocious puns may note that a building provides concrete security). The nature of net present value calculations is such that the longer-lived an asset the more its desirability is affected by interest rate changes. Buildings have the longest lives of all assets.

3.3.3   Speculative conclusions

1.   To be effective monetary policy must hurt sometimes and no technique can avoid this. Political will, even ruthlessness, is necessary to make any system work. With this, any system can work – at a price.
2.   Given existing political constraints, and the highly laudable Anglo-Saxon commitment to liberalism, direct controls probably cannot work in the UK for very long. Evasion is too easy, as is exemplified and argued above. In addition, no direct control can be effective without exchange control.
3.   Direct controls may, however, have a role whenever the authorities make mistakes. A direct control seems to play a significant short-term role while it takes time for the effects of interest rates to work through. For example, the IBELs ceiling made it much easier to restrain monetary growth in May 1978 than in autumn 1989–90 when no effective direct control was available. So long as direct controls are used infrequently and for short periods, they will be effective because it is not worthwhile evading them; evasion is not costless.

An optimist would say that the above argument is invalid because it rests on an assumption of official fallibility. A cynic would argue that it is invalid because it ignores official fallibility; no politician will accept an infrequent short-term weapon. He will make it a frequently used, permanent weapon – and so render it useless. Whether a fallible but prudent official decision taker has existed, is, perhaps, a moot point but the theory is unchanged. Direct controls are relatively quick-acting, unlike interest rates, although their effect may wear off quickly. Nevertheless, for a short period, a direct control is likely to work, especially if used skilfully by the authorities. This may be invaluable if the authorities have got policy seriously wrong, as Mr Lawson had in 1988. In similar circumstances direct controls proved useful in 1974 and 1978, whereas their absence made the conduct of monetary policy very difficult in 1979–80 as well as in 1988–89.

This is the choice concerning direct controls on credit: the fast-acting instrument against the disadvantages of black markets.

3.4 RESERVE ASSET CONTROL

It is useful to start this section by emphasizing that one mechanism has not been used in the UK: the reserve base/minimum reserve ratio system, despite many elementary textbook statements to the contrary. There have been ratios in the UK; none have been designed, or could have worked, as a textbook reserve base system/minimum reserve ratio system, one in which, for example, the authorities impose a ratio of 20 per cent and changed the base by 1 so as to change the money supply by 5, or at least 4.5 or 5.5.

The evidence for this proposition is legion. Bagehot emphasized it in his classic *Lombard Street* (1873). Both the evidence to and the report of the Macmillan Committee stressed the point in the 1930s, with Keynes, Lord Norman, Mckenna, Bradbury and Ernest Bevin in unique agreement. Radcliffe confirmed the irrelevance of the textbook model. More recently the authorities have stressed the point. The Governor' s keynote speech introducing *Competition and Credit Control* could scarcely have been more explicit:

> It is not to be expected that the mechanism of minimum reserve ratio and special deposits can be used to achieve some precise multiple contraction or expansion of bank assets. Rather the intention is to use our control over liquidity, which these instruments will reinforce, to influence the structure of interest rates. The resulting change in relative rates of return will then induce shifts in the current portfolios of both the public and the banks. Bank (1971).

The Consultative Document produced by the Bank and the Treasury in 1980 stressed the same point once more;

> The RAR was never designed to serve as an officially controlled monetary base through which the pyramid of credit created by the banks might be directly limited. Instead, in conjunction with Special Deposits, the RAR was regarded as an element in the control of short term interest rates. (Page 7, see also Annex A.) Bank (1980).

There have been a variety of ratios in the UK, including the 11 per cent cash ratio in the 1920s, 8 per cent cash ratio, 28 and 30 per cent liquidity ratios, a 12.5 per cent reserve assets ratio after 1971 and (for the clearing banks) 1.5 per cent of liabilities held as balances with the Bank of England. A 0.5 per cent cash ratio for all banks replaced it for a while in the 1980s and now these are capital adequacy ratios, a ratio of own capital to deposits.[3] All have one thing in common, causality runs from loans to reserves. *With a textbook reserve ratio, causality runs from reserves to loans.* A bank makes a loan when, but only when, it acquires extra reserves. This leads to the credit multiplier story. The alternative is the 'new view': *loans create reserves.* The slogan of this school is that banks should be analysed in the same way as other firms. Their decision about the volume of loans – output – will depend upon profit or sales maximization and so on marginal revenue, marginal cost, risk and so on. If a loan involves extra reserves these will be obtained and the cost treated approximately – in this view a reserve asset ratio is a tax on banking.

Thus, the new view of banking presents an alternative constraint on banks loans – profitability, instead of reserves. It usually assumes liability management, to use banking terminology, instead of the asset management assumed by the old view, see Gowland (1985). In the case of *asset management* a bank takes deposits as given and decides what to do with them – in the simplistic reserve base world it loans a fixed proportion and retains the rest as reserves. With *liability management* a bank decides on its asset portfolio and then obtains the necessary deposits. Of course the new view assumes that when a bank wants to it can obtain reserve assets, albeit at a price. In the UK this has always been the case; and the cost low. It is possible to argue that an individual bank can always obtain the reserve assets it needs, but the system as a whole cannot. Hence Milton Friedman, for example, would use the new view to analyse an individual bank but the old view to analyse the banking system.

It is straightforward (see appendix) to derive an identity linking the money supply to the reserve asset ratio banks' holdings of reserves and the private sector's cash: deposits ratio – the ubiquitous ratios equation. This relationship need not bear an economic interpretation. Indeed it can be absurd: a similar equation links the number of sardines eaten in York (S) to national income (Y)

$$Y = S.R.$$

where R equals Y/S, the sardine ratio. As Goodhart (1984) puts it;

> However, in order to use such an approach to explain variations in the larger total as contrasted with describing such movements, which definitional multiplier however ridiculous, can always do, some further conditions are necessary...If it is necessary to specify the structure of the system in order to understand why the multiplier works as it does, it is difficult to see what advantage is to be gained by using it as an analytical tool in the first place (pp. 132 and 133).

Figure 3.2   Money base control

(a)

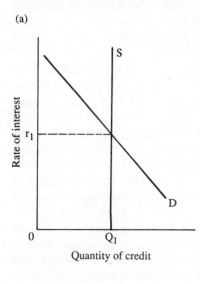

(b)

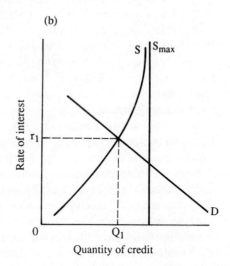

(c)

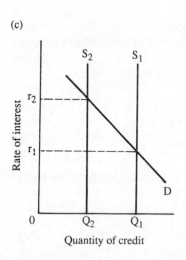

(d)

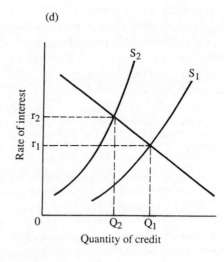

This is usually done by interpreting the ratios equation as a supply of credit function. If a bank behaves according to the credit multiplier story the supply of credit is inelastic and equal to the reserve bases times the reciprocal of the credit multiplier less one (with a reserve ratio of 20 per cent, the supply of credit is four times the quantity of reserves), see Figure 3.2 (a).

This inelastic supply of credit seems unrealistic so the next change in the model is to assume that banks hold excess reserves but that the quantity falls as interest rates rise. A bank chooses to hold excess reserves so as to satisfy customers who may come along or to operate overdrafts where customers initiate loans. If a bank holds no excess reserves it cannot respond to extra reserves nor can it offer overdrafts. However, the cost of holding reserves is not making loans so the cost rises as interest rates rise. In this case, the reserve ratio and the quantity of reserve assets determine a maximum value of credit, shown as S_{max} in Figure 3.2(b). The actual supply curve (S) is upward sloping and is asymptotic to S_{max}. The distance S–S_{max} is equal to the volume of loans not made, excess reserves times the reserve ratio. The 'new view of money' of Tobin draws an upward supply curve on *a priori* grounds and ignores all the preliminaries. The author is an advocate of the 'new view' but for a defence of the 'multiplier approach' see Coghlan (1980). It has recently been argued that banks may *increase* their loans if a reserve ratio is imposed; a reserve ratio reduces bank profits and bank respond by making more riskier loans – see, for example, Di Cagno (1990).

In the reserve base system, the authorities seek to shift the supply curve for credit, as shown in Figures 3.2(c) and 3.2(d) so as to change the quantity of credit in order to change the money supply.

An element of the case against reserve base control is that when S_{max} is changed there is no reason why the shift in the actual supply of credit should be even predictable, let alone parallel or of equivalent size.

The extent of the divergence of opinion about the reserve base system can be seen in the following quotations:

> A determined control of the monetary base, technically achievable by any central bank, is sufficient (and necessary) to ensure that no monetary aggregates can run away. (Brunner, 1981)

> This approach [monetary base control] therefore is intended to provide a means for the markets to generate the interest rates necessary [to control the money supply]. (Bank, 1980)

The Bank views the reserve base system merely as a means of adjusting interest rates, 'an interest rate control in disguise' as Lewis put it (1980), in contrast to Brunner (and Friedman) who regard it as a genuine alternative.

The Bank's argument against reserve base control can be divided into two propositions (see Bank, 1980 and Foot *et al.*, 1979):

1. At best reserve base control is the same as interest rate control.
2. In fact it is likely to be ineffective and may suffer all the problems of direct controls.

However, they concede

3. That movements in bank portfolios may act as a signal which conveys information on the basis of which the authorities may act.

1. *Base control is, at best, the same as interest rate control*

This argument can be examined best in the context of Figures 3.2(c) and 3.2(d) The effect on the money supply obtained by shifting the supply curve from S_1 to S_2 is exactly the same as, and could have been achieved by, increasing interest rates from r_1 to r_2. In the Bank's view, reserve base control is merely a means of changing interest rates. Friedman, on the other hand, accepts that reserve base control involves a change in rates but denies both that this causes the change in money and that there is a definite relationship between the change in money and that in interest rates.

Moreover, the Bank stresses the unpredictability of the shift in the supply curve in response to changes in the quantity of base assets. However, as argued in Gowland (1982–1990), if there is not perfect knowledge of the demand curve for credit, base control may lead to more certain control of money at the cost of greater variability in interest rates. It is, however, *possible* that a reserve base system could be manipulated so as to produce less variability in rates.

To summarize, the Bank argues that the authorities can move along a demand curve (for credit) more easily by changing prices than by shifting the supply curve. Brunner and Friedman argue the opposite.

2. *Base control will be ineffective*

The Bank's basic proposition is that base control is another direct control and so it is subject to evasion, inefficiency and inequity, and likely to distort statistics and so on. Basically, this is true but one crucial distinction must be noted. Direct controls, like ceilings, put a limit on each bank. The reserve base system places the limit on the banking system as a whole so banks can compete with each other for base assets. This means that in some respects the system is a half-way house between price and quantity controls. The Bank would no doubt argue, with much justice, that it combines the worst of both worlds. There are many ways in which a reserve base system can be evaded. One obvious method, also used to evade the IBELs ceiling, that some banks appear to have implemented, is to book banking transactions overseas (see p. 80). However a bank makes a loan. A loan in, say, Hong Kong dollars in Dubai is the same as a loan in sterling in London so long as the transaction can be covered by a (forward) purchase of Hong Kong dollars.

However, the bank has moved its assets outside the purview of UK monetary control. The bank can also transfer its deposits to a foreign branch. All negotiations could take place in London but the transactions would appear in the bank's books in, say, Paris (p. 80). Thus reserve base requirements would be evaded. This happened on a large scale in the 1960s to evade US reserve requirements. It is clear that such transactions would lead to both evasion and distortion of statistics. Without exchange control, reserve base control could not operate in the UK.

This danger of evasion is the main argument, to me at least, in the case against reserve base control but there are other problems. For example, it is probably impossible to combine the overdraft system with a reserve base system. Banks under a reserve base system cannot let customers have discretion about indebtedness, unless the customer pays a price equivalent to that for a loan.

In 1980 the Bank reaffirmed the position it took at the time of the *new approach* in 1971: money can be controlled only by interest rates. Any other method of control, whether by means of a ceiling or a reserve base system, can only operate if, and inasmuch as, it influences interest rates. These other methods of control are likely to produce distortion of official statistics and so render an effective monetary policy impossible. Moreover, it is probable that they will be evaded and they are likely to be inequitable and inefficient both because of misallocation of resources and the wasteful expenditure that takes place on evasion. Finally, the Bank stresses that there is a choice between interest rate stability and stability in monetary growth.

This position is intellectually impeccable but depends on:

1. There being a stable, interest elastic demand for credit, for which the authorities possess knowledge of the parameters. Moore and Threadgold (1980) re-emphasized the doubt about this.
2. The authorities having the political will to raise interest rates to the required level when necessary.
3. The authorities having the knowledge and the will to adjust interest rates quickly enough. Delay may be disastrous for the reasons discussed above: 1988 again is relevant.

Doubt may be expressed on all of the Bank's three points as in Pepper's Mais lecture. The implications are that a satisfactory method of monetary control does not, and perhaps cannot, exist in the UK.

3.5   MONETARY CONTROL IN PRACTICE

The purpose of this section is to examine two issues in the day-to-day conduct of monetary policy:

a.   the commercial bill mountain
b.   the 1981 reforms in day-to-day operations in short-term money markets

3.5.1   The commercial bill mountain

The principal change in the period was the growth of the commercial bill market and the Bank's enormous purchases of them – £87 billion gross in the year to October 1982 (by comparison they had been trivial in previous years, for example £50 million in 1977–8). The commercial bill market had been growing fast for a number of reasons. One had been the use of bills as a means of circumventing lending ceilings as bank lending in the 1960s and, more importantly, the IBELs ceiling in the late 1970s and financial innovation more generally (see Chapter 4).   The Bank's deliberate decision to use the market as a vehicle for its operations in preference to the overnight inter-bank market was also important.

The role of 'over-funding' is however crucial. When non-bank private lending to the public sector exceeds the PSBR, the non-bank private sector is a net payer of funds to the public sector. This debt can be settled by a reduction in currency holdings or by cheque in which case bank liabilities (the payer's deposit) and assets (their claims on the public sector) fall – a process described in detail above. Indeed, this is one of the primary causes of changes in the money supply. However, the operation does present certain technical difficulties when one examines which claims on the public sector the banks cease to hold. The logical possibilities are cash, Treasury Bills or gilt-edged securities. Cash holdings, whether in terms of currency or central bank deposits, were far too small and in any case a major fall in bank holdings of cash would cause massive disruption to the operations of banking. Indeed it would make it impossible for banks to function in their normal fashion and such disruption would be undesirable for both long-term structural and short-term monetary control considerations. Indeed the Bank had promised not to create or permit such a squeeze. The normal response would have to reduce the banking sector's holdings of Treasury Bills. However, these were too small – at the start of 1981–2 bank and discount house holdings of Treasury Bills were only £1 billion whereas in 1981–2 'over-funding' was over £2500 million. Moreover other factors increased the net drain on banks' holdings of public sector assets to £4.75 billion (for example, increased currency holdings by the non-bank private sector). This could not have been met even by the elimination of the entire stock of Treasury Bills. Moreover even if sufficient this would have been very undesirable as it would have reduced official leverage in short-term money markets and administered an unnecessary and unpredictable shock to the banking system. Hence the authorities chose to purchase private sector assets from the banks, commercial bills. To summarize, the normal effect of a purchase of public sector debt by the non-bank private sector is a fall in the money supply accompanied by a fall in bank claims on the public sector. Instead the process led to a fall in bank claims on the private sector.

The logic of this process is obvious but the scale was incredible. The authorities at one point held over £10 billion of commercial bills. In the circumstances it is difficult to conceive of an alternative that was practicable in the short term, given the scale of bank lending if monetary growth was to be restrained to any reasonable figure. It is possible to devise schemes involving the overseas sector but the consequences are incalculable and certainly even more risky than the acquisition of a bill mountain. Yet, however inevitable, the policy was not liked by the authorities or indeed by anyone else. It is not clear if there were genuine reasons for this distaste – it was inconvenient but perhaps no more. The root of the problem stems from the corporate sector's desire to borrow being satisfied with loans whose matching asset was a bank deposit. If instead the company had borrowed directly from the personal sector or the claim had been intermediated by a non-bank, the problem would not have occurred. The authorities, logically enough, therefore sought to encourage the growth of the commercial bond market so as to achieve this end (see p. 50, for example) by exact funding. The problem recurred throughout the 1980s and was used as an argument against the use of debt management to restrain monetary growth.

3.5.2 The 1981 reforms

On 24 November 1980 Sir Geoffrey Howe produced the monetary policy equivalent of a Budget, which introduced some longer-term, more tentative measures. More measures, many of which confirmed the November package, followed in his Budget on 10 March 1981. Further changes followed culminating in the abolition of minimum lending rate on 20 August 1981. Bank of England policy and tactics in short-term financial markets were the subject of considerable change in the 1980s because of two distinct factors. The reforms represented a continuation of the Bank's desire for a flexible, depoliticized intervention rate which had motivated the move from Bank rate to minimum lending rate (MLR) in 1972 and from MLR mark 1 to MLR mark 2 in 1978 (see Gowland, 1990). Their ideal would be for interest rate changes to be viewed as technical operations not as major acts of economic policy.

In the 1950s the authorities had welcomed the publicity surrounding a change in Bank rate because they relied heavily on 'announcement effects' as a tool of policy, the fanfare was felt to be counter-productive in the 1970s. The authorities occasionally welcomed ballyhoo in the 1980s: in 1989 (*Daily Telegraph* 8 September) and when MLR was temporarily re-introduced in 1985. Instead the Bank wanted a world in which changes in its dealing rate, whatever the name, had the same newspaper coverage as Australian rules football results – and were similarly ignored by all but a tiny band of devotees. To a considerable extent these goals were achieved. Changes in the intervention rate were frequent and never received the banner headlines of old. It would seem that political constraints on dealings were also lessened. Nevertheless, caution has to be used in any comparison of new and old systems in that more information is available about the new regime. It is possible that the old system was more flexible than it seemed, especially as the Bank could make the penalty rate as lender of last resort exceed MLR. However, the new system seemed to work more smoothly in the eyes of observers as well as participants.

The Bank certainly obtained more freedom in regard to the other objectives of the reforms; the price/quantity dilemma. Basically the 'lender of last resort' is a monopolist lending money to the banking system, usually in the UK, via the discount market, either by buying securities or making loans.[4] The new system involved less emphasis on loans against the security of bills and more on purchasing them, but the change is of no economic significance. The Bank faces a downward sloping demand curve, Figure 3.3(a). According to the elementary textbook it can choose either price or quantity but not both. Nevertheless the choice of either automatically determines the other. Hence it would not matter in Figure 3.3(a) whether the authorities announced a willingness to lend q_1 or to lend at a rate of r_1. However, in the real world the demand curve is not known with certainty, as in Figure 3.3(b), which illustrates the simple case of two demand curves with equal probability. The stochastic element may be state-contingent, for example D_1 might apply if the exchange rate were \$1.60, D_2 if it were \$1.55. Alternatively it might be purely random and D_1 would be the case on some days and D_2 on others. The problem is that on any day in advance the authorities do not know which will apply and can only operate on the basis of the expected demand curve D, the average of the other two. Traditional Bank policy was to fix the interest rate and allow quantity to be market-determined. Hence in Figure 3.3(b) the rate would be fixed at r_D, implying that q_D was the preferred quantity. Nevertheless, the actual quantity would be q_1 or q_2 depending on which demand curve was operative.

Griffiths (currently the head of Mrs Thatcher's Policy Unit) in a witty sally, said that this was being a lender of first resort rather than of last resort. This criticism in substance uses the same as Friedman's critique of the Federal Reserve. It has two elements: that the authorities should care much more about quantity than price, and that the implicit perfectly elastic supply cure encouraged undesirable bank behaviour. His preferred system, like that of Friedman and most other monetarists, is illustrated in Figure 3.3(c). The authorities fix the

Figure 3.3   Lender of last resort

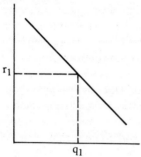

(a) Theory

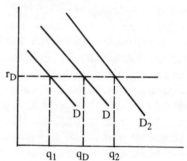

(b) Bank pre−1981

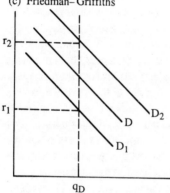

(c) Friedman−Griffiths

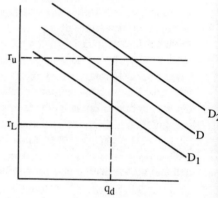

(d) Federal Reserve policy

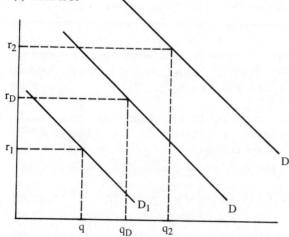

(e) Bank 1981−

quantity at q_D and let the price fluctuate according to which demand curve is operative. Other possibilities include that sometimes practised by the Federal Reserve before November 1979 (Figure 3.3(d)). They determined a target range for r (the Federal Reserve funds rate) and fixed quantity within this range so the implicit supply curve is stepped (with r_u and r_L the limits of the range).[5]

The Bank responded to the critics and sought its own goal of maximum flexibility in two ways. One involved categorizing securities according to the time remaining to maturity. The resulting categories were called bands – band 1 being less than 14 days, band 2, 15–33 days and so on up to band 4, 64–91 days. The Bank stated that it possessed the right to refuse purchase or lend against bills at any price. In American parlance it might 'close the window' and so the certainty of obtaining funds which had been the object of Griffiths's and his allies' critique disappeared. The other was not to name its price until it had elicited information from the discount houses about their desired borrowing. In effect, as illustrated in Figure 3.3(e) the Bank waited until it knew the demand curve prevailing and then allowed both price and quantity to diverge from the optimal level, but price by less than the monetarist solution and quantity by less than the old Bank method. In practice, the system is made more complex still by having two rounds of dealing. Price is fixed after the first so the Bank has not complete information about demand but it has much more than in other systems.

3.6 CONCLUSION

There are many instruments of financial policy but all have their disadvantages. The theoretically most appealing is interest rates but both practical and political considerations make it less than perfect in reality. Alternatives – reserve base or direct control – are likely to run into the black market problem. Hence, one of many consequences is that the UK is reluctant to join the EMS. Not only has the exchange rate been managed to stabilize inflation (*Economist*, 9–15 September 1989) but to maintain fixed exchange rates macroeconomic instruments have to be used since intervention in the foreign exchange market by itself is insufficient. All possibilities examined in this chapter look dubious.

GUIDE TO FURTHER READING

This chapter is intended to replace Gowland (1979) Chapter 1 and (1983) Chapter 1. Nevertheless both chapters contain much material not included here. Those who already possess one or the other should, I hope, still find them useful complements to this chapter. My views and approach can be found in Gowland (1990). Bank (1984) is essential for anyone interested in UK monetary policy.

There are a number of studies of UK monetary control in the UK – see the bibliography in Gowland (1990) – of which Artis and Lewis (1981, new edition promised) and Congdon (1982) are the most useful. Goodhart (1984) is the best of more advanced studies).

NOTES

1. The Bardepot was a law requiring those borrowing or accepting deposits from non-residents to lodge the proceeds with the Bundesbank at a negative rate of interest.
2. When borrowing from a US bank it is a normal requirement to lodge 20–40 per cent of the loan interest-free with the lending bank. This is called a compensating balance. This is partly tradition but does permit evasion of usury laws (a 10 per cent interest rate with a 50 per cent compensating balance equals a 20 per cent effective rate) and price discrimination (all pay the same rate but with varying compensating balances).
3. Banks have two sources of funds: deposits and 'non-deposit liabilities'. The latter comprise equity, including retained profits, and fixed-interest capital: bonds, preference shares etc. A capital adequacy ratio places a minimum on the latter as a percentage of gross assets and so a maximum on the ratio of deposits to gross assets. For methods of calculation and problems see Gowland (1990).
4. The Bank normally deals only with the discount houses in terms of number of deals. However its relatively infrequent (perhaps ten per annum) deals with the clearing banks are as large in quantity.
5. Shone (1984) p102 uses this diagram to illustrate the UK. This is at best an over-simplification.

REFERENCES

Artis M. J. and Lewis M. K. (1981), *Monetary Control in the United Kingdom*, Philip Allan, Oxford.

Bagehot (1965), Lombard Street, reprinted in *Collected Works, The Economist*.

Bank (1971), *Competition and Credit Control*, Bank of England, London.

Bank (1980), *Monetary Control:A Consultation Paper by H. M. Treasury and the Bank of England*, HMSO. Cmnd 7858, London.

Bank of England (1984), *The Development of Monetary Policy*, Oxford University Press, Oxford.

Bishop M. and Kay J. (1988), *Does Privatization Work?* London Business School, London.

Brunner K. (1981), 'Monetary Policy', *Lloyds Bank Review*, no. 139, (January) 1.

Coghlan R. T. (1980), *Theory of Money and Finance*, Macmillan.

Congdon T. (1982), *Monetary Control in Britain*, Macmillan, London.

Di Cagno D. (1990), *The Regulation of Banks*, Dartmouth, Aldershot.

Feinstein C.H. (1983) (ed.) *The Managed Economy*, Oxford University Press, Oxford.

Goodhart, C.A.E. (1984), *Monetary Theory and Practice*, Macmillan, London.

Gowland, D.H. (1979), *Modern Economic Analysis*, Butterworths, London.

Gowland, D.H. (1982), *Controlling the Money Supply*, Croom Helm, Beckenham, (2nd edn 1984).

Gowland, D.H. (1983), *Modern Economic Analysis 2*, Butterworths, London.

Gowland, D.H. (1990), *Monetary Control in Theory and Practice*, Routledge, London.

Gowland D.H. (1990) *The Regulation of Financial Markets in the 1990s*, Edward Elgar, Aldershot.

Lewis M. (1980), 'Is Monetary Base Control Just Interest Rate *Control* in Disguise?', *Banker* (September) p. 35.

Moore B. J. and Threadgold A. R. (1980), 'Bank Lending and the Money Supply', *Bank of England Discussion Paper No. 10* (July).

Pepper, G.T. (1990), *Money, Credit and Inflation,* Research Monograph No. 44, IEA, London.

Sayers, R.S. (1983), '1941: The First Keynesian Budget' in Feinstein (1983). (This chapter reprints part of *Financial Policy 1838–1945*, Oxford 1956.)

Shone R. (1984), *Issues in Macroeconomics,* Martin Robertson, Oxford.

APPENDIX: THE RATIOS EQUATION

Money (M)	=	Deposits + Currency	(3.1)
Currency	=	eM	(3.2)

It is assumed that the private sector holds a fixed fraction of its money balances as currency (e) and as deposits as (1–e)

Reserves	=	Z deposits	(3.3)

Banks are required to hold at least an amount equal to a fraction Z of their deposits (usually expressed as a percentage, if this were 20 per cent Z would be $\frac{1}{5}$).

If banks are short-run profit maximizers they hold no excess reserves, hence

$$\text{Reserves} = Z \text{ deposits} \qquad (3.4)$$

So

$$\text{Deposits} = \frac{\text{Reserves}}{Z} \qquad (3.5)$$

If (3.5) and (3.2) are substituted into (3.1)

$$M = eM + \frac{\text{Reserves}}{Z}$$

So

$$M - eM = \frac{\text{Reserves}}{Z}$$

So

$$M(1-e) = \frac{\text{Reserves}}{Z}$$

So

$$M = \frac{\text{Reserves}}{Z(1-e)}$$

This is the usual form of the ratios equation.

4. The Financial Revolution

D. H. Gowland

4.1 INTRODUCTION

Financial markets have been much more widely publicized in the 1980s and have assumed a larger role in popular culture than in any previous period with the possible exception of the late 1920s and the early eighteenth century.[1] There are a number of reasons for this focus of attention on a traditional Cinderella area of little interest or concern to any save a handful of *afficionados* and practitioners. One is the dramatic nature of events in financial markets, especially on the world's stock markets: the great bull market or the 1980s and the dramatic collapse of 'Black Monday' (19 October 1987). The gyrations of foreign exchange markets no doubt helped to concentrate the thoughts of media and the policy community on financial topics.

A second factor is, however, more important. This is what is often called the 'sleaze factor' – a number of well publicized scandals in both the USA and the UK.[2] Politicians and the media both felt genuine indignation and saw an opportunity to make political capital and sell newspapers. These scandals were a partial cause of a third factor: the introduction of new regulatory regimes in many countries, especially the UK; but also the USA, France, Australia and Japan.[3] In the UK this involved eight Acts of Parliament;[4] and a total of regulations, codes etc. which allegedly required over one mile of shelving to hold them. Even this new code has been the subject of much controversy and is in the process of being amended.[5] Further regulatory change has come from the European Community's move towards a single internal market, for example the second banking directive of 13 January 1988.[6] Regulatory change has been important for many reasons, one of which is that deregulation was a crucial element in both Thatcherism and the parallel American Reaganomics – that is the philosophy and policies of the right-wing governments which have transformed the two countries (for good or ill) to an extent rarely achieved by any government. Financial markets have been the theatre of much of deregulation; hence the effects of the new regulatory regimes have been viewed as litmus tests for the success of the neoliberalism of Mrs Thatcher and Presidents Reagan and Bush.

A further reason for the regulatory change has been the changes which have occurred in financial markets, notably internationalization – that is a tendency for financial markets in different countries to merge into a single international market (see p. 88). This has led regulators to collaborate and consider joint or common regulations such as the G10 banking accord.[7] Indeed change in financial markets has been another reason for the increased attention paid to them. Of such changes none was more publicized than the 'big bang'[8] in the UK on 27 October 1986. 'Big bang' was a series of reforms to stock exchange practice (and parallel but independent changes to the gilt-edged market. It had a number of causes but the initiating cause was an investigation into the (then London) Stock Exchange by the Office of Fair Trading who wished to take the Stock Exchange to the Restrictive Practices Court. The then Secretary of State for Trade and Industry (Mr Cecil Parkinson) negotiated a compromise which led to 'big bang' rather than a court-ordered restructuring. Big bang's elements were:

1. The abolition of minimum commissions, that is, the abolition of a price-fixing cartel of the sort analysed in elementary economics textbooks.
2. Conditional free entry. Previously only individuals and partnerships could act on the stock exchange, and could not also act as, for example, banks. In addition entry was only possible if a seat were bought from some existing member. After 'big bang' anyone – such as a bank – could set up as or own a stockbroker so long as he met certain conditions, minimum wealth, solvency etc.
3. The abolition of 'single capacity' – stock exchange firms previously had to choose to be 'brokers' or 'jobbers' (wholesalers or market makers). Private individuals and financial institutions alike – indeed all investors could only deal via a broker who was supposed to act only as an agent and not 'to take a position' (hold shares or go short; that is sell shares he did not own in the hope of buying them back at a lower price before he had to deliver them). The broker bought shares from or sold them to a jobber; a wholesaler who was allowed to take a position. After 'big bang' Stock Exchange firms were either agency brokers (like the old brokers except that they could take positions) or market makers, who combined the roles of the old jobber and broker. A market maker is supposed to quote continuous prices in the stocks he market makes. In theory investors can observe his prices and know that they can trade at these prices. Hence he has both to hold an inventory of stocks and have sufficient liquid funds to meet market sales. A particular feature of the (London) International Stock Exchange is that it incorporates competitive market makers in contrast to New York. In New York a market maker, called a specialist, has a monopoly in market making in a particular stock or stocks. In London, several market makers act as wholesalers in the same share, at least in leading (alpha) shares. Before 'big bang' there were thirteen jobbers, in September 1989 31 equity market makers. Problems have arisen with market making, especially around Black Monday.[9] In 1988

it seemed that the International (formerly London) Stock Exchange (ISE) might cease to be a single integrated market after Barclays de Zoete Webb (followed by other market makers) reduced the number of shares in which they were prepared to deal at the publicly quoted price. Instead all large (over 1000) share deals would be by negotiation. Arbitrage between market makers was to be eliminated, by BZW's express desire. Hence the economist's device to preserve a single market would cease to exist. The ISE inspired a series of studies. These provided a fascinating series of insights into the problems of defining the objectives of a stock exchange (such as cheap dealing, prices that reflect the true value of shares, equal treatment of all investors, services to industry). These objectives were inevitably in conflict. After contemplating these, the ISE introduced a series of devices on 15 February 1988 designed to maintain a single market, notably a right for a market maker to refuse to deal with other market makers.

4. A new electronic settlement and dealing system rather than 'pit' or floor trading, where agents make deals verbally, literally by shouting at each other. The advantage of electronic dealing is in producing records which are available to regulators and other dealers rather than to the participants. In 1988, the new system was under considerable pressure and a lot of dealing switched to telephonic trading.

The objective of this chapter is analytical, not descriptive. It is rather pointless to describe changes in financial markets since the description will be out of date before the description is read – as happened even with the authoritative Cross Report (1986). Section 4.2 analyses three myths about change in financial markets. Section 4.3 analyses the cause of change in financial markets. Section 4.4 examines the nature of change in financial markets and section 4.5 the implications of such change. An appendix provides some descriptive material.

4.2 THREE MYTHS

4.2.1 The Myth of the Cashless Society

Media features often talk about a 'cashless society' as a likely consequence of financial innovation or at least as a useful guide to the direction of change. Instead they should talk about a chequeless society. Cheques are expensive to produce and process; on average every cheque written costs the banking system about £1 to print, transport several times and process. The bank's customers often pay nothing for this facility, at least at the margin, and even those who do pay a price below cost (typically 50p for business customers and 35p for any personal customers who have to pay, usually because of having an overdraft).

Hence banks are understandably anxious to reduce the number of cheques written by almost any means – credit cards, debit cards or even cash. Banks, of course, recoup their losses in other ways; traditionally by the 'endowment' profit derived from the use of current accounts on which they did not pay interest. However these profits are rapidly disappearing, especially with the introduction of interest-bearing current accounts – a slow process which accelerated in 1989.[10] Moreover, even if they were not, it would still be in the interest of banks to eliminate a loss-making service. The alternative – of charging an economic price – would meet apparently insurmountable consumer resistance.

Cash, on the other hand, is an economically viable and very cheap method of settling small transactions. It is unlikely ever to be supplanted for bus fares, buying drinks in pubs and a myriad of other low-value (but high-frequency) transactions. The transaction costs involved with cash are all proportional to the amount spent (transport, bank charges etc.). All alternatives have a significant fixed-cost element; indeed usually resource-transaction costs depend only on the number of transactions, however they are charged for. Hence it is logical to use cash for small but not large transactions. The Chairman of one of the big four banks joked that if it did not already exist cash would have to be invented and Consumer-Anonymous Settlement by Hand would be hailed as a technological wonder. Certainly the use of cash has been encouraged by technological change; notably the invention of the cash machine (automated teller machine, ATM). The greater ease of obtaining money at any time from a 'hole in the wall' has encouraged its wider use. It may be that the UK is moving towards the position in the USA where cash and (credit) cards are normally used but cheques are relatively rare.

4.2.2   The Myth of Technology

It is not an oversimplification to say that the popular media inextricably link technology and financial innovation with the image of the Porsche-owning gun slinger sitting in front of a computer screen. In fact, technology has been relatively unimportant in changing financial products and it is necessary to be very precise about what its role has been and will be. An important form of financial innovation has been the imitation of financial products in another country. For example, mortgages in the UK have traditionally been variable-rate, that is the interest paid by the borrower varies in line with market rates over the life of the mortgage. In the USA they were always fixed-rate until the 1980s, that is the interest rate paid by the borrower was fixed when the mortgage was taken out and remained constant whatever happened thereafter to short-term interest rates. In the 1980s variable-rate mortgages were introduced into the USA and were hailed as a major innovation taking over 35 per cent of the market in five years. At the same time, fixed-rate mortgages were introduced in the UK, but with a smaller effect. Clearly this exchange was desirable in that it extended consumer choice in both countries. However, it was obviously independent of technology; either country could have copied the other in 1930 just as well as in 1980.

Similar considerations apply to financial firms entering each other's markets. Until 1980 building societies offered mortgages but not cheque books, whereas banks offered cheque books but not mortgages (in both cases there were a few exceptions). Since then each has invaded the other's market but obviously this was not dependent on technology: banks could have offered mortgages if they had wished and been allowed to in 1880 instead of 1980. Some financial innovation involves retrogression in that it involves the revival of a technique used in the past and since largely abandoned – for example the bill of exchange. In other cases genuine innovation has been independent of technology. This is well illustrated in the field of personal financial services. A good example of product innovation is the credit card, perhaps the most important of all financial innovations in the UK since its introduction in 1967. It required only one technological condition: that most shops etc. should have telephones – as was the case in London in 1910 and the provinces in1925. However, the credit card itself was not introduced for about another half century.

Most technological change has done something cheaper, faster or with less labour, that is, it has been *process innovation* rather than *product innovation*. A good example of technological change is the electronic processing of cheques, now embodied in CHAPS – clearing house automated payment system. It has been calculated that 220,000 more bank clerks would be required in the UK if this had not been introduced (Johnson, 1988). However it has not affected the consumer product at all – the method of writing a cheque and time to clear it are the same as in 1889. Similarly there were large-scale changes in credit card technology in the later 1980s but these had little effect on the consumer. In many cases hi-tech products have had little impact,such as EFTPOS – electronic fund transfer at point of sale (who wants to have their bank account debited at once if they can have six weeks' free credit with an Access card?). Such developments may eventually catch on but as Christopher Fildes (the *Daily Telegraph's* witty commentator) put it, EFTPOS is always five years in the future and has been for the last twenty. Credit card companies are becoming unhappy with the number of customers (about half) who use them to obtain free credit and then pay off the entire balance. In consequence this and the MMC report on credit cards (August 1989) will make the use of credit cards less attractive as means of payment and less usurious as a means of borrowing. This *may* make EFTPOS more attractive but I am still doubtful.

A good illustration of the process/product innovation dichotomy is on trading exchange. Those dealing in established products, like the International Stock Exchange, have introduced electronic dealing – although it may not survive. Those dealing in new products use floor or pit trading – for example LIFFE, the

London International Financial Futures Exchange. Here there has been pressure to introduce electronic trading but it has largely emanated from the regulators. Official bodies charged with supervising a market prefer electronic trading because it automatically generates a complete record of all transactions.

Thus the role of technology in process innovation has been crucial and in product innovation of secondary importance, although some product innovation has been dependent on technology for example ATMs (cash machines). However, there is an important intermediate category - where technology has reduced the price of something previously feasible to such an extent that it is almost as if it were a new product. The most important example of this is in pricing 'derivative' or 'synthetic' products – those where price is calculated from two or more other products; options, see Section 4.4, are the most important example of this. Thus, if apples are on sale in Leeds, but not in York, then a synthetic price of apples in York can be calculated from the price in Leeds and transport costs. In financial markets synthetic prices usually involve changing either the currency or the time of delivery. If Shell shares are quoted in pounds a synthetic price can be calculated in, say, Spanish pesetas – by multiplying the price in pounds by the pound–peseta exchange rate. Similarly if someone wants to buy Shell shares today for delivery in 1992 I can calculate a price for this (today's price plus the interest foregone by holding the shares until the delivery date). Many synthetic contracts involve not one but hundreds of calculations. These would have been calculable by hand machines or even pencil and paper but might have taken 15 minutes. A computer can work them out in 15 seconds. Markets in such products have mushroomed in the 1980s.

This may reflect a greater availability of such products through technology (supply curve shift) or a greater demand for them, due for example to exchange rate volatility (demand curve shift). It may be purely fashion especially as computerization can glamorize the most humdrum transaction.

4.2.3   The Myth of the Financial Revolution

Despite the use of the term *financial revolution* as the title of this chapter it can be misleading. Financial markets have always changed. Many of the phenomena analysed in this chapter began in the 1950s. However what may be different about the 1980s is the speed of change (Llewellyn, 1988) and the growing importance and the sheer size of finance in the USA and the UK. In the UK finance now accounts for 14 per cent of employment and it is a major part of the government's employment strategy to create jobs by establishing London as the financial centre of Europe.

4.3 CAUSES OF FINANCIAL INNOVATION

It is useful to analyse the causes of financial change by looking at what might have increased the demand for financial services and what might have either changed or increased supply. This leads to five causal factors, two demand and three supply.

4.3.1 Increased Variability of Interest and Exchange Rates

If interest rates were constant then variable and fixed-rate mortgages would be identical. Hence it would have been pointless to introduce variable-rate mortgages in the USA or fixed-rate ones in the UK. Growing variability of interest rates increases the attractiveness of variable-rate mortgages in the USA and of fixed ones in the UK because the products are more distinct. This example can be multiplied a hundredfold. Moreover many financial innovations offer protection against changes in the financial environment, especially changes in interest and exchange rates. Finally, the ultimate hedge against risk is flexibility and this is one of the main effects of innovation (see Section 4.4): innovation means that few decisions are irrevocable.

4.3.2 Increased Wealth and Changing Composition of Wealth

The argument is that the income and wealth elasticities of demand for financial services are high – plausible but not proven. Alternatively it is argued that increased wealth, and consequently sophistication, leads to a demand for a wider variety of financial services. Changing composition of wealth largely means the increase in house prices in the UK and USA, where the financial revolution has been centred. In consequence the personal sector is much wealthier but its wealth is largely in housing. Hence a demand for loans – to buy houses or to convert illiquid wealth into spending power (see p. 222). Moreover, the housing boom itself creates a demand for complementary financial services such as insurance.

4.3.3 Technology

This is discussed above in Section 4.2.2.

4.3.4 Changes in the Regulatory Environment

Most, especially American, authors regard this as the main cause of financial innovation. Certainly the relationship between innovation and regulation is complex and has been the focus of much attention; see Gowland (1990). Regulation leads to innovation in three ways.

First, *deregulation*. Innovations can occur when the authorities change the rules by which financial markets operate so as to permit activities previously forbidden. Strictly this is usually *re*regulation since one regulatory code replaces another even though the new regime is more liberal. Such deregulation can be either formal or informal. A good example of formal deregulation occurred in the UK in 1987 when building societies were permitted to make unsecured loans (that is loans not secured on a mortgage). This was previously illegal and became legal through a change in the Building Societies Act, 1986. Informal deregulation occurs when an informal prohibition is dropped – until 1981 UK banks believed that the Bank of England did not want them to make mortgage loans and would penalize them if they did. This prohibition was informal – that is not backed by law – and so was its removal. Credit cards were informally barred until the late 1960s through the existence of credit ceilings.

Second, *ham-fisted regulation*. Many authors have argued, for example Cargill and Garcia (1985), that the main incentive to innovate is a desire to evade official regulation. This is an application of the black market theory of elementary microeconomics: any restriction on economic activity creates an incentive to evade it. In financial markets conditions are such that evasion is usually possible – low transaction costs, homogeneous products, many economic agents, good information and the rest of the criteria listed by textbooks. Certainly innovation designed to evade regulation has been very common in the last 30 years. The Eurocurrency market, now $12000 billion, originally developed in the 1960s as a device to evade regulation (Gowland, 1979, Chapter 3; Johnson, 1983). This was a restriction on interest paid on bank deposits. Hence American banks could not pay the market interest rate to their customers if they took a deposit in, say, Dallas. If instead the deposit was made with the London branch of the same bank they could pay whatever interest rate they liked. Moreover, other regulations prevented traditional customers from borrowing from banks in the USA. These included foreign borrowers such as the Kingdom of Denmark and US firms wishing to finance overseas expansion. Hence American banks switched a large chunk of their business to London where neither deposit-taking nor lending were subject to Federal Reserve or Treasury regulations. Many institutions grew up in London in the 1960s to evade ceilings on bank lending – secondary banks for example. They aimed to perform banking business in practice but in a legal form chosen so as not to be subject to the ceiling rather as clubs often fulfil the functions of pubs while evading the restrictions on them. Evasion of the UK ceilings on bank deposits (IBELs ceiling or corset, see p. 45) in the 1970s also occurred but mainly in two other ways. One was *offshore banking*, as with the Eurocurrency market: the deposit was 'booked' to a foreign banking centre and any loan made from this branch (I can deposit money in a York bank and the amount be credited to an account with a branch in London or Paris. It is then said to be 'booked' to London or Paris). This was especially prevalent in the last few months of the ceiling, after the abolition of exchange control in November 1979. More generally, offshore banking can be used to evade a wide variety of controls on banks – reserve requirements, capital adequacy requirements, constraints on the quantity or type of lending.

Earlier in the 1970s, evasion of the 'corset' occurred via the 'bill leak' or letter of acceptance leak (named after a particular form of bill). Normally, without any controls, A deposits money with a bank and receives a security (a bank deposit in exchange). This is matched on the bank's balance sheet by a loan to B, who thereby obtains funds. Instead A may go into a bank and receive in exchange for his deposit not a claim on the bank but a bank-guaranteed claim on B (that is a bill of exchange). In reality all is the same; A has a security, B has his loan, the transaction has occurred because A trusts the bank etc. However, legally A no longer has a deposit so the control has been evaded. This was often called disintermediation in the UK but is now usually termed *off-balance-sheet lending*. More generally, disintermediation and offshore banking can be used to evade a wide range of controls on banks - reserve requirements, constraints on the quantity or type of lending, and of current significance, capital adequacy ratios. They have been introduced or increased in most countries in recent years and are part of the G10 pact mentioned above, and of the European Commission's scheme to regulate banks. The practice of off-balance sheet lending has grown enormously in the USA in response to capital adequacy ratios. Banks obtain funds from two sources: deposits and 'own capital' – equity, bonds etc. A capital adequacy ratio imposes a minimum on the latter relative to deposits, which can of course be evaded by reducing the apparent total of deposits. Such evasion could be restricted by imposing controls on the total of a bank's liabilities whether on or off-balance-sheet.

Another, much-vaunted form of financial innovation which has largely grown in response to regulation is the swap. In 1988 new 'swaps' exceeded $350 billion having been a mere $5 billion in 1984. A swap is an arrangement whereby each of two or more parties perform a transaction on behalf of the other(s). This is illustrated by what is usually said to be the first swap, involving IBM and the World Bank. The World Bank wished to borrow dollars to lend to the Third World but found Wall Street reluctant to lend because US financial institutions were already satiated with World Bank paper. IBM wished to borrow Swiss francs to finance its Swiss operations; IBM has always been reluctant to accept foreign exchange risk and normally finances its overseas operations by borrowing in the local currency. However, the Swiss regulators were unhappy at the thought of Swiss banks lending to IBM. Someone came up with the obvious solution. The World Bank borrowed Swiss francs and gave them to IBM because the Swiss regulators were happy at the thought of Swiss banks lending to an international institution. IBM borrowed dollars in New York and gave them to the World Bank; Wall Street was very happy to lend to IBM. Crucially, the two agreed to make payments to each other such that IBM was neither worse off nor better off than it would have been if it had borrowed in Swiss francs and the World Bank neither better off nor worse off than if it had borrowed dollars. Thus if (allowing for exchange rate movements) the dollar loan turned out to be cheaper than the Swiss franc one, IBM would pay the difference to the World Bank and *vice versa*. Swaps are frequently more complex; the record is alleged to involve 13 parties. All of the characteristics of a loan can be varied: currency (as in the above example), maturity, variability or otherwise of interest rates, marketability etc. A swap may be a device to evade regulation: A is forbidden to lend to B but can lend to C so he pretends to lend to C but the funds go to B. It can, however, change the characteristic of a security so as to make all parties better off, or at least happier and so be a Pareto improvement. In the above example, Wall Street institutions held a claim on IBM which they rated a better credit risk than the World Bank and *vice versa* for the Swiss banks.

In this service a swap is a form of insurance. If I borrow on a variable-rate basis and wish to insure against changes in interest rates I can swap it into a fixed-rate one. However it is possible to arrange a swap without an underlying loan. A can arrange to pay B the extra cost of a fixed-rate loan and receive from him the extra cost of a variable-rate one even if neither has borrowed. This is simply a bet on movements in interest rate; A receives money from B if interest rates rise and pays out if they fall. A High Court Judge in November 1989 compared it to the 2.30 at Kempton. The case illustrated the dangerous speculative potential of swaps. Hammersmith Council had lost about £200 million in betting on interest rates – twice its annual rate income. The Court decided the transactions were illegal. The following example was used in the case to illustrate a swap.

> On 19 May 1988, the council entered into an interest rate swap deal with Barclays de Zoete Wedd Limited. The council agreed to exchange interest payments on a sum of £10 million – which is notional and does not change hands. The Council agreed to receive these interest payments on the basis of a fixed interest rate of 9.6 per cent and to pay them on the basis of a variable rate – in this case, six month LIBOR (the London Inter Bank Offered Rate).
>
> Payments were to be made twice a year on 9 May and 9 November over a period of five years, expiring on 10 May 1993. Initially, LIBOR was lower than 9.6 per cent and, therefore, the council received a net payment of £64 356.17 on 9 November 1988. However, by the next payment date, 9 May 1989, LIBOR stood at 12.1875 per cent, which meant that the Council would have had to pay £128 311.65.

The Court of Appeal decided that such transactions were legal but only if they were used for hedging (insurance purposes). The case will finally be decided by the House of Lords.

4.3.5 Changes in Perceived Market Conditions

Much financial innovation is purely a response to changes in market conditions, as perceived by market agents. (There may or may not be an actual change underlying this; what matters is how market agents view things.) In economic terms, market agents perceive a shift in demand curves. A good example of this is that in 1980, US banks perceived the best returns to be in lending to the third world and to the energy industry, for example 'wild catters' exploring for oil in Oklahoma. By 1986, their preference was for lending to the UK personal sector to buy houses on the security of a mortgage. This difference produced innovation: a new product, or rather a new foreign supplier, in a market, and many of the entrants did offer different products either to attract business or simply because they offered US-style mortgages which were a new product in the UK.

4.4 NATURE OF FINANCIAL INNOVATION

4.4.1 Spectrum Filling

This is stressed by Llewellyn (1988) as the most important effect of financial innovation. 'Spectrum filling' means that potential products which were not previously available come on to the market and thereby fill gaps. Spectrum filling takes two forms. The first is that products previously available in one country become available in another, as with the mortgage example above, whereby US- and UK-style mortgages become available in the other country. The second, stressed by Llewellyn, was based on Lancaster's notion that goods are really combinations of primitive characteristics; for example a house is so many bedrooms, kitchen fittings, location, type (terrace, detached etc.). Products that are available are like supermarket baskets which contain various semi-arbitrary combinations of goods, that is of these primitive characteristics. One can only buy the baskets of goods, not the individual primitive ones. Spectrum filling in Llewellyn's sense occurs when the number of products is increased by rearrangement of existing characteristics, for example if terraced bungalows were devised; or by analogy if supermarkets were to offer a wider range of baskets. Loans can have various characteristics, such as long-term or short-term, fixed- or variable-rate, marketable or non-marketable, domestic or foreign currency. Combining these would create sixteen potential products. Financial innovation has increased the number from, say, six to fourteen in the UK.

4.4.2 Secondary Marketability

In the author's view this is the most important aspect of financial innovation, the creation of second-hand or secondary markets in assets which were previously not tradeable. This is of most importance in banking. Banks, and most other financial intermediaries, have traditionally 'borrowed short and lent long.' Borrowers normally want illiquid loans, that is a loan they know need not be repaid for a long time, for example a mortgagee usually obtains a 25- or 35-year mortgage. Lenders want liquid assets, that is those which can easily be converted into cash if they wish: 70 per cent of building society deposits are encashable at seven days' notice or less. Building societies can *transform maturities*, borrow for seven days and lend for 25 years because of 'the law of large numbers'. This states that if, say, 100 000 people have the right to withdraw funds at seven days' notice, only a small number will choose to do so. The financial intermediary can estimate this and hold a small reserve to satisfy this demand. For example, perhaps, 1000 people will want to withdraw funds. Hence the institution holds, say, 2 per cent of its funds in liquid form and can lend 98 per cent for longer periods.

This is traditional financial intermediation. The constraint on it is that the liquidity of a lender's asset (for example a bank deposit) is necessarily the same as the bank's obligation to him or her. If I hold a seven-day bank deposit, then I can obtain my funds within seven days but the bank is under an obligation to repay me within seven days. A secondary market breaks this link. If I can resell my bank deposit to a third party it is still liquid for me but is no longer a liquid obligation for the bank. I may hold a one-year deposit so the bank is free of any worry that the deposit will be encashed. It can still be perfectly liquid for me if I know that I can sell it to a third party whenever I wish. An important form of financial innovation was the conversion of bank deposits into a readily tradeable form, called a *Certificate of Deposit* (CD). These became very common in the USA in the 1960s and the UK in the 1970s.

A market in bank loans gives rise to similar benefits. An individual may wish to borrow for ten years and know that he will not have to repay the loan until then. This will be an illiquid asset for the bank *unless it can resell the loan*. If a secondary market is created in bank loans, then the bank's asset can be very liquid – it can recall the loan anytime it wishes – while the borrower can still have a very illiquid debt. The process of converting bank loans into a tradeable or marketable form is called *securitization*. This has been a prominent feature of banking in the 1980s.

Securitization extends not only to corporate loans but to many personal sector ones. The Bank of Scotland has pioneered the securitization of mortgages in the UK, many of which it has resold, especially to Japanese banks. In all, £13 billion of UK mortgages were in securitized form in early 1989. In the USA over 30 per cent of mortgages are in this form. Moreover in the USA most car loans are securitized; it has been calculated that the average car loan changes hands 2.1 times between the consumer buying a car and repaying the loan raised to buy it.

A particularly interesting secondary market is that in Third World Debt. This is traded at a discount reflecting the market's assessment of the chance of repayment. For example in March 1988 Peru's debt sold at 8 per cent of face value while that of Ecuador was valued at 62 per cent of face value. Normally when a bank holds a non-performing loan all it can do is hang on or seek a compromise with the debtor. Now a bank can cut its losses and sell the loan to someone prepared to take a chance. Many banks, especially small US ones, have used this market to eliminate their exposure to Third World Debt. Some UK banks, such as Anglo-Scandinavian, have done the same but in general the Bank of England has discouraged them. Purchasers may be speculators or may have arranged to use the loan to buy assets from the government concerned. One imaginative scheme involved the Midland, Oxfam and Sudan. Midland sold Sudanese debt to Oxfam at a nominal price and thereby established a tax loss. Oxfam sold the debt to Sudan at 10 per cent of face value in local currency and used the proceeds to fund its operations in Sudan. Sudan gained both from Oxfam's activities and from the elimination of a dollar debt by a small payment in local currency. Midland's donation to Oxfam was effectively costless – indeed it converted a worthless asset into a useful tax rebate.

4.4.3 Marketability

Secondary markets in hitherto illiquid securities are but one example of the general phenomenon of the creation of markets in previously untradeable constructs. London financial markets have always had a penchant for the apparently bizarre market. Since 1827, a regular auction market in 'remainders' has taken place in London. A remainder is the right to inherit under someone's will, so Spendmuch and Squanderbug could finance current consumption by selling their prospective inheritances (as the names indicate this was frequently part of the plot of Victorian novels). In the 1970s British Rail pioneered a market in tax allowances. A tax allowance is useless unless you have taxable income against which to offset it. British Rail's large investment programme gave it plenty of tax allowances but, of course, it had no profits. Hence it sold the allowances to companies with high profits and tax bills. This is generally welcomed in the UK as an investment incentive. Small fast-growing companies can solve liquidity problems by selling their allowances to mature companies.

The most important new markets are in risk. In London, FOX (Futures and Options Exchange, formerly the Commodities Market) and LIFFE (London International Financial Futures Exchange) are but two of the best known of a host of markets in which risks are traded, through options, forward markets and futures (see appendix). Trading in risk can be a means of insurance or a way of 'taking a position' as speculation has been rechristened. This is also explained in the appendix together with some other technical terms. The increase in the number of markets has excited economic theorists. The Arrow–Debreu theorem argues that for competitive capitalism to necessarily produce a Pareto optimum there must be a complete set of markets. In other words incomplete markets are a form of market failure. For example, the market in farmland may not clear optimally unless there are markets in which one can insure against drought in the year 2000. Hence general equilibrium theorists have welcomed these new markets whilst the more pragmatic have worried about the dangers inherent in the growth of speculation.

4.4.4 Rebundling

One of the most important features of financial innovation is *rebundling*. Financial services have traditionally been provided in packages that combined several services in one. In the 1970s and 1980s such packages have been broken up and the services offered separately. Moreover they have been offered in new combinations with some of the products being outside the traditional ambit of finance. This is best illustrated by banking. A bank traditionally performed at least five distinct functions. It ran the money transmission service, that is it provided a means for me to pay my gas bill, usually either by cheque or bank giro. In most cases the bank did not charge me the full cost of this but gave me some or all of the service free if I held a sufficiently large deposit. This meant that the money transmission service was inextricably linked with the second function – broker. The bank found borrowers and lenders and so acted as a broker. However, by acting as an intermediary the bank performed two further functions. It guaranteed the loan; no depositor was dependent for the security of his money on any individual loan being repaid. The bank also funded the loan in that if the original lender (depositor) withdrew his money the lender did not have to repay. Instead the bank undertook to find a new deposit. Finally the bank administered the loan, a function stressed by Llewellyn (1988) in his analogous analysis of 'disbundling'.

Now each of these functions is performed separately or in new combinations. For example, take the example of a securitized mortgage. A borrows from the Bank of Scotland and the latter combines the mortgage with others into a convenient size package and sells it to Dai Ichi. The Bank of Scotland continues to act as broker. It no longer funds the loan. It might or might not continue to administer it (usually it does). It might or might not guarantee it; in principle either Dai Ichi or the Bank of Scotland could bear the risk (some securitized loans take one form, some the other. Many mortgage-backed securitized loans pool the risk across hundreds of mortgages, providing a third form). Moreover the brokerage function could be performed by a third party such as an estate agency or solicitor (as in the nineteenth century or in France) or an independent mortgage broker. Some building societies have offered customers the choice of a mortgage directly with them or with a foreign bank (Scarborough and Portman with Allgemeine and National Bank of Saudi Arabia respectively).

Such rebundling should be more economically efficient as it should enable agents to use their comparative 'advantage rather than be stuck with a pattern based on history or accident. Banks have produced new combinations by entering new areas, for example estate agency, or by putting much more emphasis on areas that previously received little emphasis, such as stock-broking services. Rebundling has given considerable impetus to the breakdown of the bank/non-bank and finance/non-finance distinction (see Section 4.5).

4.4.5 Competition and Marketing

Financial innovation has both been caused by and been a cause of changing patterns of competition in finance. From about 1600 to 1970 non-price competition prevailed in finance in the UK and resulted in an ever-more diverse range of financial institutions - the long lists beloved of textbook writers. Competition by product differentiation was thus an important cause of innovation in this period. Such competition has continued since 1970 even though price competition has become prevalent. Moreover since 1970 marketing has become important and basic marketing concepts have led to innovation; the effect of price competition has also been to produce innovation as institutions become ever more alike, for example banks and building societies. Banks started to offer or emphasize traditional building society service products, mortgages and savings accounts whilst building societies offered 'banking' products, like cheques, travellers' cheques and consumer credit. This phenomenon occurred across-the-board in finance as the 'supermarket' replaced the 'boutique'. However, it is not yet clear whether the generalist firm offering a wide range of services will replace the specialist firm; in many areas the specialist is doing well, for example in corporate finance.[11] Conflicts of interest between divisions of a firm may handicap its competitive force.[12]

In any case the growth of the generalist gives rise to 'niche' marketing which also creates innovation. 'Niche marketing' is the identification of and provision of services to a small group where interests are neglected by general supplies, for example D H. Evans (clothes for women with fuller figures) or High and Mighty (its equivalent for tall or stout men). Many financial products have been designed for equivalent groups; for example variants of foreign exchange options for small travel agents who organize one-off tours, for example a trip to the Holy Land for a church-based group.

It is a favourite adage of marketing men that a product can only be sold if it is 'new' or provides something 'free'. This gives rise to bogus innovation, when

products are relaunched with minimal change to give an illusion of newness -
perhaps teabags with larger holes. In finance, a new name for an old product may
increase its appeal or cost – renaming a bill of exchange, for example. Combining
two products into one (as with a 'swap') may offer convenience or may be a
marketing device. A perpetual floating-rate note may be regarded as either. In
essence it is a perpetual bond on which the interest rate varies with short-term
market rates. Before the collapse in the market in December 1986, they were
apparently overpriced compared to equivalent bonds, which suggested successful hyping by the promoters. More often, however, marketing strategies aim to
add a genuine new feature to a product and to make a large profit on it – 'adding
value-added'. The high-margin extra feature is certainly common in finance.
Finally a reputation for innovation may itself be a valuable marketing tool:
Goldman Sachs and First Boston for example value their reputation as pioneers.

This makes it possible to analyse a difference between innovation in finance
and elsewhere: innovations in finance are rarely patented (see the discussion in
Johnson, 1988). There are three possible reasons:

(a) it is impossible for legal reasons, Llewellyn (1988);
(b) firms innovate as a marketing tool so patenting is seen to be unnecessary –
     what matters is to be first. Indeed to be copied may be a virtue for Goldman
     Sachs if it emphasizes that Goldman Sachs is a pioneer.
(c) patenting is undesirable for 'network' reasons, as with cassette players or
     telephones – no one would want a telephone if no one else would ever have
     one. The value of a phone increases as the number of users rises[13]. A new
     security may only be attractive to both borrowers and lenders if it will
     become widely used, for example to ensure marketability. Hence the
     optimum strategy for a firm may be to market products which are not yet
     provided by other firms but soon will be.

4.4.6   Internationalization

In many countries, expansion of financial firms is or has been limited by either
legal barriers or by quasi cartels. Moreover, expansion may not be attractive for
many other reasons. Hence financial firms have often found that expansion
abroad was more attractive or easier than at home. In some cases institutions who
were unwilling to compete with each other at home have competed with each
other abroad, as predicted by oligopoly theory. Such cross-national expansion
has been common in recent years and so internationalization has been an
important aspect of financial innovation.

Internationalization can take two forms, of product and of supplier, and it is
important to distinguish between them. Internationalization of product is the
creation of services where the *raison d' être* comes from international factors

such as travellers' cheques or devices to finance international trade. There has been some innovation of this form, especially involving foreign exchange risk. However, in many ways it is surprising how slow it has been rather than how fast it has been. Of course there has always been a wide range of international financial products, at least since the Phoenicians. Indeed international financial services have always been the most sophisticated and highly developed aspect of finance. Hence, it is perhaps not surprising that it is not possible to detect the sort of rapid acceleration of financial innovation that has occurred elsewhere.

Internationalization of supplier occurs when it becomes possible to purchase the same (domestic) product from either a foreign or a domestic supplier. For example, a UK citizen can choose whether to have a mortgage from a US or a British bank – this is internationalization of supplier. On the other hand the option to have a mortgage denominated in Swiss francs or ECUs is internationalization of product. Such internationalization of supplier should lead to the unification or integration of markets. The economist judges that a market is unified when a single price prevails within it. The European Commission's 1992 study, shows the range of price variation within the EEC and possible scope for gain by integration. This study also reveals that the opportunities for UK firms to profit from 1992 seem much less than is often assumed in Whitehall or the City.

When assessing the scale of internationalization it is worth remembering the extent to which it is a return to the state of affairs prevailing in 1900. Two world wars, socialism and dirigisme more generally, and the consequent widespread exchange control provided many barriers to international finance. Internationalization since 1957–8 (when most European countries made their currencies convertible into dollars) has undone many of these effects but it is difficult to find international services now available that were not available in 1900, though they may now be available faster or cheaper. In turn this is relevant to the issue of the importance of technology in promoting internationalization, compared to regulatory forces: the arguments in 4.2.2 are especially relevant here.

The patchiness of internationalization is worth emphasis – some products in some countries are much more internationalized than others. Even within a market a mixed pattern prevails. In the UK personal (retail) market, the mortgage market has become internationalized in the 1980s. On the other hand, there is only limited internationalization of either deposits or other credit. Moreover, the degree of international competition in these areas has not changed much in recent years. Finally, there may seem more competition when viewed from one side of the market than the other! Most UK banks would judge that a firm wishing to borrow £1m was in an international market with equal access to Japanese, American and British banks. Most firms – judged by surveys – do not feel this to be so and perceive themselves as having little choice even within the UK.

4.5   EFFECTS OF FINANCIAL INNOVATION

1.   Banks are no longer 'special'
Many of the features which traditionally differentiated banks from other financial sectors are growing less important. As described above, for example, banks
such as the 'big Four' in the UK, are now performing a much wider range of non-
banking transactions and are publicizing these services to a wider extent than in
the past – insurance, estate agency, share purchasing, etc. Similarly, non-banks
of various sorts are offering the services which were traditionally the prerogative
of the banks such as credit cards and cheque books. In the past the basic banking
services required the maintenance of branches and, in many cases, a large chain
of branches, for example over 5000 for Barclays. Basic cash provision and
deposit services can now be provided by machines which do not require any
branch; they could be located in, for example, supermarkets. Midland now
operates a subsidiary which provides all retail banking services by telephone,
mail and machine card. Some have suggested that banks are potential dinosaurs,
with large now-redundant branch networks. The more likely alternative is that
they use the space for other purposes, including some unconventional ones. Bank
customers either possess assets (depositors) or have a penchant for spending
(borrowers). Hence they are attractive to sellers of a wide range of goods
including money outside finance. Suggested or rumoured links include Italian
fashion, fine art and antiques.

2.   The capital and money markets are no longer distinct
'Securities houses', investment banks and deposit banks can no longer be clearly
distinguished from one another. It has been argued that the special feature of a
bank was that it provided loans to the non-market sector, that is to those
companies and persons who did not have direct access to securities markets. This
distinction is becoming less important with 'securitization' and the development
of secondary markets in which loans can be resold. If, as in the USA, loans to
consumers for the purchase of cars are resold on an active secondary market, then
there is no longer anything distinctive about a bank's customers, nor about the
distinction between 'bank' and 'capital' market finance.

Ironically, this means that one of the 'hottest' developments in Anglo-Saxon
financial innovations has brought them back to what prevailed in Italy and other
Latin European countries. In these countries bill finance never disappeared, so it
never had to be resurrected under fancy new titles.

3 Finance no longer distinguishable
One big department store, Sears Roebuck, is also the third largest financial
intermediary in the USA. In the UK department store chains, notably Debenhams,

have experimented with financial innovation on a large scale and have in certain respects, such as credit cards, become large financial institutions.

Marks and Spencer have both obtained a banking licence and started to market investment products, especially unit trusts. Such developments had been predicted by economists from the early 1970s. Indeed the surprise was not retailers' entry into finance but that it had not occurred earlier. Reputation and trustworthiness are the *sine qua non* in finance. There is little doubt that most people in the UK trust and regard, say, Marks and Spencer and Sainsburys, at least as highly as any financial institution and more highly than almost all. Some developments are not restricted to the personal sector. BP have become one of the ten largest banks in the UK through a similar effect. Their corporate cash management division found that it could profitably intermediate funds because of the high repute of BP. Internationalization has increased the scope of such cross-entry. Large multinational corporations, like BP, are almost certainly better known to, say, an investor in Brussels or Rome, than is a UK building society: even Abbey National has had problems of lack of recognition, according to press reports. The profit of finance has made it an obvious candidate for diversification – for example BAT's purchase of Eagle Star and Farmers (US), although BAT is now reversing this following an absolute takeover bid. Some entry into finance has been purely opportunistic (in the favourable sense), for example Ford's purchases of bankrupt Savings and Loans Associations, the US equivalent of building societies.

Thus it is becoming more difficult to distinguish between financial and non-financial firms. This is not surprising since the division largely evolved as an historical accident and was by no means immutable. It may be that other divisions are more logical, for example, many marketing experts believe in the desirability of provision according to the customer rather than according to the goods or services provided; hence shops have emerged which provide all the services required by a particular type of customer (for example teenager) rather than a particular type of good. In this case, instead of a shop selling a wide range of clothes for all age groups, it would sell everything which it perceived teenagers wanted, namely clothes, records, sports equipment, etc – and in the future financial services? Similar developments would lean to an even more radical restructuring of the financial system than has already occurred.

4. *Financial firms are more willing and able to compete with each other*
This has been both 'on price' and by invading each other's markets by offering to provide services that are traditionally the preserve of another type of institution.

5. *International competition*
A UK citizen can now choose to transact with a UK bank in London, with a UK bank in Milan, with an Italian bank in Milan or with an Italian bank in London.

6. *Economic agents can to a much greater extent than in the past, choose both the nature of the financial service and the provider*
This freedom is especially open to corporate and wholesale users of financial markets but is available, to a considerable extent, to personal and retail users.

7. *The size of the financial sector has grown enormously*
This is so both in the USA and UK.

8. *Some countries have chosen to deregulate their financial markets*
In effect the problems of regulation discussed above have tipped the balance in favour of liberalism (Gowland,1990). This has implications for all other regulators.

9. *Financial markets are now more volatile*
Hence rapid price changes are more likely.

10. *There is now a much greater emphasis by governments on international trade in financial services*
This has occurred as a consequence of the above points, as exemplified by the GATT Uruguay Round, and of the employment consequences of finance.

11. *The nature of the lender of last resort problem has changed*
When acting as lenders of last resort, central banks have traditionally been concerned with an illiquid but solvent bank – a bank whose assets are worth more than its liabilities but are temporarily unsaleable. With secondary marketability this is less likely to occur but solvency problems are more likely. Moreover, the focus of the problem may have changed from the institution (bank) to the market which provides liquidity. Corrigan, of the New York Federal Reserve, has suggested that the fulcrum of the system is now the clearing house, whether of banks or securities exchanges or any other market. The regulator should seek to preserve the integrity of the clearing house at any price.

12. *The conflict of objectives has sharpened*
Central banks have not only macro-monetary goals of policy, such as inflation, but also structural ones: efficiency and stability. The effect of innovation is to sharpen this conflict.

13. *It is much harder to interpret financial data*
Any series of data is likely to change its significance as a result of financial innovation. However, while this may make monetary policy harder to implement, it neither makes it impossible nor justifies the abandonment of broad money targets (see p. 30).

14. *World liquidity has grown tenfold in the 1980s*
The liquidity of an asset is a measure of how easily it can be converted into purchasing power – speed, cost, certainty and collateral value. All assets are much more liquid than in 1980. In addition the volume of financial assets has grown rapidly. Hence Benson (1989) has calculated that the effective world money supply grew by 930 per cent between 1979 and the end of 1988.

GUIDE TO FURTHER READING

On big bang: Clarke (1981), Hamilton (1986), Plender and Wallace (1986), Reid (1988), Strange (1987), Thomas (1981), Welsh (1986). Of these Reid is the most incisive.

On the theory of innovation: Silber (1983) is the seminal work. Goodhart (1989) and Llewellyn (1988) the best synthetic analyses.

Finally for those seeking an insight into markets (or an amusing read) Mackay's (1841) analysis of the Dutch Tulip boom is still unsurpassed.

NOTES

1. Galbraith (1954) makes a similar point about the 1920s; pp.101–3. He argues that what was different about the 1920s compared to before and after was not a greater objective role for Wall St nor greater popular involvement, both were small:'rather it was the way it became central to the culture'. My view of the 1980s bull market is similar although privatization issues did lead to a peripheral involvement for millions. For the 1720s (South Sea Bubble) see Casswell (1961). For bull markets in general the classic is still Mackay (1841).
2. Notably, Ivan Boesky, E.F. Hutton, Miliken (of Drexel Lambert) in the USA, Johnson Matthey, Guiness, Barlow Clowes, Blue Arrow, various insider trading cases and a long list of scandal at Lloyds. For details and references see Gowland (1990).
3. See Cargill and Garcia (1985) (USA), Cerny (1988) (France), for Australia, Hall (1987) for Japan Okuda (1990). For the UK see the Guide to Further Reading.
4. Lloyds Act (1982), Police and Criminal Evidence Act (1984), Corporate Securities (Insider Trading) Act (1985), Financial Services Act (1986), Building Societies Act (1987), Banking Act (1987), Criminal Justice (Number 1) Act (1987), Criminal Justice (Number 2) Act (1987).
5. The controversy is discussed in Gowland (1988) and (1990). Of crucial importance was the effective sacking of Sir Kenneth Berril as Chairman of the Securities and Investments Board (SIB) on 20 February 1988. His replacement, David Walker of the Bank of England, has made it clear that he intends drastic amendments to a regulatory regime that he regards as excessively dirigiste; on one occasion he castigated its 'East German type' rules. The main fruits of this are

over 300 amendments to the 1989 Companies Bill and a new SIB rule book (8 August 1989). The problems the latter caused for the AFBDA, who regulate future brokers and dealers, was discussed in the *Independent*. They had just completed that rule book after four years' effort and had to start again.

6. For a detailed analysis see Llewellyn (1988a) and Gowland (1988).

7. An agreement to have the same (risk-weighted) capital adequacy ratio in all ten countries; see Haberman (1987) and Bank of England *Quarterly Bulletin*. vol. 27, no. 1 (Feb 1987) pp. 85-93, vol. 28 no. 2 (May 1988) pp. 220–2, vol. 28, no. 3 (August 1988) pp. 212–4. These cover the G10 pact and its predecessor the Anglo-American banking accord.

8. Big bang has been extensively analysed; see the Guide to Further Reading.

9. The problems of market making are discussed in Gowland (1988, 1990). In Barro (1988) Telser argues in favour of the London system, compared to New York. This does not contradict the argument in Gowland that market makers need greater privileges (or exemption from disclosure requirements).

10. In 1984, the total of interest-bearing sight deposits exceeded non-interest-bearing ones for the first time and the proportion of the former continued to grow. Personal (retail) customers could obtain interest-bearing current accounts only in special circumstances, such as if they held a minimum balance of £1000. Even so in October 1988 such accounts (£14 billion) exceeded orthodox, non-interest-bearing ones (£12 billion). In October 1988, the Midland followed by the other 'High Street' banks introduced interest-bearing current accounts which did not involve minimum balances or other restrictive features. It was estimated that the change would reduce Nat West's profits by 14 per cent. The precise means used to evade ceilings in the 1960s are now of only historic interest; see Gowland (1978) and Zawadski (1981).

11. This has been much discussed in the financial press. The success of firms like Barings and the establishment of take-over specialists like Wasserstein are cited as evidence that many clients prefer specialists.

12. For example, Barclays advised Adelmann in his acquisition of Storehouse shares. In consequence Storehouse fired Barclays as corporate registrar (in favour of Lloyds) and as the bank in which the group's takings were placed (Midland being the beneficiary).

13. The calculations can become complex. Phillips seem to have got it wrong both ways. With cassette recorders, which they invented, they allowed other firms to make them. The network principle suggests that sales of cassettes and recorders increase according to the availability of both. They decided that the gains from this were less than if they had exploited a monopoly on cassette players and cassettes. Thus they believed they had made a mistake. Faced with a similar problem with video recorders they patented their invention. This inspired Sony to invent a rival format.

REFERENCES

Barro, R. J. *et al*. (1988), *Black Monday and the Future of Financial Markets*, Dow Jones–Irwin, New York.

Benson, J.G. (1989), 'Effective monetary growth', *Financial and Economic Review*, vol. 27, no. 6, pp. 216–22.

Cargill, T. F. and Garcia, G.G. (1985), *Financial Reform in the 1980s,* Hoover Institution Press, Stanford, California.

Casswell, J. P. (1961), *The South Sea Bubble*, Crescent, London.

Cerny, P. (1988), 'The Little Big Bang in Paris', *European Journal of Political Research*, vol. X, p. Z.

Clarke, M. (1981), *Regulating the City*, Open University, Milton Keynes.

Cross Report (1986), *Report on Recent Innovations in International Banking*, Bank of International Settlement, Basle.

Galbraith, J. K. (1954), *The Great Crash*, Hamish Hamilton, London. (English edition, also Pelican, 1961).

Goodhart, C. A. E. (1989), *Money, Information and Uncertainty*, 2nd edition, Macmillan, London.

Gowland, D.H. (1978), *Monetary Policy and Credit Control*, Croom Helm, London.

Gowland, D.H. (1979), *Modern Economic Analysis*, Butterworths, Sevenoaks.

Gowland, D.H. (1988), 'Il Processo di deregolamentazione finanziaria alla luce della recente crise dei mercati borststici Moniali' *Economia Italiana*, Banco Di Roma, no. 3, pp. 389–410.

Gowland, D.H. (1990), *The Regulation of Financial Markets in the 1990s*, Edward Elgar, Aldershot.

Gowland, D.H. (1990a), 'Financial Innovation' in Llewellyn (ed.) (1990).

Haberman, G. (1987), 'Capital Requirements of Commercial and Investment Banks: Contrasts in Regulation', in *Quarterly Review*, Fed. of New York, vol. 2., no. 3, pp. 1–11.

Hall, M. (1987), *Financial Deregulation*, Macmillan.

Hamilton, A. (1986), *The Financial Revolution*, Penguin, Harmondsworth.

Johnson, L. T., (1988), *The Theory of Financial Innovation*, Institute of European Finance, Bangor.

Johnson, R. B. (1983), *The Economics of the Euromarket*, Macmillan.

Llewellyn, D. T. (1988), 'Financial Innovation: A Basic Analysis' in *Paeles De Economica Espanola*, (Feb).

Llewellyn, D. (1988a), 'Integration of European Financial Markets', *Economia Italiana*, Banco Di Roma, no. 3.

Llewellyn, D. (1990), *Financial Markets and Institutions*, Money Study Group Surveys, Macmillan.

Mackay, C. (1841), *Extraordinary Popular Delusions and the Behaviour of Crowds*, Richard Bentley, London.

The present title was adapted for the second edition (1852), National Illustrated Library. The most accessible modern edition is an abridgement (1973) Unwin Books, London.

Mauro, G. (1990), 'Italy' in Gowland, D. H. (ed.) *Bondmarkets and Debt Management*, Routledge, London.

Okuda, G. (1990), 'Japan' in Gowland, D. H. (ed.) Bond Markets and Debt Management, Routledge, London.

Plender, J. and Wallace, P. (1986), The Square Mile, Hutchinson, London.

Reid, M (1988), *All-Change in the City*, Macmillan, London.

Silber, W. (1983), 'The Process of Financial Innovation', *American Economic Review*, Papers and Proceedings, pp. 89–95.

Strange, S. (1987), *Casino Capitalism*, Blackwell, Oxford.

Thomas, W. A. (1981), *Big Bang,* Philip Allan, London.

Tobin, J. (1984), 'On the Efficiency of the Financial System' in *Lloyds Bank Review*.

Welsh, F. (1986), *Uneasy City*, Weidenfeld and Nicolson, London.

Zawadzki, K. K. F. (1981), *Competition and Credit Control,* Basil Blackwell, Oxford.

APPENDIX: FUTURES, FORWARD MARKETS AND OPTIONS: FORMS AND FUNCTIONS

The purpose of this appendix is to explain what forward markets, options and futures are. In addition their function will be considered for three economic agents: Heslington (Tours), John the Prophet and Metrobank.

Heslington Tours has arranged a one week holiday in Italy for 100 people in nine months' time. At this point it will have to pay out 100 million lire to various hotels, restaurants. It will receive £100 000 at the same time from its UK customers to pay these bills and its other liabilities, air fares etc., which will total £40 000. It therefore has lire obligations and sterling assets and wishes to eliminate the consequent foreign exchange risk.

John the Prophet believes he can predict the future and hopes to profit from his prophecies.

Metrobank, with apologies to Alex of the *Independent*.

Forward markets

A *forward* contract is the simplest of the three. Two parties agree now that they will trade in the future at a price fixed today. Student A is taking some exams. He might agree that after the exams were over he would sell his textbooks to B for £20. This is a simple forward contract. Similarly Heslington Tours might now arrange to buy 100 million lire for delivery in nine months' time, at a rate of 2000 lire to the pound. It therefore now knows that in nine months' time it will receive 100 million lire and will pay out £50 000. This is the essence of a forward contract. The agreement today about price with delivery in the future can act as a form of insurance for Heslington Tours. Its profits are no longer dependent on movements in the exchange rate. Added to its other bills and receipts it will then have a clear profit of £10 000: the lire it receives will pay the hotel bill and it will face outlays of £90 000 in sterling – £50 000 for the lire and £40 000 for its other bills. Hence Heslington Tours has eliminated the foreign exchange risk implicit in its operations.

John the Prophet can use the forward market to back his judgement. If he can forecast the pound: lire exchange rate in nine months' time he can transact and profit accordingly. If he thinks the rate will exceed 2000, say 2500, he should buy pounds forward. If he buys £50 000 forward, he will commit himself to delivering 100 million lire in exchange for £50 000 (the reverse of Heslington Tours' transactions). If in nine months' time, the rate is 2500 lire, he can buy the 100 million lire for £40 000 and make a profit of £10 000 – the difference between his receipts of £50 000 and his outlay. If his forecast is wrong, he will make a loss – if the spot exchange rate is 1000 lire to the pound he will have to pay £100 000 to buy the lire and will lose £50 000. Contrariwise, if John expected the lire to appreciate he would buy forward lire.

Hedging is a term used to describe a financial transaction designed to eliminate a risk. *Speculation* (or *taking a position*) is a transaction which increases risk but undertaken in the hope of profit if the speculator's view of the future is correct. Thus the terms describe the motives of the agent, not the form the transaction takes. Heslington Tours and John may both buy forward lire. Heslington Tours is hedging because it already has an obligation in lire and seeks to match this by buying forward. John would be speculating because he thought he could sell the lire for a higher price when he received them. Metrobank can use the forward market to hedge (like Heslington Tours) or to speculate (like John). Metrobank, however, also has a third option – it can supply the forward exchange to either profitably. This possibility can best be understood by considering another choice open to both Heslington Tours and John: borrowing, converting and lending, the most common method of foreign exchange transaction in the 1970s for hedgers and speculators alike. Heslington Tours could have borrowed pounds and converted them to lire at the spot exchange rate. It could then have deposited these for nine months in an Italian bank. In nine months' time it would have been in the same position as with the forward contract– an obligation in pounds (to pay off the loan) and a receipt in lire from the bank. It could have used the lire to pay the hotel bill and used its income to pay off the loan. Hence it could have hedged in this way. The cost of doing so would have depended on the interest it paid and received on its loan and deposit. Similarly John could have taken a position in the same way.

Hence a forward position can be created by borrowing, converting and lending. Metrobank can – and will – use this device to make it possible to offer forward exchange contracts to either Heslington Tours or John. Keynes (1923) pointed this out and showed that there is an equilibrium relationship amongst the spot exchange rate, forward exchange rate and the domestic and foreign interest rates– the interest parity theory: Gowland (1983a) pp. 121–5 or Gowland (1979) pp. 52–4.

Options

An *option* is the right to buy at a specified price on a specified day but the holder has no obligation to do so. For example, I might pay £100 for the right to buy a house for, say, £100,000 in six weeks' time as one builder currently offers. If I do not choose to buy the house, I will merely forfeit £100. Hence, an option is a form of insurance– I have insured myself against a rise in house price or the possibility that I might want a house. On financial markets options are usually for standard commodities – that is those that meet some clear-cut definition, such as a 20-year bond with a coupon of 10 per cent. Moreover, they are usually traded options, that is they can be bought and sold. In the above example, if in six weeks' time the house is worth £104 000 I could sell my option to someone for say £3000 since it will be cheaper to pay me £3000 and the builder £100 000 than to pay the builder £104 000. Of course the option might be worthless – if the value of the house falls to £95 000.

Moreover, trade can take place over the life of the option. If after three weeks, the house has risen in value I might then sell the option. Options which appear worthless are called *out of the money* options (that is when the option is to buy at above the current price or sell at below the current price).

For the sake of example, assume Metrobank offer Heslington Tours the following option: for £1 000 you can, if you wish, purchase 100 million lire in nine months' time for £50 000. Now Heslington Tours know that they can settle their hotel bill for £51 000: the cost of the option plus the sterling they pay out to acquire the lire. If, however, the pound: lire exchange rate rises they may not wish to exercise the option. If in nine months' time the exchange rate is 2500 they will buy the lire in the spot market for £40 000, and their profit will be £19 000 (receipts £100 000 option £1000, hotel bill £40 000, sterling costs £40 000). If the exchange rate is 1000 lire they will exercise the option. John the Prophet can obviously use the option market to profit from his judgement. Metrobank can calculate the cost of options as with forward contracts. Alternatively they are betting on the variability of rates when they offer ('write') options. If they write options both ways – that is for pounds to be bought and to be sold – then they will lose only if exchange rates fluctuate in either direction. As they charge a fixed fee for each option they will profit unless the variability in rates is sufficient to offset this income. Hence their decision about whether to write (supply) options depends on their view of the likely variability of rates relative to the fixed price. The latter is determined in a competitive market so the supply of options curve is the marginal opportunity cost, that is expected variability. The potential loss from miscalculation is enormous. One trainee accountant with an annual income of £6000 was allowed to write options on share prices by the National Westminster Bank. His losses after Black Monday were £3 million.

Futures

A future is like an option except that the holder is obliged to exercise it. A future might therefore be an obligation as well as a right to exchange 100 million lire for £50 000 on a specified date. A future is therefore similar to a forward contract but, like an option is for a standard commodity at a standard price. The price of a future then depends on the difference between the standard price and the forward market price. Imagine the forward price of Shell Shares for delivery in three months' time is £4.78. The equivalent future may be to buy one share at a price of £4. Hence to buy such a future I would have to pay 78 pence, ignoring interest. The advantage of futures is that they can be traded easily. Moreover they are usually traded on organized exchanges which allow them to be *cleared*, that is balanced by a subsequent deal. If John expected the lire to depreciate he would happily have sold forward lire to Heslington Tours. However he might subsequently wish to reverse the deal, either because he changes his view or to take a profit, if the lire falls before the contract expires. Heslington Tours will not wish to undo the contract. Hence John is in a quandary. He might try to find an Italian firm organizing a holiday in the UK and try to reverse his deal in that way. However it is unlikely that he would succeed and moreover either Heslington Tours or the Italian firm might default. With futures he can buy the opposite futures, present them to the exchange and take his profit or accept his loss.

Caps, collars and all that

There are two basic loan contracts: fixed and variable (or floating). If I borrow money for 20 years to buy a home the mortgage could incorporate a fixed rate of interest, say 12 per cent. Alternatively the rate could fluctuate over time as short-term rates change – the classic variable-rate loan. However, one could incorporate into the latter a provision that the interest rates could never exceed 14 per cent. This would be a *cap*. Normally the rate would be slightly higher at other times: in effect the borrower would pay an insurance premium to avoid the risk of having to pay a high rate. Similarly, a *collar* could be written into the contract, a provision that the interest rate would never fall below, say, 8 per cent.

5 Inflation

D.H. Gowland

5.1 INTRODUCTION

It is easy to argue that inflation is the most important problem in both politics and economics not only in the UK but throughout the industrialized world. In the UK inflation seems to be the issue which topples governments, occasionally reinforced by industrial militancy itself partially generated by inflation: 1951, 1970, 1974, 1979. Indeed only in 1964 has inflation not been the key issue in an election in which a government lost power. The Conservative decline in 1988–9 seems to have had a similar cause. Moreover, throughout the 1980s Mrs Thatcher and her ministers reiterated that the primary target of their policy was the reduction and elimination of inflation. Inflation is as crucial a political issue in other countries as in the UK. The damage caused by inflation is examined in a separate chapter (7). Economists are divided about how to analyse inflation let alone about how to control it. This chapter seeks to elucidate the key issues involved.

Conventional macroeconomic theory is a theory of the determination of nominal, or current price income.[1] This, often referred to as Y, is equal to price multiplied by output. A nominal income of £1000 might represent 10 000 loaves of bread at 10p, or 1000 loaves at £1 each or any of any almost infinite number of other combinations. Nominal income can change if output changes or if price changes or if both change. The Keynesian and monetarist models (at least in their strict sense) are equally restricted since both explain Y but do not offer an explanation of the breakdown into changes in the price level (P) and the aggregate output (Q). This limitation was called the 'missing equation' by Friedman and the 'fatal ambiguity' or 'great fault' by Keynes. Sometimes an *ad hoc* addition is made to a model so that it can be presented as a model of either inflation or output and, so implicitly, employment. In the 1960s many Keynesians assumed a fixed (exogenous) level of prices so that a theory of the determination of nominal income could be presented as a theory of output. Similarly, classical monetarists assumed a fixed level of output so that the quantity theory of money could be presented as a theory of the price level. Nevertheless, both theories were and are, essentially, theories of nominal income.

There are obvious limitations to the value of a theory which explains nominal income. To know that nominal income will rise by 10 per cent is of little value unless one knows whether this is a 10 per cent rise in output or a 10 per cent rise in prices or a 3 per cent rise in both. Moreover, it is possible that a 10 per cent rise in nominal income could conceal a fall in real income together with a rise of more than 10 per cent in prices – as in the UK in 1980. It is the purpose of inflation theory to explain the breakdown of changes in nominal income into changes in price and changes in output (and employment).

Moreover, concentration on this ambiguity of conventional macroeconomics highlights the crucial problem of policy making: can governments influence the division between price and output or must they accept whatever an apparently arbitrary fate determines? This issue provides one of the sharpest distinctions between the Labour government of 1974–79 and the present (1979–) Conservative government. The Labour government believed that it could influence the price/output split and, in particular, used incomes policies to try to achieve a higher level of output, and a lower level of prices, at each level of nominal income. Mrs Thatcher, on the other hand, believes that governments are powerless to influence the mix of price and output at each level of income, at least in the short term. Such a division of opinion continues to lie at the heart of the difference between Mrs Thatcher and her opponents.

The traditional theory of inflation is set out in section 5.2. The implication of this theory seems to be that governments face a choice between unemployment and inflation, the classic trade-off. Currently many of Mrs Thatcher's opponents accept the existence of such a choice, whereas the government denies it. This is the other crucial difference in economic theory underlying the contrasting approaches to economic policy of Mrs Thatcher and her rivals. The government believes that the trade-off is, at best, a short-term phenomenon. *Accelerating* (not just a higher level of) inflation would be necessary to maintain a lower level of unemployment if the government sought to reduce unemployment by demand management (Gowland, 1989). The reason for this belief is inherent in the modern, expectational theory of inflation discussed in Section 5.7. The government has gone further and argues that inflation in the short run causes unemployment in the longer term. This issue is also examined in section 5.8 and in Chapter 10.

To summarize, there are three critical issues in inflation theory and policy:

1. What determines the level of price and output at each level of nominal income?
2. Can governments influence the mix of price and output?
3. Is there a choice between inflation and unemployment or does the one cause the other?

In this chapter, Section 5.2 sets out the traditional theory, and Section 5.3 the modern aggregate supply–aggregate demand theory which is designed to remedy some defects in the conventional models. Together these comprise the post-war orthodox economic approach to inflation, the successor to Samuelson's 'neo-classical synthesis' – Section 5.4. Section 5.5 presents the Thatcherite critique of the post-war orthodoxy, and the associated analysis of the effects of a government commitment to full employment. Section 5.7 presents the expectational theory of inflation. Section 5.8 considers alternative approaches to reflation, that is Thatcherism and the alternatives. Section 5.9 looks at alternative theories and in particular, the monetarist analysis of oil price increases. This is one of the more interesting and useful, but ignored, areas of monetarism. It denies that OPEC price increases of 1973 and 1978 caused inflation. Section 5.10 presents some conclusions. Throughout the chapter, especial attention is paid to the scope of government policy in general and to the possible role of an incomes policy in particular, since in some form this is still the centrepiece of any viable alternative to Thatcherism, if one exists.

5.2 THE TRADITIONAL MODELS

There are two simple traditional solutions to the problem of determining the level of prices and of output. The first is to assume that prices are fixed, or at least exogenous, that is determined independently of income. The usual term applied to this approach is the 'cost push' theory of inflation. It is assumed that prices are fixed by cost factors, usually either import prices or wages, which are, in turn, often thought to be fixed by union behaviour. The rationale for this is some form of 'cost plus pricing' whereby firms determine prices by using a fixed mark-up over average cost at some normal level of output.[2] Whatever the merits of this approach to the analysis of firms' behaviour, its macroeconomic implications are clear. A change in the level of nominal income will mean that output has risen by the same amount.

Indeed, any cost push theory of inflation transforms the monetarist and Keynesian theories of the determination of nominal income into theories of output, as in 'French monetarism'. French monetarism is an amalgam of the quantity theory and of cost push inflation. Many self-styled 'Keynesian' models in the 1960s combined the determination of nominal income in a similar way, by injections and withdrawals with fixed prices, to produce a theory of output.[3] Within this model the role of incomes policy is both obvious and clear. Its aim is to reduce costs below the level at which they would otherwise have been and so ensure a lower price level. It is worth emphasizing that the theory of cost push inflation would also justify 'union-busting'. A South American dictator who tortured trade union leaders could appeal just as much to the cost push theory to justify his action as a pale pink advocate of incomes policy.

The other simplistic extreme theory is that output is fixed, or at least exogenous. A theory of nominal income has been transformed into the classical theory of the price level. The best known of such theories is classical monetarism; a form of 'demand pull' inflation. This regards output as fixed in the short run at some full employment level, usually called 'Say's Law' in elementary textbooks. This level is determined by technological factors, available resources and other structural factors and is normally thought to rise over time. The microeconomic rationale of this theory is a special form of perfect competition.

There are a number of problems with both of these theories. One is that they are both extreme, simplistic and implausible. For example, there is considerable evidence that the mark-up varies according to the pressure of demand, so the simple cost push theory is hard to sustain. More seriously, the two theories are presented in a form which is not susceptible to analysis, still less to determining which is right. The art of the economist is to pose a question in such a way as to highlight the factors upon which the answer depends. Thus, it is necessary to put cost push and classical monetarist theory into some appropriate context. It seems that the most appropriate is the aggregate supply–aggregate demand model.

5.3 AGGREGATE SUPPLY AND AGGREGATE DEMAND

The aggregate demand–aggregate supply model has many advantages as a framework within which to analyse the cost push–demand pull debate, and to try to resolve it. One of these is familiarity. The resolution of price and output is normally solved in economics by supply and demand analysis and exactly the same method can be used to analyse the aggregate price level and aggregate demand. Moreover it seems to highlight both the merits and limitations of monetarism and Keynesian demand management theories if they are viewed as theories of aggregate demand.

When the government uses the tools of fiscal or monetary policy to influence the economy it is determining the total of expenditure. Moreover, the government can only determine the *value* of *nominal* expenditure not the volume of *real* expenditure, in other words it determines current price income. The value of nominal or current price expenditure (or income) is equal to the volume of real output times the price level. Thus in an economy in which baked beans were the only good produced, a nominal income of £1000 could consist of 1000 tins at £1 each, 10 000 tins at 10p each or even 1 tin at £1000 or any of a myriad of other combinations. Macroeconomics assumes that economies can be analysed as if they produced only one good, so similar problems arise in analysis of all economies. Something is needed to explain what determines which pair of values of output and price correspond to the level of nominal income determined by

Figure 5.1 Aggregate demand

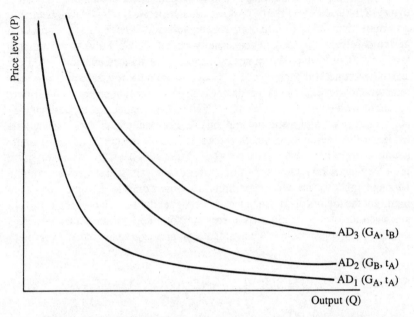

Note: The government can shift the aggregate demand curve from AD^1 by either
increasing expenditure from G_A to G_B or cutting the tax rate from t_A to t_B.

government policy: Friedman's 'the missing equation' and Keynes's 'great
fault' and 'fatal ambiguity', above.

The government, in effect, determines aggregate demand when it determines
the level of the tools of fiscal exchange rate and monetary policy to determine
nominal income. This can be shown as in Figure 5.1 by representing this as an
aggregate demand curve. Moreover, in simple models the aggregate demand
curve must be unit-elastic, since expenditure is constant: the definition of unit
elasticity. Each aggregate demand curve is drawn for a particular set of values for
the policy variables: money supply (m), exchange rate (e), level of government
expenditure (G) and tax rate (t). Thus if any of G, m, the exchange rate or tax rates
changes the aggregate demand curve shifts. There are a large number, indeed an
infinite number, of aggregate demand curves, each corresponding to a different
level of G, m, e and t, as in Figure 5.1; for simplicity only two variables are
considered. When government spending is increased or tax rates reduced the
aggregate demand curve shifts outwards, for example a reduction in the tax rate
from t_A to t_B causes the aggregate demand curve to shift from AD_1 to AD_3. Thus
the 'theory of demand management' is a theory that the government can choose
the aggregate demand curve it wants.

Alternatively the AD can be derived as follows. In an elementary Keynesian model it is usual to assume a fixed price level (say P_1) and then calculate the level of output (Q_1) for given values of G, t etc. This gives one point (P_1, Q_1) on an AD curve. Then assume another fixed price level (P_2) and repeat the exercise to derive a second point (P_2, Q_2) and so on *ad infinitum*. In a monetary economy, AD curves must slope downwards.

To complete the model an aggregate supply curve is needed so that the price level and output can be determined. It is easy to see, as in Figure 5.2, that if aggregate supply is horizontal, then the cost push model above is valid. An outward shift of the aggregate demand curve does lead to a rise in output but not in price – indeed this is the definition of perfectly elastic, horizontal supply. For example the shift of the aggregate demand curve from AD_1 to AD_2 causes the level of output to rise from Q_1 to Q_2 while the price level remains at P_1. Moreover, output is indeed demand-determined – the aggregate supply curve has no effect on output. Indeed, cost push inflation can be defined in terms of the slope and shift of aggregate supply.

Many advocates of activist demand management in the 1950s believed in this model as part of the theory of 'cost push' inflation. They argued that the

Figure 5.2   A horizontal aggregate supply curve

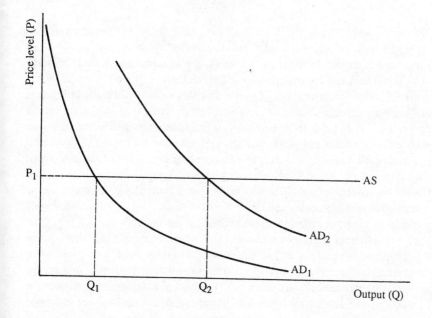

Figure 5.3   Cost push inflation

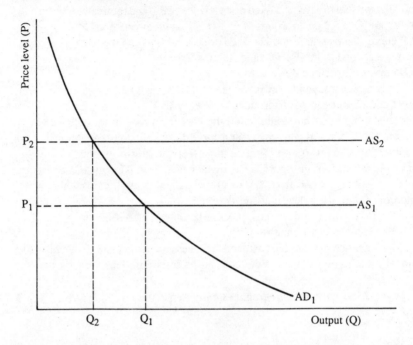

aggregate supply was horizontal but was liable to be shifted upwards by exogenous cost factors such as import prices or trade union inspired wage demands. This model is illustrated in Figure 5.3 where aggregate supply shifts from AS_1 to AS_2 causing prices to rise from P_1 to P_2. Cost push inflation is therefore a particular theory of the shape and movement of aggregate supply curves and can be analysed accordingly. It is important to realize that such cost push inflation necessarily leads to a fall in output from Q_1 to Q_2 and therefore a rise in unemployment unless the government shifts the aggregate demand curve outwards and so ratifies or accommodates the cost push inflation. The leading UK economist in the 1960s, Harry Johnson (for example 1973), stressed both the role of government acquiescence in cost push inflation and the implausibility of prolonged cost push inflation, as an explanation of the 1950s and 1960s. Cost push inflation has been reinterpreted as inflation generated by a movement of the AS curve and demand pull as that generated by a movement of the AD curve (for example Curwen, 1976). However, it must be emphasized that, while such a definition may be useful, most of the basic textbooks' statements about cost push inflation do not apply to this version. In particular, demand factors influence prices even when there is an exogenous shock to costs such as OPEC.

Figure 5.4   The Keynesian model

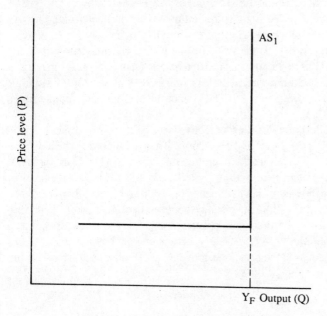

Figure 5.5   Inflationary and deflationary gaps

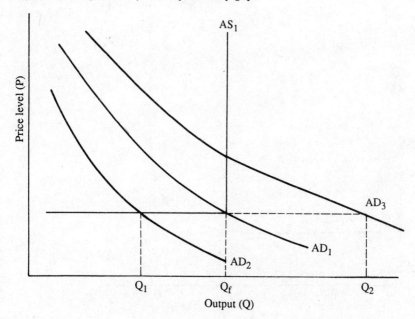

However most neo-Keynesian economists, and nearly all elementary exposi-
tions of the model assume that the aggregate supply curve is a reverse 'L' shape,
like AS_1, in Figure 5.4. The logic is that output is demand-determined up to a
certain point: full employment. Similarly, up to this point changes in demand
have no effect on price. Thus the AS schedule has an elastic portion up to Y_F.
However, beyond this point, increases in demand do lead to increases in price as
output can increase no more. Hence there is a perfectly inelastic supply schedule
at this point, as in a classical model. The kink of the curve is at the point termed
'full employment': Y_F.

Within this model the authorities' objective is to choose the aggregate demand
curve which touches the 'kink' of the AS curve. Thus in Figure 5.5, the objective
is to use fiscal policy such that the operative AD curve is AD_1. If instead AD_2
were selected by government action, there would be an inadequate level of
demand; hence, in the Keynesian parlance of the 1940 and 1950s, there would be
a *deflationary* gap of $Q_2 - Q_F$, the distance between the actual and full employment levels of AD. Similarly, if AD_3 prevailed, there would be excess demand
and an *inflationary gap*, $Q_2 - Q_F$. Clearly, activist demand management works
as well in this model as in the basic one above. One calculates the AS curve and

Figure 5.6   Bottlenecks

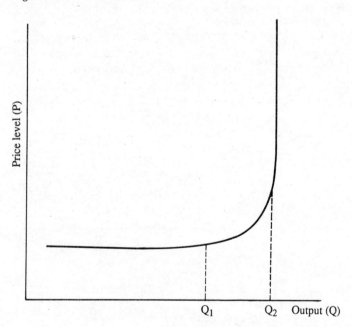

so the position of the 'kink'. The authorities then select the values of G and tax rates so that the consequent AD curve passes through the kink.

In the later 1950s, many Keynesians accepted Keynes's own notion that the effective aggregate supply curve was as in Figure 5.6 with a rounding off of the corner of the 'L'. The idea was that within the region $Q_1 - Q_2$ some industries could not increase output and so increased price when demand rose whereas others still had spare capacity and increased output (the former industries sometimes being called 'bottlenecks' for obvious reasons). Thus the 'full-employment' level of output was no longer clearly defined. Nevertheless the general outlines of the model still applied. From the above analysis the extreme nature of the cost push inflation argument is obvious and so is the fact that the aggregate supply curve can have other slopes. In contrast to the Keynesian and cost push theories are the classical and neoclassical theories. The classical theory is that aggregate supply curves are vertical, Figure 5.7(b). This means that increases in demand increase the price level but not output. In Figure 5.8 a shift of the demand curve leaves output unchanged at Q_1 but increases price from P_1 to P_2.

A neoclassical hard-liner would say that Keynes has arrived at an upward sloping supply curve by a very tortuous route. The neoclassical proposition is that aggregate supply curves slope upwards because all supply curves are assumed to slope upwards unless there are strong arguments to the contrary. At the aggregate level, there are none. It is always possible to increase output – at a price. More and more unsuitable labour can be employed, the hours of work can be increased, the life of plant can be stretched and so on. Hence, the neoclassical supply curve slopes upwards over all relevant ranges (see Figure 5.7 (e)). However, if diminishing returns apply it will become steeper as one moves along it.

Aggregate supply and aggregate demand analysis provides a framework within which to determine price and output. Different aggregate supply curves provide different predictions about the impact of monetary and fiscal policy. In particular, many economic debates hinge upon the elasticity of aggregate supply: see Figure 5.7. This became clear in the debates between Keynes and other economists and policy makers around 1930 (see Clarke, 1988). In the 1950s and 1960s economists used the closely related concept of a Phillips' curve to analyse this elasticity. In fact a Phillips curve can always be derived from an aggregate supply curve and *vice versa* (see Gowland, 1983, pp. 96–8). Nevertheless, it seems much simpler to follow both Keynes (Patinkin and Leith, 1977, pp. 39–64) and modern fashion and use AS/AD analysis rather than Phillips curves.

Figure 5.7   Aggregate supply curves

(a) Cost push

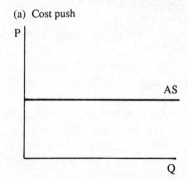

(b) Classical

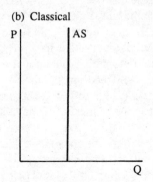

(c) Textbook Keynesian

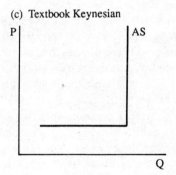

(d) Keynes's

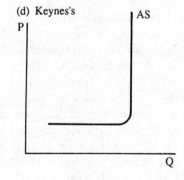

(e) Neoclassical

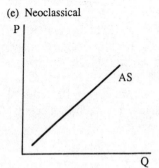

Figure 5.8   The classical model

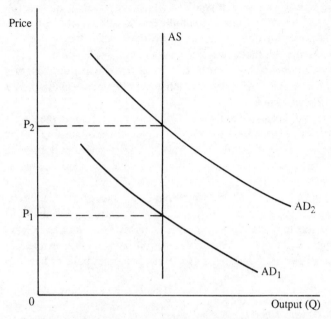

5.4 THE POST-WAR ORTHODOXY

One of the advantages of the aggregate supply–aggregate demand model is that it is easy to analyse the role of government. The authorities ought to be able to determine the aggregate demand curve by monetary and fiscal policy. Unfortunately, manipulation of the level of aggregate demand produces the classic trade-off between unemployment and inflation – the post-war orthodoxy.

The post-war orthodoxy is encapsulated in Figure 5.9. This is an aggregate supply – aggregate demand diagram with a fixed upward-sloping AS curve, AS. By a combination of monetary and fiscal policy the government (the monetary authorities) can determine the aggregate demand curve. For example, it would be AD_1 when government spending equalled G_1, the money supply M_A and tax rates were at a particular level (t_A). If instead the government chose to increase government spending to G_2 and the money supply to M_B, the AD curve would shift outward to AD_2. In fact, the government could choose from an infinite number of possible AD curves, each one generated by a different set of values of G, t and M. Here, however attention will be restricted to the choice between AD_1 and AD_2. If AD_1 is selected, output will be Q_1. Employment can also be marked along the horizontal axis and will equal E_1, the number of workers required to produce Q_1. The authorities will then be faced with unemployment equal to the labour force less E_1. If this is 'too high' it can be reduced by selecting

AD_2 instead. Output rises to Q_2 and employment to E_2 so unemployment falls by $E_2 - E_1$. However, a price must be paid, literally, since prices are higher at P_2 instead of P_1 so the reduction in unemployment has caused inflation. Macroeconomic policy involves a choice of evils, or rather the choice of a mixture of evils. Hence this model was known as the *trade-off model* in the UK; governments had to choose how much inflation to have when the cost was inflation – they had to trade-off inflation against unemployment. In the USA it was called the *dilemma model*.

This dilemma could be avoided if the authorities could influence the aggregate supply curve (or, alternatively, the Phillips curve), either by shifting it or by changing its slope. If the authorities could cause the aggregate supply curve to shift outwards, they could have both a lower price level and more output, as shown in Figure 5.10.

The $64000 question is whether government can induce such a beneficial change, and, if so, how. Incomes policies, and price controls, proved almost universally attractive to western governments as devices with which to endeavour to shift aggregate supply curves in the period before 1979. In the UK governments of all parties introduced 13 variants of incomes policies between

Figure 5.9   Post-war orthodoxy

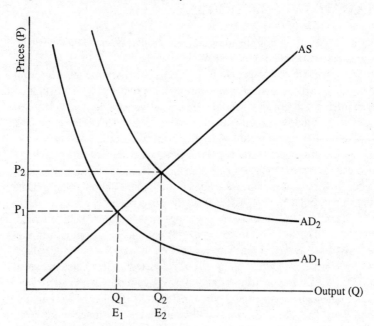

Figure 5.10 A successful supply-side policy

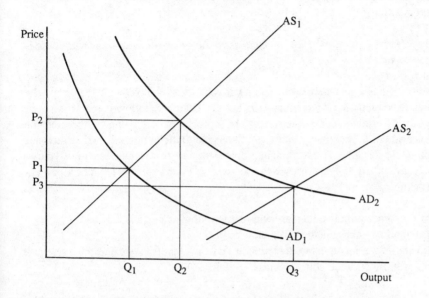

1948–79 (see Gowland, 1989, p.28). During this period the standard rationale for an incomes policy was to shift the AS curve.

Incomes policies are not the only means of shifting aggregate supply curves. Some of President Reagan's advisers toyed with the old idea that a suitable tax policy might induce greater output (and so lower prices) at each output by providing incentives to work, save and invest: 'supply-side economics'. In addition, it has been argued frequently that governments may inadvertently shift aggregate supply curves in a malevolent fashion, especially by over-generous unemployment pay and social security, such as the changes introduced in 1967 which included earnings-related supplements (see Chapter 6). However, the theory is more widely applicable and includes a strongly argued view that it was a major problem in the 1930s, an opinion which most people find incredible.[4] Minford has argued that shifts of the aggregate supply curve are the major cause of increases in unemployment (for example in Minford and Peel, 1981). (Supply shifts are discussed more fully below and in Chapter 6.)

5.5 THE ECONOMICS OF THATCHERISM

It is now convenient to examine the analysis of demand management put forward by Mrs Thatcher and those economists who support her (this is discussed more fully in Gowland, 1989). Mrs Thatcher's essential point is that demand management is counter-productive. Her argument can be analysed as a series of propositions:

1. *There is no hope that an incomes policy can shift the aggregate supply outwards*
It was explained above that all previous governments since 1945 had hoped to shift the aggregate supply curve outwards by means of an incomes policy. The evidence on their effects in unclear, but the Thatcherite view is that, if after 30 years of effort success has not yet been achieved it is time to abandon the experiment of incomes policy. Moreover, the Thatcherite view is that incomes policy has an adverse effect on aggregate supply – that is it causes the AS curve to shift inwards not outwards as the post-war orthodoxy suggested. The argument is simple:

(a) incomes policies interfere with the workings of market forces
(b) market forces ensure efficiency
(c) therefore, incomes policy reduce efficiency, that is they cause the aggregate supply curve to shift upwards.

2. *Governments have concentrated on a short-term demand policy rather than on a long-term aggregate supply policy*
If it is accepted that short-term demand policy does not work, this is self-evident; indeed it is one of the slogans of 'supply-side economics'.

3. *Governments aggregate demand policy has caused the aggregate supply curve to shift upwards*
This proposition is based upon both Friedman's arguments (below) and upon the adverse effects of a belief in full employment (Gowland, 1989 and below). The effect is clear, illustrated in Figure 5.11: Mrs Thatcher's variant of the post-war orthodoxy shown in Figure 5.10. As before the government can choose which aggregate demand curve it wants. Suppose that output were originally Q_1 where AS_1 and AD_1 intersect. To reduce unemployment the government increases its spending and the money supply so as to shift the aggregate demand curve from AD_1 to AD_2. Both orthodox and Thatcherite analyses agree that the effect will be to increase output to Q_2 and so reduce unemployment, albeit at a cost of $(P_2 - P_1)$, that is, of inflation. However while this is the end of the post-war orthodox story, Thatcherite analysis has a further crucial stage: the aggregate supply curve shifts upwards to AS_2 so that *output is lower at Q_3 than it was originally*. Mrs Thatcher's analysis, in other words, rejects the view that aggregate supply and aggregate demand are independent of each other. Shifting the AD curve outwards

Figure 5.11   Mrs Thatcher's analysis

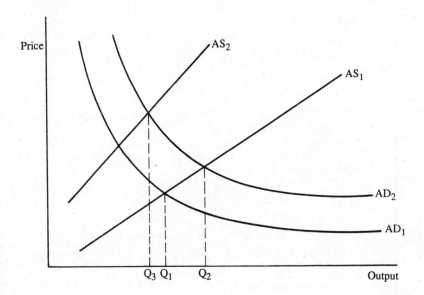

causes the AS curve to shift inwards; this point is expanded below. In consequence:

4. *The real trade-off is over time, not between unemployment and inflation*
Governments can reduce unemployment in the short term but the cost is not only inflation but higher long-term unemployment. Unemployment has therefore been high in the 1980s as a consequence of misguided efforts to reduce it in the 1950s and 1960s. Moreover, only by reducing aggregate demand in the short term, and so increasing short-term unemployment, can the aggregate supply curve be shifted outwards and so unemployment be reduced. This is illustrated in Figure 5.12. The government reduces aggregate demand from AD_1 to AD_2 and so output falls from Q_1 and Q_2 and unemployment rises, but the aggregate supply starts to shift outwards so that in the end output is higher at Q_3 and unemployment lower. Few economists would disagree that this will happen 'in the end' or indeed that it has happened in the UK but the issues are about how long before the full benefits are obtained and whether they are worth the cost.

Figure 5.12   Deflation increases output in the long run

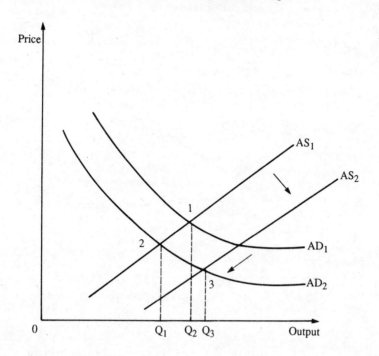

5.6 A BELIEF IN FULL EMPLOYMENT

In the previous section a reference was made to the effects of a belief in full employment. In many ways this is alleged to be the key to the post-war economic history of the UK. First of all, it is the explanation of why unemployment was on average less than 300 000 in the mid-1950s and over 3 million in the mid-1980s. Keynesians and anti-Keynesians alike agree that unemployment was not low in the 1950s because of direct government manipulation of the economy, the fiscal demand management of so many exercises. Instead there was full employment in the 1950s because the private sector believed that the government would maintain full employment. In consequence of this belief the private sector altered its behaviour such that there was full employment.

In particular, businessmen invested more. Full employment implied that demand and expenditure (that is future sales) would remain high. Thus it would be profitable to invest to satisfy this demand. Moreover, a belief in full employment boosted such intangible forces as business confidence, and so caused a further rise in investment.

One category of investment does not depend in any way on expectations of future sales. This is house building which is of especial importance because some studies suggest that it was a significant cause of the high levels of employment experienced in the late 1950s (Matthews, 1968). In Keynesian terms, it was the injection which kept the economy at a high level of demand. However, the house building boom depended in large part on the enormous personal sector demand for housing which was matched by a willingness to accept long-term mortgage commitments to finance house purchase. Keynesian economists plausibly argue that the belief in full employment was at least a necessary condition for people being prepared to do this. If someone takes out a mortgage they are committing themselves to making repayments over a period of at least 20 years. No-one would do this if he or she feared that they were likely to lose their job in the near future; nor for that matter would any building society (who had a monopoly of mortgage lending in the 1950s) lend to him or her. Moreover, house purchasers have to consider the prospects of resale which depend on both the state of the economy in general and other people's willingness to take out mortgages in particular. Hence, the belief in full employment was again one of the causes of extra demand.

Finally, in the 1950s employers started to hoard labour, that is they did not dispense with spare labour because they believed that they would not be able to find labour in the future when they did require it. Hence in the 1950s the government's commitment to full employment was self-fulfilling.

In the 1960s, less favourable consequences of the belief in full employment became clear – the so-called English disease. In particular, because trade union leaders believed in full employment, they ceased to believe that the threat of unemployment need constrain wage demands. Hence they asked for large-scale wage increases. Employers acceded to these demands, in part because their belief in full employment meant they thought they would be able to pass the wage increases on as price increases and consequent high demand. Hence the belief in full employment led to cost increases, and so to upward movements of aggregate supply curves.

Moreover, a belief in full employment generates the inefficient use of resources in the longer term in other ways. In fundamental arguments for capitalism, it is argued that if firms seek to maximize profits the result will be a minimization of costs and an economically efficient allocation of resources (at least under certain circumstances, see Gowland, 1983, Chapter 8). However, it is acknowledged that in reality those running firms may be interested in other goals – sales, prestige, leisure, perks and so on – besides profits. The presence of many of these will lead to excessive costs and so to economic inefficiency (this sort of economic inefficiency is often called X inefficiency, see Leibenstein (1976)). Advocates of market capitalism rely upon competitive pressures to restrict such activity by forcing managers to aim to minimize costs and maximize profits. A belief in full employment weakens the strength of such pressures and so generates inefficiency. Less formally, the effects of a belief in full employment on management is to induce complacency. The belief in buoyant demand (which generated extra investment) meant that firms believed that they could sell their products at home irrespective of price, quality, design or reliability. The growing success of imports in the UK revealed and reveals the hollowness of this belief. Indeed the belief, by generating complacency, is counter-productive. Adeney (1989) describes this process in graphic detail in the motor industry.

On the arguments presented above, a belief in full employment generated changes in behaviour which reduced efficiency and so shifted the aggregate supply curve upwards and leftwards. The consequences are obvious in terms of output and price. Moreover, by this argument, many of the UK's longer-term problems can be attributed to those malign effects of full employment policies. In summary, inefficiency was generated by the effect of the belief in full employment on the behaviour of both trade union leaders and businessmen. In consequence the AS curve shifted inwards.

Almost all commentators would agree with this diagnosis of the problems of the UK economy in the 1970s. What is less obvious is the solution. Marxists would argue that it showed capitalism to be inconsistent or at least only possible with a 'reserve army of the unemployed'. Social democrats would cite the necessity of planning and an incomes policy. Mrs Thatcher took the view that it was necessary to end the commitment to full employment (Fforde, 1983). In the 1980s it may be that once more businessmen reacted before trades union leaders and thereby produced a worst of all worlds short-run scenario that was the mirror image of the 1950s. (See Gowland, 1989, pp. 30–3 and 58–60 for a fuller discussion of this hypothesis.)

5.7 THE EXPECTATIONS MODEL

The traditional approach described above in this chapter has two major defects. The first is that, in the 1970s, inflation and unemployment rose together, at least on a medium-term basis. The other is that the traditional theory is really a theory of the price level, not of inflation. This is ironic as all textbooks have always emphasized that inflation is not just a once and for all rise in the price level but a persistent rise in prices:

> a process of continuously rising prices, or equivalently, of a continuously falling value of money. Its importance stems from the pervasive role played by money in a modern economy. (Laidler and Parkin, 1975)

Neither cost push nor demand pull nor any of the other theories sketched above explains a process of continually rising prices. Some attempts have been made to produce a pseudo-dynamic model. The wage–price spiral is the best known of these models where, in a cost push model, a rise in prices generates a rise in wages and so a rise in costs, causing a rise in prices and so on *ad infinitum*. However, this is not satisfactory in itself. Both theory and evidence suggest that the rise in prices would be less than the rise in wages, even in a rigid mark-up model, because of imported raw materials. A rise in prices does not necessarily generate a rise of the same size in wages. Thus the spiral would produce decelerating inflation; using plausible values a 10 per cent cost push would generate a 7 per cent price increase and this in turn would produce a 4 per cent wage change, thus generating a 3 per cent price change, etc. In other words, the spiral would quickly come to an end. The 'spiral', in its simple form, is probably better seen as a description of disequilibrium adjustment to a higher price level than as a theory of inflation. Moreover, the spiral should produce ever-falling output and, so, ever-rising unemployment, as in Figure 5.3. Such a process might well be part of the story of the 1950s but not the crucial element. The cost inflation would have to be ratified by a subsequent government decision to increase aggregate demand, a point originally made by Johnson (for example 1973).

Whether they are monetarist, Keynesian, or neither, nearly all economists now base their theory of inflation on Friedman's (1968) insight. Friedman argued that if everyone expects prices to rise then they will rise. Firms make decisions about their pricing decisions on the basis of costs and demand (marginal and average revenue). However, all of these have to be based on their beliefs about these variables since in the real world they cannot be known with certainty. In many cases, prices are fixed for a period of time so these beliefs are expectations about the future. For example when Hoover are deciding what price to charge for washing machines, they need to determine the demand for their product. This will depend on the price of substitutes (Hotpoint, etc.). If Hoover believe Hotpoint are going to increase their prices then their perceived demand curve is further to the right. Thus Hoover's expectations about price increases by rivals will determine the position of their demand curve and so their price. If every firm expects every other firm to charge more, the belief is self-fulfilling. Moreover, a higher price for the same output is a definition of an upward shift in a supply curve, aggregate or otherwise.

The argument is even simpler in the labour market. The perceived shift in the demand for goods causes a shift in the demand for the labour (marginal value or revenue product). A higher expected level of prices causes a fall in perceived real wages and so an inward shift in the supply of labour. Supply moves in and demand moves out hence wages rise at each level of employment. All of these shifts can be represented at an aggregate level by a shift of the AS curve. In other words, higher inflationary expectations lead to an upward shift of the AS curve.

Friedman's argument is that higher inflation leads to a higher expected level of inflation and so to an adverse shift of the AS curve. Hence a change in the price level can be divided into two components (1968). The first is the expected change; the second the change predicted by the traditional theory, especially by demand factors.

Change in price level = expected change in prices + demand effect

This theory can easily be used to produce a theory of inflation if the additional assumption is made that expectations of price changes are based on past price changes. In this case a change in prices generates expectations of further changes and so causes further changes and so on, that is a process of inflation. Formally:

Inflation   = expected inflation + demand inflation
Expected inflation = last year's inflation
So inflation   = last year's inflation + demand inflation

In other words, Friedman had produced a theory of inflation as a process by linking price changes in each year to previous years'.

The expectations model provides the best argument for an incomes policy. If an incomes policy reduces inflationary expectations, it will reduce inflation. Moreover, a short-term incomes policy may reduce inflation permanently by eliminating, or reducing inflationary expectations. If there is no subsequent demand inflation, a lower level of inflation will be permanent. This argument can be restated in terms of reducing the unemployment cost of lowering inflation, as Mr Healey argued so often during the period 1975–9. If demand inflation is reduced, there is the cost to be paid in terms of unemployment, but if expectational inflation can be reduced, this cost is avoided. This whole argument is crucially dependent on an incomes policy which influences expectations favourably. The whole case for an incomes policy depends on its impact on expectations and so will depend on circumstances. Hence, in 1970 Friedman accepted the case for an incomes policy, although he was worried about its effect on resource allocation. In 1974, he thought that incomes policy was futile because expectations would not be affected. By 1980, he thought that incomes policy would have the apparently perverse effect of increasing inflationary expectations. This can be justified either by popular scepticism about the success of official policy or by a belief that people will react to an incomes policy by regarding it as a sign that inflationary prospects are bad.

Friedman derived three much publicized and enormously influential propositions about inflation and unemployment (1968). All three depend on the assumption that expected inflation is precisely equal to inflation in the previous period:

Expected inflation$_t$ = last year's inflation

which leads to

Inflation   = last year's inflation + demand inflation

The three propositions are examined in this section and the modifications to the propositions, required when the special case is relaxed, are discussed in the next section.

Proposition 1: A higher rate of inflation will not reduce unemployment permanently; only accelerating inflation will achieve this
This proposition is known also as the vertical Phillips curve hypothesis because it denies, in the long run, the Phillips trade-off between inflation and unemployment.

Friedman's proposition can be explained in various ways. The simplest uses his basic relationships:

Inflation$_t$ = demand inflation + last year's inflation

There is a negative relationship between demand inflation and unemployment, not total inflation. The government can utilize this in the short run to reduce unemployment at a cost in terms of demand inflation. However, demand inflation means that inflation exceeds last year's: in other words it accelerates. Moreover, the higher level of inflation increases inflationary expectations the following year so, with unchanged demand inflation and unemployment, inflation will be higher in the following year and so on; in other words it continues to accelerate.

Proposition 2: To maintain a constant rate of inflation unemployment must equal the natural rate and if unemployment equals the natural rate inflation will be constant
This proposition follows directly from Friedman's two basic assumptions:

Inflation$_t$ = last year's inflation + demand inflation.

If unemployment is at the natural rate, demand inflation is equal to zero; this is Friedman's definition of it.[5] Hence, inflation is equal to inflation in the previous year, that is it is constant. Similarly, if inflation is constant, demand inflation must be zero and, hence, by definition, unemployment is at the natural rate.

If the coefficient on past inflation is not unity, the proposition does not hold. If the coefficient is less than unity, that is if expected inflation is less than previous inflation, then when demand inflation is zero, inflation will obviously decelerate. If the coefficient is greater than unity, inflation will accelerate even if demand inflation is zero because expected inflation is greater than last year's inflation.

Proposition 3: To reduce inflation, it is necessary and sufficient for unemployment to exceed the natural rate
This third proposition follows from Friedman's basic model.

Inflation$_t$ = last year's inflation + demand inflation

If inflation is to fall, that is be less than in the previous year, demand inflation must be negative. Since, by definition, this means that unemployment must be above the natural rate, it is essential for a reduction in inflation that unemployment exceeds the natural rate. Similarly, by definition, if unemployment is above the natural rate, demand inflation will be negative, and so inflation will be less than in the previous year, that is the condition is sufficient for a reduction in inflation. These propositions can also be derived geometrically or algebraically, see Gowland (1983) pp. 103–8 and 114–8.

5.8 THREE STORIES OF REFLATION

From 1982, *Private Eye* and other papers started to refer to Mrs Thatcher as 'Tina' because of the frequency with which she stated 'There is no alternative' to her long-term strategy for reducing unemployment. (Mr Lawson revived the slogan at the Tory Pary conference in 1989). On the other hand her political opponents and many (but by no means all) economists argued that there was: the Keynesian method of reflation. The debate about the merits of reflation as a cure for unemployment became so central to British politics that Neil Kinnock, now leader of the Labour Party, described the 1983 General Election as a referendum on economic theory. In this section, the consequences of reflation are contrasted. In particular, the object is to see what would happen if the putative alternative reflation had been introduced in 1983 or 1987. To do this, three basic analyses are presented:

a. Friedman's
b. the version advanced in 1983 and 1987 by the Labour Party which accepted some of Friedman's analysis but still left a role for demand management.
c. Mrs Thatcher's; this is a variant of Friedman's analysis.

The third political group in the 1983 and 1987 elections (the SDP–Liberal alliance) argued that Mrs Thatcher's analysis was correct unless there were a successful incomes policy introduced in which case the Labour Party analysis was operative. Thus, as no group has changed its views since 1983 it is possible to analyse in this section the policies of all the major political groups and to examine their relationships to economic theory.

The contrasting analyses are presented in Figure 5.13. In 1987, the economy was at point 1 where aggregate demand curve AD_1 intersects aggregate supply curve AS_1. Thus output was Q_1 and inflation P_1 – for convenience, in this analysis inflation rather than the price level is marked on the vertical axis.[6] All parties to the debate about reflation are agreed that if the government had chosen to reflate it could have shifted the aggregate demand curve to AD_2 by increasing both government spending and the rate of growth of the money supply. In consequence the economy would have been at point Q_2 in 1988, that is the intersection of AD_2 and AS_1. Thus whilst inflation would have risen to P_2, unemployment would have fallen because output would have been higher at Q_2 so more workers would have been employed to produce this output.[7]

Figure 5.13   Three stories of reflation

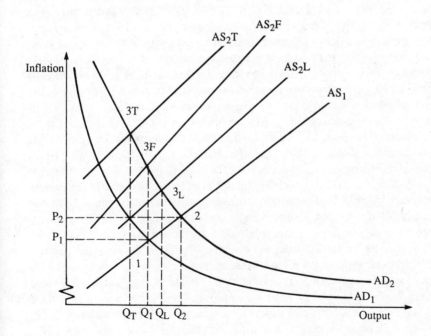

Thus far, the analysis is identical for all three schools – Friedmanite, Labour and Thatcherite. Moreover, they agree on the next step. The higher level of inflation (P_2 instead of P_1) would cause an upward shift in expectations of inflation. This is a reasonable view: if inflation in 1988 had been both higher than in 1987 and higher than expected, then consumers, trade union leaders and businessmen would all have revised upwards their expectations for the level of inflation in 1989. Moreover, everyone agrees that this would have caused the aggregate supply to shift upwards for the reasons discussed in Section 5.7.

The disagreements between the various analyses arise as to how far the AS curve will shift upwards. Friedman argues that it will shift upwards to AS_2F so that in 1989 output would have fallen back to Q_1 – its 1987 level. The reason why the shift in AS was exactly enough to generate this result was explained in detail in Section 5.7: it was because the rise in the expected rate of inflation for 1989 was exactly the same as the actual increase in inflation in 1987, that is $(P_2 - P_1)$. This is both necessary and sufficient to generate Friedman's result.[8]

The Labour Party analysis, by contrast, was that the curve would shift upwards by less than in Friedman's analysis – to AS_2L so that in 1989 and thereafter the economy would be at point 3_L. *Critically unemployment would be permanently lower, as output is permanently higher at Q_L.* The argument as to why the AS curve would shift by less than in Friedman's analysis was partially dependent on the effects of the other elements of the Labour Party's economy policy, especially the *National economic assessment* which was described as an incomes policy by Labour's opponents and a substitute for it by the Labour Party. Mainly, however, the argument is based on the econometric evidence that when inflation rises by 1 per cent the rise in the expected rate of future inflation is less than 1 per cent; perhaps about 0.7 per cent. As the shift in the AS curve depends upon how much inflationary expectations rise in 1989 as a consequence of the rise in inflation in 1988, this is sufficient to generate the 'Keynesian' result: reflation can reduce unemployment permanently.[9]

Thatcherite analysis is in stark contrast. The AS curve shifts by *more* than in Friedman's analysis: to AS_2T. Thus the effect of a reflation in 1987 would have been a short-term rise in output in 1988 (from Q_1 to Q_2) but a long-term fall to Q_T in 1989. The AS curve will shift by sufficient to ensure that reflation reduces output so long as a 1 per cent rise in inflation generates a rise in expected inflation of more than 1 per cent. Thatcherite economists point out that this is very likely because it only requires the plausible belief that economic agents look at the trend as well as the level of inflation. For example, if inflation in year X is 5 per cent the expected rate in both the Friedmanite and Labour analyses, the expected level for X + 1 is independent of its value in X – 1. For Thatcherite analysis, this value is crucial. For example, the expected value might be 7 per cent for year X + 1 if inflation had been 3 per cent in X – 1 but 3 per cent if it had been 7 per cent in X – 1. If agents extrapolate trends in this way, then the upward movement of the

AS curve is sufficient to produce the key Thatcherite result: reflation destroys jobs, because it reduces output.

Other views are possible. Centre groups such as the Alliance and SLD have argued that the Thatcherite view would be right unless there were an incomes policy. With an incomes policy, the Labour view could be correct. Hence their enthusiasm for an incomes policy. New Classical economists would argue that a point to the left of Q_1 was as likely as one to the right even in year 2.

To summarize:

a. reflation will shift the aggregate demand curve to the right
b. this will reduce unemployment in the short term *but*
c. cause the aggregate supply curve to shift upwards. However
d. it is a matter of fierce controversy whether this shift is enough to render reflation futile (Friedman), counter-productive (Thatcher) or to still leave it effective (Labour).

5.9 SOME ALTERNATIVE THEORIES

Orthodox economic explanations of inflation all depend upon some form of inflationary expectations mechanism. There are alternatives to this, sometimes lumped together as 'sociological theories'. This characteristic is misleading as most of them incorporate some form of economic analysis. One theory, however, is purely sociological. This is the argument that inflation is a 'disease of western civilization', a phrase used in this context by Andre Malraux, Noble Laureate, de Gaulle's Minister of Culture. The hypothesis is that western civilization is in decline and that all declining civilizations suffer from prolonged and substantial inflation. The syllogism can be completed simply: therefore the western world will suffer from inflation. One can challenge the underlying historical theory; not all declining civilizations are bedevilled by chronic inflation – even if it is accepted that western civilization is doomed. Moreover, the hypothesis need not rule out any other theory, for example declining civilizations might all produce excessive monetary growth because their governments spend too much and are too weak to finance their spending by taxation. So, if Malraux were right, it would still be worth analysing *why* inflation is endemic. Finally, the theory leaves no apparent role for anti-inflation policy, a very unwelcome prospect. However, the real issue is methodological: is one's preference for a sweeping untestable theory or for a conventional economic theory?

A much publicized theory is the 'frustration hypothesis' accepted *inter alia* by the New Cambridge School and Bacon and Eltis; see Gowland (1983). The theory was first tested by Johnson and Trimbell (1973). The basic notion is that if workers do not receive as big a *real* wage increase as they hoped for, they (and their unions) will respond by making very high *nominal* wage demands. These are, more or less, acceded to, so there is a substantial rise in prices. This, in turn, means that real wages are unsatisfactory so the 'frustrated' workers put in very large nominal claims once more. There are variants of the theory: for example, all workers, or only unionized workers or only workers in the market sector may be those whose 'frustrations' matter. Moreover, it maybe a deficiency of real income, of real consumer expenditure or total consumption, including some 'social wage', which induces frustration. Some theorists incorporate a threshold, for example frustration is felt only if an expected wage rise of 3 per cent is not achieved.

The theory of frustration suggests that some orthodox policy prescriptions may be wrong. For example, most orthodox economists consider an income tax increase anti-inflationary because it shifts the aggregate demand curve leftwards. However, since it reduced real personal disposable income, it increases 'frustration'; in orthodox terms, this shifts the aggregate supply curve and, as most believers in frustration believe in a very elastic aggregate supply curve, this effect dominates. This view was accepted by the Government in 1972, when income tax was reduced in order to try to buy off union wage claims. The results were disastrous and an incomes policy was introduced quickly. In fact, all major wage explosions have followed abnormally large increases in real PDI and consumer expenditure, namely 1969–70, 1973–75 and 1979–81; and 1988–9 to some extent. The 'winter of discontent' in 1979–80 followed the largest annual increase, 8 per cent in real consumer expenditure for 20 years. Hence it seems that 'frustration' cannot be the main cause of union wage claims.

Finally, there is a class or group of 'conflict' theories. These argue that society is riven by conflicts, between unionized and non-unionized workers, public and private sector workers, traded and non-traded goods sector workers, as well as the classic class struggle between capital and labour. Wage claims are the weapon used in these battles because there is no alternative method by which public sector workers can seek to make themselves better off in relation to private sector workers. This theory is interesting and plausible but untestable. It would be rash to claim that economic models provide a complete explanation of inflation, although they perform surprisingly well when tested. Clearly, there are socio-political factors at work and, for example, a complete theory would need to explain union militancy. Nevertheless, the orthodox analysis seems superior to all alternatives.

It is conventional to attribute some of the acceleration in inflation to the OPEC oil price increase of 1973. In fact, some models of inflation ascribe considerable importance to the international transmission of cost increases. For example, in the two-sector Scandinavian model, prices in the competitive traded goods sector are determined by world costs and prices in the sheltered sector by the increase in the competitive sector. Monetarism, on the other hand, has always denied that an increase in the price of one good could cause inflation, arguing that it would cause only a change in relative prices. This argument is as follows:

1. The money supply determines nominal income, price (P) and output (Q). This is true either at world level or for a single economy.

    $$M \alpha \ P.Q$$

2. Nominal income (P.Q) may be divided into expenditure on oil (price of oil P_o and quantity Q_o) and expenditure on everything else ($P_r Q_r$). For this purpose expenditure on oil includes the energy or oil component of other goods – 80 per cent of the price of tomatoes in the UK was oil, for example.

    $$M \alpha (P_o Q_o + P_r Q_r)$$

3. If oil prices rise, the effect depends on the price elasticity of demand for oil. If this is greater than one, expenditure on oil will be reduced and so expenditure on other goods will rise so that the total P.Q is unchanged. If, as is usually assumed, the elasticity is less than one, expenditure on other goods will fall if oil prices rise, expenditure on oil ($P_o Q_o$) rises so ($P_r Q_r$) must fall. Hence, either the price or the output of other goods will be less than it would otherwise be. Hence Q_o and Q_r are both lower, so Q must fall.

Thus the monetarist predictions of the effect of oil price increases are that the effect on the aggregate price level is unclear; oil prices are higher but other prices are lower; and output falls in the non-oil producing countries. *Therefore the effect of an oil price increase is felt on unemployment rather than on inflation.* For completeness, it is necessary to add that oil price increases caused deficits in many countries' balance of payments. As these were not fully sterilized; their money supplies were reduced in comparison with the level at which they would otherwise have been. OPEC's money supply did not increase sufficiently to offset this so world monetary growth was lower. This was a further factor which was added to the forces working to reduce output and offsetting any inflationary pressure.

Monetarist analysis, therefore, suggests that the OPEC price increases of 1973 and 1978 did not cause an increase in inflation but led to an increase in unemployment instead. Some evidence supports this. First, world inflation was lower in 1974 than in 1973. This is also true if the price increase is measured from September 1973–September 1974 when inflation was less than in the previous twelve months. Second, profit margins were squeezed worldwide. This suggests that prices rose less than costs, that is that prices rose less than they would otherwise have done, because of demand pressures. This analysis is relevant to

the gyrations in oil prices in 1986 and 1990. It is obviously even more relevant
to the sharp increase in oil prices which followed the Iraqui invasion of Kuwait.

5.10   CONCLUSION

It seems to the author that the aggregate supply–aggregate demand approach
provides the best framework within which to analyse inflation. Any analysis of
inflation must give a key role to inflationary expectations. Inflation does seem to
be largely the result of errors in government macroeconomic policy. Hence
Coleridge's seems the best conclusion:

> If man could learn from history, what lessons it might teach us. But passion and party
> blind our eyes.

GUIDE TO FURTHER READING

This chapter is intended as a bridge between elementary cost push–demand pull
treatments and modern texts such as Parkin and Bade (1985). Anderson (1989)
is a superb modern survey. It is available free on request from the BIS.

NOTES

1. See Brittan (1981) who argues that insufficient emphasis on this point is responsible for most
    of the confusion in the monetarist–Keynesian debate. A similar point is made in Gowland
    (1979), Chapter 5.
2. The latest in a long time to argue this is Sawyer (1983).
3. This was the model styled 'Keynesian' by Friedman in his attempt to reconcile Keynesians and
    monetarists; see Gordon (1974).
4. Benjamin and Kochin (1979) inaugurated this debate; see, for example, Hatton (1983) for the
    opposite view. A debate on the topic can be found in the *Journal of Political Economy*, vol. 90,
    no. 2 (April 1982), pp. 369–436.
5. Hence the natural rate is sometimes rechristened NAIRU, non-accelerating rate of inflation.
    The natural rate is that at which inflation is equal to expected inflation or that at which demand
    inflation is equal to zero: in Friedman's model the two are identical. The issue is discussed in
    Chapter 6.
6. See Dornbusch and Fisher (1987, p.510ff) for an account of how to transform AS/AD diagrams
    into this form.
7. Indeed it might be argued that it did happen, because Mr Lawson's policies were closer to the
    opposition's than to Mrs Thatcher's. Nevertheless, the opposition would have reflated by much
    more than Mr Lawson did. Hence as well as explaining Thatcherism this analysis is also a
    contrast what happened with what might have happened.
8. The position shown is the new long-run equilibrium, which would have been achieved by 1989.
    The AS curve would have shifted several times to achieve this point.
9. See Wallis (1988) pp. 52–72 which reveals an unemployment–inflation trade-off after five
    years in the Bank of England model (3.3 per cent inflation per million reduction in unemployment

if government spending is raised), LBS model (1.9 per cent), Treasury model (2.6 per cent) and National Institute model (1.6 percent); no long-run trade-off exists in the Liverpool model.

REFERENCES

Adeney, M. (1989), *The Motor Makers*, Fontana, London.

Anderson P.S. (1989), *Inflation and Output*, BIS Economic Paper, no. 24, Bank for International Settlements, Basle.

Benjamin D.K. and Kochin L.A. (1979), 'Searching for an Explanation of Unemployment in Inter-war Britain', *Journal of Political Economy*, vol. 87, no. 3, pp. 441-78.

Brittan S. (1981), 'How to End the Monetarist Controversy', *Hobart Paper No. 90*, IEA, London.

Clarke P. (1988), *The Keynesian Revolution in the Making 1924–36*, Oxford University Press, Oxford.

Dornbusch R. and Fisher S. (1987), *Macroeconomics*, Fourth Edition, McGraw-Hill International.

Feinstein C.H.(1983), (ed.),*The Managed Economy*, Oxford University Press, Oxford.

Fforde J.S. (1983), 'UK-Setting Monetary Objectives' in Meek (1983).

Friedman M. (1968),'The Role of Monetary Policy', *American Economic Review*, vol. LVIII (March) p.1.

Gordon R.J. (1974), (ed), *Milton Friedman's Monetary Framework*, University of Chicago Press, Chicago.

Gowland D.H. (1979), *Modern Economic Analysis*, Butterworths, Sevenoaks.

Gowland D.H. (1983), *Modern Economic Analysis II*, Butterworths, Sevenoaks.

Gowland D.H. (1989), *Whatever Happened to Demand Management?*, RJA Books, Bedford.

Hatton T.J. (1983), 'Unemployment Benefits and the Macroeconomics of the Inter-War Labour Market', *Oxford Economic Papers*, vol. 35, no. 3, pp. 486-505.

Johnson H.G. (1973), *Macroeconomics and Monetary Theory*, Gray Mills, London.

Johnson J. and Trimbell J.C. (1973), 'A Bargaining Theory of Wage Determination', Manchester School, vol. XLI (June), p. 141.

Laidler D.E.W. and Parkin J.M. (1975), 'Inflation – a Survey', *Economic Journal*, vol. 85 (December).

Leibenstein (1976), *Beyond Economic Man*, Harvard University Press, Cambridge Mass.

Matthews R. (1968), 'Why has Britain had full employment since the war?' *Economic Journal*, vol. 78, no. 3, pp. 555-69, reprinted with a critical commentary in Feinstein (1983).

Minford P. and Peel D. (1981), 'Is the Government's Economic Strategy on Course?', *Lloyds Bank Review*, no. 140 (April).

Parkin J.M. and Bade R. (1988), *Modern Macroeconomics*, 2nd edition, Philip Allan, Oxford.

Patinkin D. and Leith J.C. (1977), *Keynes, Cambridge and the General Theory*, Macmillan, London.

Sawyer M.C. *et al.* (1983), *Business Pricing and Inflation*, Macmillan, London.

Wallis K.F. *et al.* (1988), *Models of the UK Economy* (4th Review), Oxford University Press, Oxford.

6. Unemployment

Melanie Powell

6.1 INTRODUCTION

The nature and causes of unemployment have been controversial issues throughout the development of economics. Some of the many methods of analysing unemployment found in the current literature stem from early Classical theory and others from Keynesian macroeconomic theory. These methods can be described as either equilibrium or disequilibrium wage theories,[1] but both have a common focus in the microeconomic foundations of the macroeconomic problem of unemployment. In a micro-foundations approach, unemployment is explained in terms of the factors which affect demand and supply in the labour market of a capitalist economy. The focus of the analysis is on the type of choices made by firms who demand labour and by people who supply labour.

One group of micro-foundations models was developed from the work of Clower (1965) and Leijonhufvud (1968) in the reassessment of Keynesian economics. In these models, unemployment is explained as the result of market failure which necessarily arises in a monetary economy. Any disequilibrium in the goods markets is passed on to the labour market as constrained labour demand, leading to unemployment at the equilibrium market-clearing real wage.[2] Another group of micro-foundations models developed from the neo-Classical theory of the Chicago school associated with Friedman (1968). Unemployment in these models also occurs at equilibrium real wages and is known as the natural rate of unemployment.[3] More recently, economists have looked at the rate of adjustment of employment (and therefore unemployment) to changes in the real wage rate within the labour market. These 'wage stickiness' models attempt to explain the persistence of disequilibrium unemployment which occurs when the real wage is above its equilibrium market clearing rate. Unemployment in this case is not caused by adjustment problems in the labour market but results from optimal behaviour.[4]

The labour market focus of the micro-foundations approach to unemployment has drawn attention to the practical problems of measuring unemployment and changes in the labour force. Since 1979, a number of important changes in the method of calculating unemployment in the UK have been made. The problems of measurement are examined in Section 6.2. The changing pattern of UK unemployment over time and differences in unemployment patterns between countries are examined in Section 6.3. The main features of microeconomic models of unemployment are outlined in Section 6.4 using demand and supply analysis in the labour market, and the implications for unemployment policies are discussed in the final section.

6.2   PROBLEMS IN THE MEASUREMENT OF UNEMPLOYMENT

Total unemployment is usually measured in one of two ways:

1. The stock concept (in thousands) measures the difference between the size of the workforce and the size of the workforce in employment at any point in time. However, it is easy to think of the stock as a 'stagnant pool' of unemployment, and to forget that there is a flow in and out of unemployment over time.
2. The percentage rate measures the number unemployed (numerator) relative to the size of the workforce (denominator), multiplied by 100 to derive a percentage.

Both measures capture the impact of the factors which affect the demand and supply of labour. Supply factors alter the size and composition of the workforce who are either in work or looking for work, while demand factors affect the size and composition of the workforce currently employed. Figure 6.1 shows how demand and supply factors have changed over time. The workforce of the 1970s increased steadily until 1980 as the children of the post-war baby boom and more married women entered the labour force and increased supply. The downturn may reflect an increase in the number of discouraged workers who left the workforce during and after the recession. Notice the sharp increase in the size of the workforce after 1982 which appears to set the workforce growth rate back on its pre-recession trend path. The workforce in employment is determined by demand and the downturn between 1979 and 1982 indicates a sharp recession. The gap between the two lines measures the stock of unemployment, but gives no indication of how the duration of unemployment and demographic structure of the unemployed may have changed.

6.2.1   Workforce Projections to the Year 2000

Looking to the future, estimates from the 1988 Labour Force Survey suggest that by the year 2000, the civilian labour force in the UK will be 1 million higher than the estimated mid-1988 level of 27.6 million (*Employment Gazette,* April 1989).

Figure 6.1   Workforce and workforce in employment

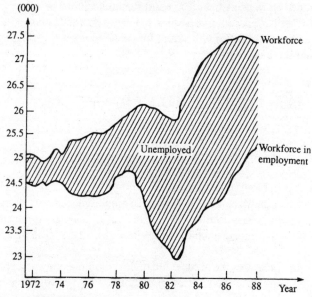

Source: *Employment Gazette*

In addition, the projections suggest that 90 per cent of the increase will result from increased participation by women. The labour force change is likely to consist of an increase of 2.3 million people aged between 25 and 54 years, and a decrease of 1 million workers aged under 25 years. These changes may affect the rate and type of unemployment for any given change in aggregate demand.[5] A continuation of the expanding employment trend in the service sector will probably accommodate the growth in female labour. However, between 1973 and 1988, employment in the predominantly male, full-time manufacturing sector declined by 35 per cent, whereas employment in the non-manufacturing sector which attracts female labour increased by 16 per cent.

6.2.2   Claimant Count and Survey Measures

In practice, the number of people unemployed can be estimated by counting those who register as unemployed and/or claim benefit, or by using a survey. Both methods are used in the UK.

1. The claimant count (Row 7 in Table 6.1) is derived from statistics provided by the Unemployment Benefit Offices and includes those unemployed people claiming unemployment benefits, supplementary benefits or national insurance credits on a given day each month.

2. The Labour Force Survey figure is derived from an annual survey of 60 000 adults in Great Britain (a similar survey is undertaken in Northern Ireland). Since 1987, the Labour Force Survey has asked a question which uses the International Labour Office/OECD definition of unemployment. The question asks whether the respondent is without paid work but is available to start work and has sought work in the past four weeks, or is waiting to start a job already obtained.[6] The ILO/OECD measure has been designed to aid international comparisons, but is also more consistent with the theoretical concept of labour supply derived from economic theory.

Table 6.1   A comparison of claimant and Labour Force Survey measures of unemployment - SPRING 1988 (Millions)

	All	Men	Women
1. ILO/OECD definition of which:	2.37	1.40	0.98
2. not in claimant count	0.75	0.24	0.52
3. claimants	1.62	1.16	0.46
4. Claimants not unemployed under ILO/OECD definition of which:	0.79	0.52	0.28
5. inactive	0.63	0.41	0.22
6. employed	0.16	0.10	0.06
7. Claimant count	2.41	1.68	0.74

Source: Employment Gazette, April 1989.

Figures in Table 6.1 shows the difference between the two measures of UK unemployment. The UK claimant count is the sum of the claimants under the ILO/OECD definition of unemploymnt and the claimants not unemployed under the ILO/OECD definition (row 3 + row 4). Overall, the claimant count is higher than the survey measure, but the claimant count records a lower rate for women and a higher rate for men. The survey measure shows that 0.75 million people were unemployed but not claiming benefits, and are therefore excluded from the claimant count (row 2). This group includes many women who are not eligible for benefit. But 0.79 million claimants are excluded from the survey measure because they are either employed or have not sought work in the last four weeks (row 4). Of these, 0.63 million people were not actively seeking work (row 5). They include the long-term unemployed who are described as 'discouraged workers' and would accept work at the going wage (or even lower), but do not believe they will find work. The survey measure suggests that the claimant count may underestimate the number of unemployed. Unemployment could include the survey count of 2.37 million plus up to 0.63 million discouraged workers.

6.2.3   Changing the Measurement of the Unemployment Rate

The percentage measurement is made up of two parts: the numerator measures unemployment and the denominator measures the workforce or labour force. An increase in the value of the numerator and/or a decrease in the value of the denominator will increase the unemployment rate measure and *vice versa*. The official method of measuring the numerator and the denominator has been changed several times since 1979. As a result, the new unemployment rate measure gives a lower value than earlier measures. The changes shown in Tables

Table 6.2 Main changes to the unemployment count measure from 1979

Date of change	Type of change	Estimated effect '000)
Oct 1979	Switch to fortnightly benefits payment and signing on	+20
Nov 1980	School leavers not entitled to claim until September	−100
Nov 1981	Men aged over 60 in receipt of benefit for more than 1 year, switched to new benefit and not required to sign on	−37
Oct 1982	Clerical count of registered unemployed at job centres replaced by computer count of benefit claimants at benefit offices	−190
Apr 1983	Men aged over 60 gained additional benefits but not required to sign on	−162
Jul 1985	Changes to Northern Ireland count	−5
Mar 1986	Two-week delay in publication of monthly figures to eliminate those who were no longer employed	−55
Oct 1986	Abolition of right to claim partial benefit for those with insufficient contributions	−57
Jun 1987	Maximum period of disqualification from benefit extended from 6 to 13 weeks	−2
Oct 1988	Those under 18 years defined as in education, training or employment so removed from labour force	−100

Source: Adapted from Glaister (1988) and *Employment Gazette*

Figure 6.2   Changes in male and female unemployment rate using April 1989 definition

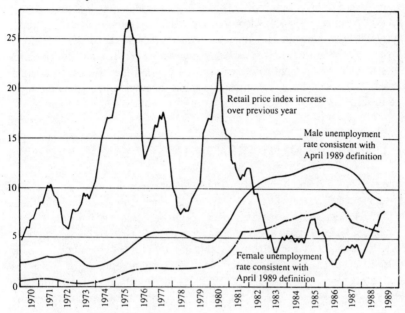

Source: Department of Employment

Table 6.3   Changes in the workforce measure

Definition	Components
Employed labour force	Employees in employment + self-employed + H.M Forces
Workforce in employment	Employed labour force + government training schemes
Working population	Employed labour force + unemployed + unemployed school leavers
Workforce	Workforce in employment + unemployed + unemployed school leavers

6.2 and 6.3 have reduced the unemployment count by approximately 690 000 while increasing the workforce measure.[7] Before July 1986 the denominator measure was employees in employment plus the unemployed (including school leavers). After July 1986 the denominator was changed to the working population plus unemployed, and then subsequently changed to the workforce measure plus unemployed. Whichever measure is used, a consistent series shows that unemployment rose steadily to 1986 and then started to decline. Figure 6.2 shows the changes in male and female unemployment using the April 1989 definition.

6.3 UNEMPLOYMENT TRENDS AND CHARACTERISTICS

At the turn of the century, the UK unemployment rate was about 4 per cent, but the rate increased sharply after 1921 to above 15 per cent. The unemployment rate then declined steadily to 8 per cent until the depression of the 1930s, when the rate rose sharply again to exceed 20 per cent. After 1932, the rate declined slowly towards 1940, and remained stable at around 3 per cent until the early 1970s. Much of the increase in unemployment seen in both the UK and in the main trading partners of the UK after 1970 has been attributed to recession. UK recession may have resulted from any one or a combination of the following factors:

1. UK monetary policy (restrictive or inflationary)
2. The impact of inflation derived from external factors such as rising oil prices and high import costs
3. Low levels of investment and the relative decline of the manufacturing base
4. Low levels of productivity and industrial competitiveness
5. The nature of the 'business cycle' or cyclical trends in international production and trade.

Explanations of demand-led unemployment may combine several of these features.[8] The time trend in Figure 6.2 shows how the unemployment rate has varied with the rate of inflation, as measured by the percentage change in the retail price index. Although upturns in the rate of unemployment appear to follow sharp increases in the rate of inflation (the classic augmented-Phillips curve), high levels of unemployment persisted despite the decrease in the rate of inflation after 1980. The number of notified vacancies was widely accepted as a reliable indicator of the pressure of demand during the period, but vacancy figures showed little variation after 1980 (*Employment Gazette*, monthly updates).

6.3.1 International Comparisons

A comparison of unemployment patterns in developed countries also provides some evidence that the persistence of unemployment in the 1980s was created by factors other than recession. From the graphs in Figure 6.3, it is clear that countries have experienced substantially different average rates since the 1950s as well as different trend and dispersion patterns around the average. Low and high average rates of unemployment are found in countries operating tight fiscal policy. Cross-national studies have also shown that where people are paid unemployment benefits over long periods, the average spell of unemployment tends to be longer (Layard 1986). Unemployment duration appears to account for the majority of variation in the rates of unemployment between countries.

6.3.2 Characteristics of the Unemployed in the UK

Patterns of unemployment tend to vary according to individual characteristics such as gender, age, ethnicity, qualification and experience, occupation and where people live. Evidence from the 1988 Labour Force Survey shows that higher rates of unemployment were experienced in the northern regions relative to the south, amongst the young, minority ethnic groups, and amongst the least well qualified. Between 1974 and 1984, the average regional unemployment rate increased from 2.3 per cent to 11.5 per cent, but the dispersion between regions declined.[9] By 1988, the regional average had fallen to 9.1 per cent, but the measure of regional disparity had increased above the 1979 level. The distribution of unemployment rates by type of qualification shows a similar pattern. Although the average unemployment rates by age and ethnic groups vary in the same way as regional rates over the period, the degree of disparity between groups continued to decline after 1984. In addition, not all groups experiencing higher average rates also experience the longest duration rates. The evidence suggests that policies which reduce total unemployment may affect the degree of disparity in groups in different ways. As a result, a fall in total unemployment may be accompanied by a rise in the rate of unemployment for one age group or one ethnic group.

6.4 MICROECONOMICS AND THE LABOUR MARKET

6.4.1 Unemployment and Market Failure in the Labour Market

Deficient demand may explain why unemployment rates increased in many OECD countries, but it does not fully explain why unemployment persists after periods of recession. Many economists have begun to look at the labour market

Figure 6.3   *International unemployment rates (OECD standardized rates)*

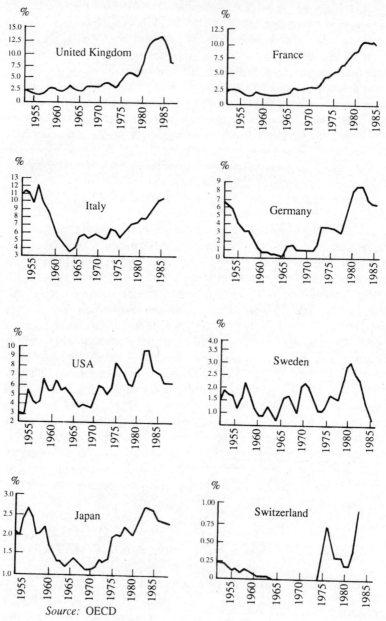

Source: OECD

with a view to explaining unemployment as the result of traditional market failure. If the labour market fails, the impact on unemployment of demand-based policy would be limited, and unemployment might be more effectively reduced by policies targeted directly at the source of failure.

The labour market can be modelled using a partial equilibrium approach, with demand and supply representing the optimal preferences for employment in the market at different real wages. Labour demand is derived from the demand for output as labour is a factor in production, and labour demand will shift outward (other things constant) as output increases. At any level of output, producers may also substitute other factor inputs for labour if labour becomes relatively expensive. Labour supply is derived from the optimal choices of individuals between hours in work and hours in non-work or leisure activities, at given real wages. Labour supply will shift with changes in the conditions of supply such as education, training, job search costs and the level of benefits.

Figure 6.4 shows a simple labour market equilibrium. Labour demand equals labour supply at the real wage W_1/P, and the amount of employment is N1. Unemployment is defined as an excess supply of labour at any real wage. Unemployment can only exist, therefore, if the market is restricted to maintain the real wage at a point like W'/P, above the equilibrium wage. This might happen if either government or trades' unions imposed price floors on wages to ensure a minimum wage above the equilibrium. Unemployment could be eliminated by removing the price floors. In most microeconomic analysis of markets, it is assumed that demand and supply schedules reflect social values at the margin as well as individual values when there is no market failure. However, macroeconomic definitions of unemployment are often described as equilibrium rates, as voluntary or involuntary, but these concepts are not directly comparable to the equilibrium in Figure 6.4.

There is a great deal of debate over whether unemployment is an equilibrium or disequilibrium concept, over the precise definition of voluntary and involuntary unemployment, and whether trade unions generate voluntary or involuntary unemployment. Much of the confusion stems from the assumption that the labour demand and supply schedules incorporate market failure associated with trades union activity, the existence of an unemployment benefit system, lack of information for job search, etc. The Classical economists and both Keynes and Friedman assumed that demand and supply of labour should include market failure. However, their definitions of market failure and equilibrium differed. These differences, and hence the confusion, can be found in the literature which has been developed from their work. The differences between the microeconomic equilibrium and disequilibrium approaches to unemployment, and their relationship to demand deficient unemployment are examined below.

Figure 6.4   Labour market equilibrium with no market failure

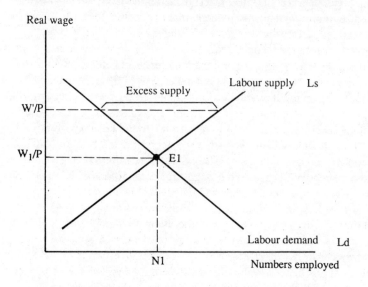

6.4.2   Microeconomic Approaches to Unemployment

Two microeconomic explanations for persistent unemployment have been
widely debated which emphasize the factors influencing labour demand and
supply and the nature of market failure. They are:

1. Labour supply may have altered if the workforce have decided to change the
    terms on which they accept employment because of changes in the structure
    of unemployment benefits or trade union membership.[10]
2. Labour demand may have altered if employers have changed the terms on
    which they offer work and appoint employees because of a rise in wage and
    non-wage labour costs and/or a decline in the competitiveness of UK
    industry.[11]

In order to determine which of these two explanations has been the most
important, economists have adopted either an equilibrium or a disequilibrium
approach to unemployment in the labour market. The equilibrium approach
examines the factors which affect the equilibrium rate of unemployment and may
therefore have caused it to rise. In this case equilibrium is defined as the market-
clearing level of employment and real wage in the presence of market failure.

The disequilibrium approach examines the factors which cause unemployment to fluctuate around the equilibrium level (market-clearing level with market failure), allowing disequilibrium unemployment to continue. The disequilibrium in this case is a type of equilibrium (because it persists), but it is defined as the level of employment and real wage with market failure where there is no tendency for change.

6.4.3   Equilibrium Rate Theories

Equilibrium rate theories model changes in the long-run rate of unemployment, or the rate which exists when price expectations are fulfilled. The long-run rate of unemployment is the level of unemployment at full-employment output or at the market-clearing equilibrium. According to Friedman (1968), this is the natural rate of unemployment which occurs if all the elements of market failure, including those derived from uncertainty and imperfect information in the labour market, are 'embedded' in the demand and supply functions. Persistent unemployment may arise if the equilibrium rate increases because of disturbances outside the economy, or because of structural changes in the technical and institutional framework of the economy which determine how quickly the labour market adjusts to equilibrium. These theories explain shifts in the natural rate of unemployment or the non-accelerating inflation rate of unemployment (NAIRU).

The natural rate can be illustrated as the level of unemployment at the equilibrium real wage and employment level N* in Figure 6.5 but only if we assume that the demand and supply schedules include market failure. Demand and supply schedules and the resulting equilibrium in Figure 6.5 are not comparable to those shown in Figure 6.4 The impact of introducing market failure is shown in Figure 6.6. Labour demand, Ld, and labour supply, Ls, are the schedules shown in Figure 6.4 which represent the optimal choices people would make when there is no market failure. The additional labour supply schedule, Ls*, represents the optimal choices people make when market failure such as job search costs exist and unemployment benefits are paid. The Ls* schedule is the same as that shown in Figure 6.5, and shows the number of people who are willing to accept (rather than want) work at the current real wage offered. The two labour supply schedules converge because it is assumed that the marginal value of a fixed level of unemployment benefit is smaller at higher real wage levels. For simplicity, it is assumed in Figure 6.6 that there is no market failure in labour demand so that Ld = Ld*.

Equilibrium in Figure 6.6 occurs at E^* at the market-clearing real wage W*/P, and employment level N^*. The distance between the two supply schedules $(Nx - N^*)$ at the equilibrium wage represents the natural rate of unemployment. Any factor which causes the Ls^* schedule to shift to the right, other things being constant, will reduce market failure and hence the natural rate of unemployment.

Figure 6.5 Equilibrium unemployment and the labour market

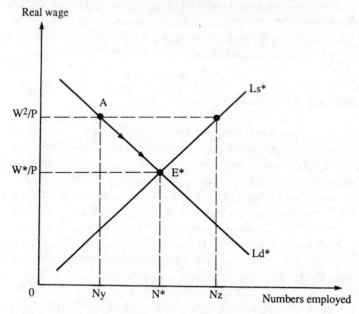

Figure 6.6   The impact of market failure on the labour market

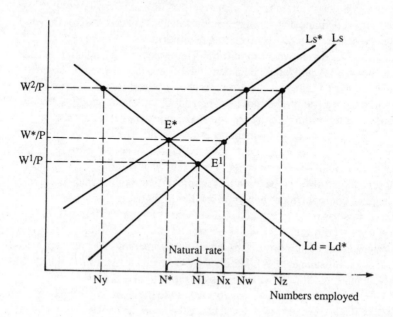

Classical unemployment could occur at the real wage, W^2/P, in Figure 6.6, where the unemployment $(Nz - Ny)$ is voluntary, but only $Nw - Ny$ is due to the high real wage. The Classical economists did not use diagrams, but in terms of Figures 6.5 and 6.6 they argued that the real wage should be reduced to W^*/P. Unemployment, however, could still occur at the equilibrium real wage because the Classical economists accepted that market rigidities or market failure existed at the market-clearing real wage.

Because the unemployment shown at W^2/P in Figures 6.5 and 6.6 does not occur at the market-clearing equilibrium real wage, it could be described as disequilibrium unemployment or involuntary unemployment. In fact Keynes described involuntary unemployment as the unemployment that existed when people were willing to accept a wage below the existing real wage.[12] The involuntary unemployment at W^2/P could be caused by a change in aggregate demand which alters the general price level, forcing up the real wage. A Keynesian response would be to shift the labour demand schedule. Keynes argued that the Classical response would not work. If nominal wage were to be reduced, for example, the labour market moves from point A towards point E^* in Figure 6.5. However, the movement down the labour demand schedule could cause a shift in aggregate demand, which could then cause the labour demand schedule to shift, and the target equilibrium to shift.

Most textbooks identify two types of unemployment: voluntary and involuntary. Involuntary unemployment is usually equated with Keynesian demand-deficient unemployment. For Keynes, frictional unemployment existed because of 'natural' market failure such as lack of information in the labour market, and voluntary unemployment existed because of 'institutional' factors such as trade unions and governments. Both types of non-demand-deficient unemployment caused by market failure in the labour market are usually included in the term 'voluntary unemployment' in modern analysis. Voluntary unemployment can therefore be described as: *all unemployment corresponding to the natural rate or the market-clearing rate; those people who are looking for work but would only accept work at a higher wage.* This may be caused by:

1. Frictional unemployment due to market failure caused by poor information and job search;
2. Structural/mismatch unemployment due to market failure caused by the immobility of labour and capital, and institutional factors such as trades unions which lengthen the time industry takes to adjust to changing demands.

Those who are voluntarily unemployed are strictly not in the labour force at the equilibrium wage because they would only accept employment at a higher wage (Minford *et al.*, 1985). Using this definition, the actual unemployment rate measured in the market can be assumed to be the natural rate. It exists because unemployment benefit payments and the black economy provide a buffer zone above the equilibrium wage.

Search theories have been developed from the natural rate equilibrium analysis.[13] Everyone who looks for a job is assumed to make a personal assessment of the likelihood of getting the wage rate wanted. In order to find the highest wage being offered, the person looking for a job will have to spend time and money gathering information. The cost of looking for a job at the margin is the value of the best wage offered minus the value of any government benefits which could be claimed. The benefit at the margin is the present value (or discounted stream) of best wages expected, minus the best wages offered. Each person looking for a job will have to decide on their 'reservation wage': the lowest wage which will be accepted because it just balances the marginal benefits and marginal costs of looking for a job. Because the reservation wage tends to decline as the job search continues, most people will accept any job offered with a wage which exceeds the reservation wage. An important prediction derived from the job search model of the natural rate of unemployment is that the equilibrium rate will increase if unemployment benefit rates rise relative to the wage rate (replacement ratio), and if trades unions increase in strength.

The impact of unemployment benefits and trade union activity on the natural rate can be shown with a simple model. Assume that the total workforce is limited and that the economy only produces two goods. One good, cars, are produced with unionized labour and the other good, services, are produced with non-union labour. The trades union in the car sector can raise wages by restricting employment, but the union would like to have both higher wages and more unionized labour. If the demand for union labour is exogenous, the union will maximize its goals for higher wages and more labour, given the constraint of the demand for union labour in the car sector. The result will be that the unionized sector will determine how much of the total labour force is used to make cars. Given the demand for non-union labour, if there are no unemployment benefits, the wage in the non-union sector must adjust to attract the rest of the labour force looking for work. Otherwise there may be unemployment. If unemployment benefits become available, the reservation wage will increase amongst those looking for work in the non-union sector. Jobs will be available but only at a wage lower than the reservation wage, and voluntary unemployment will arise. Similarly, an increase in national insurance contributions will tend to lower demand in both union and non-union sectors with the same size labour force, increasing the amount of voluntary unemployment.

Search models predict that equilibrium unemployment will rise if unemployment benefits rise, if taxes on employment rise, and with an increase in trade union ability to raise wages for a given level of union employment. Unemployment will also rise with a fall in the rate of productivity growth or with less favourable terms of trade, affecting labour demand. In addition, structural changes which increase the mismatch of jobs and job searchers, or demographic changes which increase the proportion of difficult to employ groups, may also increase the equilibrium rate of unemployment.

Estimates of the natural rate of unemployment in the UK suggest that the rate has risen sharply in recent years. Layard and Nickell (1986) estimate that the average long-run natural rate between 1980 and 1983 was 9.0 per cent, four percentage points below the actual rate. The average long-run natural rate during the period 1955–66, however, was 1.96 per cent, equal to the actual rate. However, empirical studies use different models with different data sets. As a result, the estimates of the importance of trade union power and unemployment benefits in explaining unemployment gained from these studies vary widely. For example, Minford estimates the values of the elasticity of unemployment with respect to the real value of unemployment benefits and trade unionization as 3 and 5.5 respectively. Nickell and Andrews find that these variables have very little impact on employment and unemployment (Greenhalgh 1983).

In fact, changes in the level of unemployment benefit since the mid-1970s have caused the replacement ratio to fall. This should have reduced unemployment rates. In addition, the groups who experience higher unemployment rates in the 1980s form a smaller proportion of the workforce than similar groups a decade earlier. On the demand side, the decline in the manufacturing sector, the increase in raw material prices, and the rise in real wages relative to productivity have tended to increase unemployment. Where profits have suffered, employers have tended to shed labour in order to move away from labour-intensive techniques.

6.4.4 Disequilibrium Adjustment Theories

Unemployment persistence can also be explained by modelling market failure caused by wage stickiness. Because the labour market adjusts slowly, quantity or employment tends to adjust rather than price or real wages. Disequilibrium is defined as a point where the labour market comes to a temporary or permanent rest above the market-clearing real wage. If the rest is permanent, the equilibrium is defined as a position where there is no tendency for change. Most disequilibrium adjustment models are based on a combination of the following types of market failure which stop the labour market reaching its market-clearing equilibrium:

1. Labour market segmentation, which occurs when employers discriminate because of skills, gender and age
2. Trade union practices
3. Pay bargaining methods and employer practices
4. Mode of production and type of good produced
5. Size of the public sector (Bacon and Eltis hypothesis)
6. Labour mobility problems.

In *insider/outsider models* (Blanchard and Summers 1986), the labour market is segmented into two sectors:

1. The primary sector – where employees and employers have the power to bargain over wages and employment, so that wages can rise above the market clearing equilibrium,
2. The secondary sector – where wages are set at the market-clearing level.

Those in work in the primary sector are called insiders. If a demand shock reduces employment in the primary sector, the people who are laid off may become outsiders, and the smaller number of insiders will continue to set wages and employment to protect the smaller insider group. In the extreme case, when all the unemployed immediately become outsiders, temporary shocks to labour market equilibrium may persist, resulting in permanent disequilibrium. This form of disequilibrium is known as hysteresis. It occurs when the current level of unemployment becomes the equilibrium level.

Insiders may be able to maintain the real wage above the market-clearing level because they have union power. However, primary workers need not be unionized. They may gain the power to raise wages if the costs of hiring and firing for specific skills are very high, if long-run employment contracts reduce the risks for both the employer and employee, and if they threaten unionization and output disruption.

Search-related models have been developed to investigate the persistence of unemployment under variations in demand conditions by introducing the concept of the segmented market.[14] These models show that if unemployment benefits are available for longer periods, the long- and short-term unemployed will look for work with different intensity. In this case, Bean and Layard (1988) argue that a demand shock which increases unemployment will mean that more people are unemployed for longer. A larger pool of ineffective job searchers will put even less downward pressure on wages in the primary sector, leading to persistent unemployment.

Timing and persistence models are derived from economic models of human capital which look at the decisions people take over their whole life. Modern classical macroeconomic models explain cyclical fluctuations in unemployment by assuming that leisure is easily substituted across different periods, affecting the timing of the decision to participate in the labour force.[15] This assumption is known as intertemporal substitution. People who work are assumed to time their participation to coincide with temporary periods of relatively high real wages. If aggregate demand decreases suddenly, people will reduce their participation rates and unemployment increases initially. However, most people soon revise their participation decision upward to maintain their average lifetime participation level, causing labour supply to rise.

Alternatively, persistence models assume that those who are employed for longer accumulate more human capital, raising the marginal value of their work and hence the opportunity cost of their leisure. For most people, their current employment status is determined by their past work experience, and so persistence implies that a decrease in aggregate demand results in an increase in unemployment and lower labour supply.[16] These models show that labour markets will not return to market-clearing equilibrium levels in the medium term.

Efficiency wage models are derived from organizational theory and the cost of monitoring productivity when two parties, the employer and the employee, do not have the same type of information. In most cases, it is assumed that employers have less knowledge about marginal productivity than individual workers and that workers will tend to shirk when paid a standard wage rate. If the costs of monitoring workers are high, the firm may decide to raise the wage above the equilibrium market-clearing level. A higher real wage will increase the impact of the threat of dismissal and will discourage shirking. If other firms follow suit, the wage in that sector will increase, generating excess supply above the market-clearing wage and unemployment will continue. This sector can then be seen as a primary wage sector, and unemployed workers are effectively queuing for access.

6.5   POLICY IMPLICATIONS AND CONCLUSIONS

The labour market models outlined above indicate that the natural rate or labour market failure should be the target for policy action to reduce persistent unemployment. A reduction in voluntary unemployment can be achieved by reducing the impact of market failure in the labour market. In terms of Figure 6.6, many of these policies will result in a shift to the right of the Ls* schedule. They include the following:

1. Reduce mismatch by raising the chance of finding a job at the reservation wage via government training schemes and actions such as those detailed in the 1989 White Paper, *Employment for the 1990s*.
2. Reduce the marginal rate of tax which holds the perceived real wage below the equilibrium real wage.
3. Reduce the replacement ratio by reducing size, duration and coverage of benefit schemes.
4. Increase labour mobility by improving information flows and reducing regional disparities generated by market failure in other sectors.
5. Reduce the monopoly power of unions who raise wages in union sectors, resulting in lower relative wages in non-union sectors and subsequent unemployment.

Reductions in labour market rigidities will reduce wage stickiness and fluctuations around the natural rate. In some cases, however, market rigidities may result in permanent disequilibrium unemployment. In these models, it is possible to argue that not all unemployment derived from market failure is voluntary, although the friction is derived from the labour market and not the goods market as in the modern Keynesian case. The impact of demand shocks can result in a permanent or persistent change in the nature of unemployment. As a result, classical Keynesian policy responses may reduce unemployment if market frictions cannot be affected. The difference between Keynesian involuntary unemployment and all the definitions of voluntary unemployment depends on the nature of market failure. Keynes accepted that market failure would lead to unemployment, but the type of failure that results from uncertainty in a money economy was not to be classified as standard market failure. Search models, however, tend to model uncertainty in the same way as all other market failure in the labour market.

In the case of search unemployment, Diamond (1982) argues that expanding demand can create new vacancies and increase the chance of finding a job, without raising the reservation wage to the extent that the likelihood of leaving unemployment is unchanged. Timing and persistence models imply that expansionary policy can have a longer-run effect on unemployment without rational economic agents being consistently wrong. However, efficiency wage models imply that expansionary policy may reduce unemployment, but also reduce productivity. Despite the sophistication of the micro-foundations approach, the two strands of analysis from which it was derived are still in contention and the evidence suggests that involuntary unemployment is still a significant policy issue.

One reason why the theories continue to proliferate but the contention remains is that the micro-foundations approach has not tackled the underlying problem of the relationship between money prices and money wages. To assume that employment levels are determined in the labour market is to assume that money wages and the price level can be determined independently. However, prices are an element in wage determination, and wages are a cost of production and enter into price determination. With this in mind, all the micro-foundation theories can be categorized as natural rate theories because attention is focused on equilibrium market clearing rather than on the dynamic problems of how to reach market-clearing equilibrium.

NOTES

1. For a classic survey of unemployment theory see Malinvaud (1977) and more recently see Johnson and Layard (1986).
2. For an overview of the Keynesian reappraisal see Chapter 7 of this volume, Gowland (1985), Chapters 7 and 8, Gowland (1983), Chapter 3, and Gowland (1979), Chapter 6 by G. Davies. Also see Coddington (1983) and Chick (1983) for a more detailed discussion.
3. For a general discussion of modern extensions see Minford *et al.* (1985).
4. Two good general references on unemployment theories are Layard (1986) and Minford *et al.* (1985).
5. Long-run models usually assume that the unemployment rate is independent of the size of the labour force and changes in technical progress, for example see Johnson and Layard (1986).
6. Before 1987, the ILO/OECD definition was reported concurrently with the old Labour Force definition which covered those without a job who were seeking work in the survey week or were prevented from doing so by temporary sickness or holiday, or were waiting to start a new job already obtained.
7. Changes in the measurement of unemployment are discussed in more detail in a recent article by Glaister (1988) and the *Employment Gazette,* August 1988.
8. For a general discussion of demand theories and the links between these factors see Chapter 1 in Prest and Coppock (1988) and Part 1, Coates and Hillard (1986). An intermediate but clear introduction can be found in Creedy (1981), and for a quantitative approach see Part I of Greenhalgh *et al.* (1983).
9. Dispersion here is measured by the coefficient of variation, the standard deviation relative to the mean.
10. A study by Dilnot and Morris (1982) showed that between 1968 and 1978, the overall impact of changes in the tax and benefit system led to an increase in the replacement ratio such that in 1980, 11 per cent of employees could expect to receive 90 per cent of their earnings as benefit in the first two weeks out of work.
11. For a general discussion on the macroeconomic implications of wage formation see Calmfors and Horn (eds) (1986).
12. See page 209 of the *General Theory.* The author would like to thank her colleague Brendan Sheehan for his ideas and useful comments in this section.
13. For a review of the recent developments in search theory see McKenna(1985), and for a discussion of quantitative applications and empirical modelling see Blundell and Walker (1986).
14. A survey of the use and implications of a variety of search models in segmented markets is provided by Dickens and Lang (1988).
15. The classic paper exploring initial empirical applications of intertemporal substitution is Lucas and Rapping (1970).
16. Empirical analysis and a comparison of the two hypotheses with respect to female participation and labour supply is examined by Clark and Summers in Greenhalgh *et al.* (1983).

REFERENCES

Bacon, R. and Eltis, W. (1978), *Britain's Economic Problem: Too Few Producers* (2nd edition), Macmillan, London.

Blanchard, O.J. and Summers, L.H. (1986), 'Hysteresis and the European Unemployment Problems', in S. Fischer (ed.), *NBER Macroeconomics Annual,* MIT Press, Cambridge, Mass.

Blundell, R. and Walker, I. (1986) (eds), *Unemployment, Search and Labour Supply,* Cambridge University Press, Cambridge.

Calmfors, L. and Horn, H. (eds) (1986), *Trade Unions, Wage Formation and Macroeconomics Stability*, Macmillan, London.

Chick, V. (1983), *Macroeconomics After Keynes*, Philip Allan, Oxford.

Clower, R.W. (1965), 'The Keynesian Counter-Revolution: A Theoretical Appraisal' in F. Hahn and E. Brechling (eds), *A Theory of Interest Rates*, Macmillan, London.

Coates, D. and Hillard, J. (1986), *The Economic Decline of Modern Britain*, Wheatsheaf Books, Brighton.

Coddington, A. (1983), *Keynesian Economics*, Allen and Unwin, London.

Creedy, J. (1981), *The Economics of Unemployment in Britain*, Butterworths, London.

Diamond, P.A. (1982), 'Aggregate demand management in search equilibrium', *Journal of Political Economy*, vol. 90(5), pp.881–94.

Dickens, W. and Lang, K. (1988), 'The Reemergence of Segmented Labour Markets Theory', *American Economic Review: Papers and Proceedings*.

Dilnot, A.W. and Morris, C.N. (1982), 'Modelling Replacement Rates', Institute of Fiscal Studies, Working Paper 39, October.

Friedman, M. (1968), 'The Role of Monetary Policy', *American Economic Review*, vol. 58 (March).

Glaister, K. (1988), 'Measuring the Rate of Unemployment', *British Economic Survey*, vol. 18(1).

Gowland, D.H. (ed.) (1979), *Modern Economic Analysis*, Butterworths, London.

Gowland, D.H. (ed.) (1983), *Modern Economic Analysis 2*, Butterworths, London.

Gowland, D.H. (1985), *Money, Inflation & Unemployment: The role of money in the economy*, Harvester Press, Brighton.

Greenhalgh, C.A., Layard, P.R.G. and Oswald, A.J. (eds) (1983), *The Causes of Unemployment*, Clarendon Press, Oxford.

Johnson, G. and P.R.G. Layard (1986), 'The Natural Rate of Unemployment: Explanations and Policy', Chapter 16 in O. Ashenfelter and P.R.G. Layard (eds), *The Handbook of Labour Economics*, North-Holland, Amsterdam.

Layard, P.R.G. (1986), *How to Beat Unemployment*, Oxford University Press, Oxford.

Leijonhufvud, A. (1968), *On Keynesian Economics and the Economics of Keynes*, Oxford University Press, Oxford.

Lucas, R.E. and Rapping, L. (1970), 'Real Wages, Employment and Inflation', in Phelps, E. *et al.*, *Microeconomic Foundations of Employment and Inflation Theory*, W.W. Norton, New York.

Mckenna, C.J. (1985), *Uncertainty and the Labour Market: recent developments in job-search theory*, Wheatsheaf, Brighton.

Malinvaud, E., (1977), *The Theory of Unemployment Reconsidered*, Blackwell, Oxford.

Minford, A.P.L., Ashton, P., Peel, M., Davies, D., and Sprague, A., (1985), *Unemployment: Cause and Cure* (2nd edition), Basil Blackwell, Oxford.

Prest, A.R. and Coppock, D.J. (eds) (1988), *The U.K. Economy, A manual in applied economics* (12th edition), Weidenfeld & Nicholson, London.

7   The Costs of Inflation

D.H. Gowland

7.1   INTRODUCTION

As stated in the chapter on inflation (5) it is clear that electorates view inflation as the one unforgiveable sin in governments not only in the USA (for example, Carter in 1980) and the UK but also in Japan and continental Europe, especially Germany. Moreover, throughout the 1980s Mrs Thatcher and her successive chancellors have stressed that the reduction and elimination of inflation was and should be the overriding goal of economic policy; inflation was 'public economy number one' as it was put in one Budget speech. In pursuit of this goal, Mrs Thatcher was prepared to suffer both electoral unpopularity (especially in 1981 and 1989) and to pay a high economic price, in terms of unemployment and lost output (albeit in her view this was a short-term price, see p. 114). However, elementary economics textbooks are at a loss to explain why it is such an evil. The purpose of this chapter is to examine and assess the arguments that have so far been advanced as to why inflation is a problem. In other words, why is it regarded as so evil and is it correct to regard it as so damaging?

The view that inflation is evil has become inextricably, if illogically, linked with monetarism. Amongst the twelve tenets of Mayer's definition of the monetarist creed is a proposition that inflation is a major policy problem and that its control should usually be given priority in economic management (Mayer 1978, p. 2). Brunner, in his comment on Mayer (Mayer 1978, p.59–60) argued that it was absurd to include a value judgement or policy preference amongst the defining characteristics of a school of economics, characterizing Mayer's dictum as a 'widespread misconception'. If monetarism is viewed only as an economic doctrine, Brunner's argument is obviously right. There is no logical relationship between a view of how an economy works and a preference for one economic goal rather than another. Nevertheless, since positive and normative are rarely totally separable where monetarism is concerned if only because anti-monetarists tend to view monetarism as a much broader creed than its supporters. Thus Mayer has a point. Moreover monetarism has usually gained credence as an anti-inflationary creed, at least in the last 100 years. Virtually all anti-monetarists treat this as being a litmus test for monetarism and argue that elimination of inflation should not be the overriding goal of economic policy (Desai, 1981, p.8-

151

10; Hahn, 1982, p.13; Kaldor, 1982, p.3; Tylecote, 1981, p.21). Many self-styled Keynesians seem to argue that an incomes policy should be relied on to control inflation. They accept a risk of failure and so of high inflation because they feel it is outweighed by the benefits of being able to use demand management policies to reduce unemployment. Keynes himself disagreed with this – he felt that the control of inflation should be the first priority of economic policy, unemployment coming second in a lexigraphic ordering (Keynes, 1923). Moreover, he decried incomes policies as undesirable and ineffective (1971, volume XXII). It is indeed difficult, in practice, to find a self-styled monetarist who does not share Keynes's phobia about inflation. Hence there seems in practice to be a difference in attitude which a political economist cannot ignore. Certainly, nearly every commentator links the resurgence of monetarism in part to an increasing concern about inflation in the 1970s, for example, Foot (1981), p.20; Desai (1981, p.8); Friedman (1977) sceptic, critic and high priest alike. Most important of all, all avowedly monetarist governments have been very anxious in both theory and practice to eliminate inflation – for example Thatcher (UK), Reagan (USA) and Fraser (Australia). Indeed some cynics have argued that monetarism is only an excuse for deflation, or defended it on such grounds: Fforde (1983). It has similarly been argued that Volcker's switch to monetarism in 1979 was merely 'camouflage' for high interest rates (as a Keynesian member of the Federal Reserve Bank termed it); see the discussion in Gredier (1987). No doubt it is true in some quarters but there does seem to be a genuine link between changing political attitudes, monetarism and opinions about inflation. In these circumstances, no study of monetarism would be complete without an analysis of the costs and benefits of inflation.

Leijonhufvud in brilliant polemical papers (1981, Chapters 9 and 10) has argued that only economists doubt that inflation is an evil. He tartly linked this position to the fact that they were uniquely protected from the effects of inflation because as intellectuals their main asset was human capital, immune from the ravages of inflation. In the UK, moreover, economists have the prospect of index-linked pensions whether employed by government or in academia. This is a good personal argument but while it is true that virtually all non-economists believe inflation to be evil this does not mean that they are right. Popular opinion can be wrong. Self-interested economists might be right! It is an economist's task to analyse beliefs and see if they are well founded (as Leijonhufvud does). Accordingly Section 7.2 presents the standard textbook argument that inflation is relatively harmless or, at worst, that its evils are remediable by suitable government action. The usual remedy is indexation, discussed in Section 7.4 after a discussion (Section 7.3) which presents the counter-case, that inflation is evil, together with rebuttals of these arguments.

7.2 THE LESSER EVIL

Economists usually assume that an individual's welfare is a function of his consumption of goods over time, or of real income. Keynes for example put it as follows:

> Consumption is – to repeat the obvious – the sole end and effect of all economic activity. (Keynes, 1936, p. 104).

In this case it is very difficult to show that inflation is harmful, although not impossible. Hence the battleground is defined by most economists so as to make it much harder to demonstrate the case that inflation is evil. Inflation, it is usually argued or assumed in elementary textbooks, cannot lessen the quantity of goods available for distribution and so it cannot lessen welfare. The distributive consequences may be undesirable but they can be offset: for example, if inflation hurts the elderly, old-age pensions can be increased.

Moreover it is often argued that inflation (or the price level) will be positively correlated with output. This argument is usually based on a Phillips curve, or aggregate supply curve argument that inflation and unemployment are alternatives (see p. 109). Alternatively, it is argued that inflation greases the wheels of industry such that higher output is generated. The mechanism for this is rarely stated but it is usually taken to be through offering incentives to entrepreneurs or by facilitating relative price movements. These arguments are usually stated rather than demonstrated. The simplest is that inflation reduces real wages because prices rise by more than wages. Lower real wages increase the demand for labour. Moreover lower real wages should imply higher profits and so provide inducement to increase output. The assumption that inflation lowers average real wages is no longer valid and in any case even if effective such regressive redistribution is rarely desirable. The argument about relative price movements is that it is assumed money prices cannot fall. Hence if for example it is necessary for the (relative) price of wine to fall in terms of beer this can only be achieved by a rise in the price of beer. These arguments and their consequences are considered below in the context of the anti-inflation case. However, if it is the case that a trade-off between inflation and unemployment exists, for any reason, this virtually settles the argument for viewing inflation as a necessary evil. The nature of utility functions assures this result: if only goods enter utility functions and the acceptance of inflation increases the quantity of goods available, inflation must be a 'good thing'.

It is conventional, moreover, to divide inflation into 'anticipated' and 'unanticipated' and to argue that only the latter is undesirable. The system can adjust to expected inflation. This is usually extended to a proposition that while accelerating inflation may have harmful side-effects, because it is unpredictable, any *stable* level of inflation will be anticipated and so adjusted for. For example, it is argued that nominal rates of interest will rise by the amount of the expected rate of inflation. Similarly, contracts will be written so that both parties are aware of their prospective real obligations and benefits. With minor exceptions, inflation will be a harmless feature of such a model. Inflation will certainly cause problems for the tax system. If indirect taxes are specific and direct taxes progressive then inflation will reduce the real yield of the former and increase that of the latter. For example if prices double the real yield of a tax of £1 per gallon of beer is halved. If an individual's pre-tax real income is unchanged, the proportion taken as tax will rise with inflation. For example, if the tax rate is 25 per cent above an allowance of £2000 an individual with an income of £5000 will pay £750 income tax: 15 per cent. If prices double his nominal income would have to rise to £10000 to leave his real income unchanged – but his tax bill of £2000 would be 20 per cent of income. This effect is usually called 'bracket creep' in the USA and 'fiscal drag' in the UK. Fiscal drag increased the proportion of direct taxation to total taxes by about 10 per cent in the UK in the decade of high inflation 1969–79. However tax rates can be adjusted to leave their real impact unchanged. This can be done automatically by some form of indexation, for example by linking the £1 per gallon and £2000 allowance in the above example to the price level (so that both the taxes would be doubled if the price level doubled). This was done in the UK in 1977 by the Rooker-Wise amendment[1] and in the USA by the 1981 Reagan tax reform. Similar problems arise with corporate taxation and indeed the drawing up of corporate accounts. Accountancy theorists and practitioners have debated for years how to prevent meaningful company accounts in an inflationary era: the inflation accounting debate.[2] Nevertheless it seems the problems arise from changes in relative prices as much as inflation and the changes in the absolute price level. The indexation of tax rates is an example of a general theme, since it is argued that indexation can eliminate any problems. The advantages and disadvantages of inflation are considered in Section 7.4. So far as the evils of indexation are concerned the argument runs: if inflation is a problem, indexed contracts will emerge through market forces, or that governments can ensure they will, if markets fail. The debate about indexation is a long-running one. Suffice it to comment that virtually all economists regard it as desirable but are divided about how much of the ill-effects of inflation it can remove. Leijonhufvud (1981) is the best argued of the sceptics.

In brief, the standard textbook argument is that high and growing output should be the main goal of economic policy. If inflation is a by-product of this, its effects must be accepted and ameliorated if possible. Certainly it is never worth paying very much in terms of the economic costs of loss of output or the social costs of unemployment to avoid inflation. In contrast, Friedman's views of the role of indexation and the evils of inflation stand starkly clear:

I know of no other (expedient)...that holds as much promise of both reducing the harm done by inflation and facilitating the ending of inflation...(it is necessary) to end inflation before inflation ends not only the conventional wisdom but perhaps also the free society. (Friedman 1977)

7.3 THE CASE AGAINST INFLATION

The arguments that inflation should be eliminated even at a very high cost are as follows. Inflation is immoral because of the effects it produces. These arise in part from uncertainty and in particular because inflation redistributes income and wealth in a highly undesirable fashion. Moreover, uncertainty hinders the working of the price mechanism and, at the least, means that there is a welfare loss through inefficiency and at the worst that the survival of capitalism is endangered. This welfare cost is intensified because sub-optimal holdings of money are held. Crucially, inflation is the cause of unemployment, not the alternative. This argument has been used extensively in the UK by Mrs Thatcher (see p. 114). Finally, this school observes the negative correlation between output and inflation and observes that this proves that one or other of the above arguments must be right. As this is a powerful case with many more ramifications than the textbook case it will be scrutinized in detail.

In 1990 a resolution was introduced in the US Congress to make the elimination of inflation the sole goal of US Monetary Policy, backed by five of the 12 Federal Reserve District Presidents. One of them, Black, argued that it was desirable because of the negative correlation between output and inflation. He went on to cite the redistribution, uncertainty and signal arguments referred to above. This is a typical example of the use of this argument by powerful policy makers as well as academics.

Many writers argue that inflation is *per se* immoral and that 'sound money' as a moral absolute should be an end in itself. This view is widely and sincerely held, sometimes in a moderate form as by Mrs Thatcher, sometimes in a hyperbolic one – for example Justice Douglas, who regarded it as 'the end of Western civilization' when the USA left the gold standard because it would lead to inflation (Schlesinger, 1969, p.201). By their very nature such moral absolutist positions cannot be debated or scrutinized, especially where the position is universalizable except on logical grounds.[3] Fortunately for the analyst the position is often stated in utilitarian fashion which is amenable to scrutiny. Inflation, it is sometimes argued, leads to an upsurge of sexual immorality although the connecting links in the argument are weak (see for example in Stein and Stein's brilliant monetarist novel, 1978). More plausible, inflation is linked with the breakdown of political order, usually citing Rome and Weimar Germany. Neither example is very persuasive since Roman inflation was at a peak in the third century and its external political weakness was still 150 years in the future whereas internal political chaos was recurrent throughout its history.[4] The history of Weimar Germany is very complex but once one has taken note of national humiliation, the First World War, the French occupation of the Ruhr and the incompetence and intransigence of virtually all non-Nazi politicians, it is difficult to link directly the alleged cause of inflation with the effect of Nazism.[5]

The proposition that inflation renders it impossible for a government to fulfill some of its basic functions is more impressive. One of the core functions of a liberal state is to provide an environment in which contracts can be made and enforced. The uncertainty generated by inflation makes it much harder to draft fair contracts over time. Indeed in some cases it is impossible. Equally, however, it does not render contracts totally unmakeable so this argument is better combined with the efficiency arguments below. However, inflation does deny to individuals the right to plan for the future. An individual cannot make provisions for retirement or in general plan consumption over time. In summary, inflation generates uncertainty and the effects of this are objectionable on equitable as well as efficiency grounds. The main argument that inflation is unjust must rely on its redistributive effects. The basic effect of inflation is to transfer wealth and income from creditor to debtor, although uncertainty may render both worse off than in a world of price stability. The largest debtor, in money-denominated assets, is the government. Any gain by this is usually called the inflation tax. Its composition and size are much debated but in general it is usually agreed to be an arbitrary and unfair tax, however small. Some governments have also gained by the fact that if a progressive tax system is expressed in nominal terms then its real yield will rise with inflation, 'fiscal drag' or 'bracket creep', as the real value of allowances and lower rate bands fall. Inflation, in practice, often increases direct and reduces indirect taxes so that their real value changes with inflation. Such effects can be removed by indexation, as in the UK, but they may be significant in the real world, however irrational this may be. For example, it was (wrongly) assumed in early 1983 that Congress would abolish the indexation clause of the Reagan tax 'cuts' because this would have been a simple way of increasing taxation. Moreover many politicians seemed incapable of realizing that it was a tax increase at all or, rather, many Congressmen and Senators, especially Democrats, seemed incapable of realizing that indexation is not a tax cut. One may conclude that at the least the effect of inflation is to lead to confusion in making tax policy which is likely to lead to a less desirable outcome. Nevertheless the interaction of political processes and inflation is so complex that general conclusions about its effects are impossible to make.

The other main debtor in the UK, apart from the government, has traditionally been the rich. It may seem paradoxical that the rich gain by inflation and perverse that this is because they borrow from the poor. Nevertheless this is the case. One reason is that the opportunity to profit from inflation is only open to the relatively well-off and, except for owner-occupation, to the rich. The way to make a profit out of inflation is to borrow funds, use these to buy real assets and pay off the debt with depreciated money. However, in practice, this is an option only open to the wealthy. There are prohibitive transaction costs on small dealings. Diversification is necessary, since no asset is guaranteed to rise with inflation. Indeed to profit from inflation one usually needs sophisticated advice and a large portfolio. Finally to be able to borrow presupposes collateral and therefore wealth. Hence it is not as surprising as it may seem that the only group in the UK who did not possess net monetary assets were the richest 10 per cent. The credit boom of the 1980s has modified this picture somewhat, but borrowing is still highly income and wealth-elastic.

Less well-off groups have sought inflation hedges in a variety of forms, the cult of the equity in the 1950s being the first, as it was assumed that ordinary shares (equities) would protect their holder against inflation. However, some forms of these, such as insurance policies, fared very badly and the value of ordinary shares in real terms fell by 70 per cent between 1960 and 1980. They recovered in the 1980s, of course, but only when inflation was low. The only asset which served as an inflation hedge was owner-occupied property. Even here the benefits of rising house prices to an owner-occupier are debatable. The benefit is only encashable when the owner moves to a smaller house. Indeed those owner-occupiers planning to 'trade-up' are probably losers. Nevertheless even illiquid wealth or the prospect of wealth is better than none at all, so that it is reasonable to view most owner-occupied as gainers from inflation. The benefits, such as they were, were gained by those of above average income who obtained mortgages, at the expense of building society depositors. The typical building society depositor has a deposit of £6000 so, in miniature, three depositors lend money to one house purchaser – the average mortgage outstanding is £20 000 and building societies hold 15 per cent reserves. This in itself suggests the depositor is less well off. Only 2 per cent of mortgagees have incomes below the tax threshold whereas about 20 per cent of depositors do. Hence the savings of the poor as well as of reasonably well-off people are lent to the reasonably well-off. (An added complication is that some people are both mortgagees and depositors.) In fact the main redistributive effect of mortgage lending is horizontal, from old to young, but it is regressive in so far as it is vertical. Local authorities have borrowed to build council houses and the resulting gains are distributed across all tenants within a local authority by pooling. Hence the gain is arbitrary by area even though perhaps more equitably by income and age, than in the private sector.

The old, especially the private sector pensioner, lose by inflation to the young. However, the old gain by house price inflation. The private sector employee also loses out to the public sector worker since the variance of wage settlements is much higher and so is the risk of a fall in real income. Public sector employees are fairly well protected against falls in real income. Finally in the UK the South (a net borrower) gains at the expense of the North (a net saver). However, the redistribution from poor to rich, old to young and private to public sector employee is much less than the capricious and random redistribution within each group. It is undeniable that inflation does produce undesirable changes and that fear of its ravages does cause suffering.

The most serious form of maldistribution in the eyes of most observers may be that the unscrupulous are permitted to profit by what are at least perceived to be anti-social activities such as asset-stripping at the expense of the thrifty and honest. This is also the basis of the first of the efficiency arguments. Inflation distorts the incentives which are necessary for a capitalist or mixed economy to function satisfactorily. Any argument for market forces from Adam Smith's invisible hand onwards has used the idea that by maximizing self-interest, individuals indirectly maximize the public good. For example, Henry Ford became the world's richest man by satisfying the demand for cheap and reliable cars. However, pursuit of profit from inflation yields no such social return. In this it is akin to rent seeking rather than profit maximization, to use (the extreme pro-marketeer) Buchanan's terminology. There is no difference from the point of view of the individual but there is in the social return. If an individual makes money by buying an office block with borrowed money no-one else gains. If, however, he had had to invest in a cheaper or better computer to make a fortune others would have benefited. An extreme but interesting form of this is Cagan's model (1972) in which monopoly banks both cause and profit from inflation. At best the social return is zero, at worst significantly negative. There will be a bias towards certain industries, for example, housing, but, more seriously, towards wheeler-dealing at the expense of productive or useful activity. The diversion of the nation's entrepreneurial talents into attempts to protect themselves against or to profit from inflation is serious. This danger has been stressed by both Friedman and Keynes. Keynes indeed emphasized the point by attributing to Lenin the view that 'the way to destroy capitalism is to debauch the currency' (1923).

The blunting of incentives that most worried Keynes arose from a confusion of relative price changes with absolute ones. At a casual empiricist level, the evidence suggest that this has been a major problem in the UK over the last 40 years. If an individual observes that a price has risen he does not know whether this is a rise relative to the price of other goods or merely part of a general rise in prices. In the former case he should respond by considering a change to another good but not in the latter case. For example, a university lecturer could observe in 1977 that he could increase his income by £2000 per annum by becoming a polytechnic lecturer instead. This could have arisen from a deliberate policy to encourage academics to seek polytechnic posts or from an accident due to different calculations of expected inflation having been built into the two salaries (or even from 'overlapping contracts' made at different dates). It was not clear which, so the individual could not make a rational decision, nor consequently could the government rely on price incentives to facilitate job mobility. The problem is worse where one is responding to prices. If one's usual supermarket raises the price of goods, one does not know whether it is worth shopping around or not. So it is worth it if other supermarkets have not raised prices (that is a relative change) but not if they have (that is an absolute change). Deaton (1977) has argued that individuals will tend to assume all changes are relative; Keynes and Friedman that they are absolute. In either case the workings of the price mechanisms are hampered. Friedman (1977) followed Keynes by arguing that this was the main economic disadvantage of inflation. It blurred the signals and distorted the incentives on which a market economy depends.

One could restate this problem by saying that inflation increases uncertainty and reduces the amount of information available. In this way it will necessarily produce a less efficient allocation of resources. Garfinkel (1989) called this 'the confusion effect'. Jansen (1989) has recently denied its practical relevance. However, extra search costs will be incurred in these circumstances. Some writers have thought that these are amongst the more important costs of inflation (Friedman, 1969). To these search costs can be added additional transaction costs in the form of printing of catalogues, new price tags and alterations to cash registers unable to ring up the new total.

In practice inflation seems to redistribute income from profits to wages. This is very much a modern development; until the Second World War the opposite was a 'stylized fact' in the UK and was incorporated into trade cycle models etc. The change was almost certainly a product of increased trade union power. Indeed trade union power may be linked to inflation; the resurgence of strikes in the UK in 1989 coincided with inflation accelerating to 8 per cent. This redistribution may in itself be either desirable or undesirable, but it has been argued that it has serious efficiency effects because it reduces investment to a sub-optimal level. Through reducing the real rate of return on capital, inflation again distorts the price mechanism. This effect might, however, be offset by inflation reducing the real rate of interest; interest rates seem to rise by less than the increase in expected inflation, at least when inflation accelerates. Garfinkel estimates this welfare loss at 0.7 per cent of US GDP when inflation is 5 per cent (1989). He stresses that this problem is reinforced by other effects of the unattractiveness of fixed-interest debt in an inflationary age. One is that lenders will only be prepared to provide short-term finance. Another is a rise in the debt: equity ratio. The impact of inflation of financial markets is analysed in the next section.

Friedman analysed one particular loss of efficiency in some detail (1969). This is the welfare loss induced by sub-optimal holdings of money. This argument has been scrutinized in minute detail and is sometimes treated as if it were the only argument against inflation (Desai, 1981; Hahn, 1982). The argument rests on the assumption that money does not pay interest, based on legal constraints in the case of demand deposits and practicality, *pace* Gessell, in the case of currency. This obviously became less true in the 1980s. As inflation increases the opportunity cost of holding money, then less will be held. This reduces consumers' surplus some of which is gained by producers of money – banks or the government – but some is a deadweight loss. To this should be added the loss of part of producers' surplus. This 'welfare cost' of inflation is in principle calculable and so estimates have been made by various authors (Garfinkel, 1989).

None of the estimates are very large and all are subject to enormous margins of error. Not surprisingly, self-styled monetarist politicians have ignored this aspect of the case against inflation. Instead, they have attempted to deny the trade-off between inflation and unemployment. Indeed, the present Conservative government in the UK has argued that inflation, far from being the alternative to unemployment, is the cause of it. Both theoretical and empirical evidence supports this view. There are two strands to the argument. The simpler relies on the relationship between saving and inflation, p. 157 above.

Thus the following processes can be traced.

1.	A rise in inflation which causes
2.	a rise in the average propensity to saving, the savings ratio. This causes
3.	a fall in output and so
4.	a rise in unemployment.

This mechanism certainly seems to have operated in the UK in the 1970s. Mrs Thatcher and Sir Geoffrey Howe put considerable reliance upon its working in reverse to reduce unemployment. Theoretically this is less certain but the fall in inflation in 1982, with other factors, did cause a consumer boom and a rise in real spending (see Chapter 10).

The other way in which inflation may cause unemployment depends on the inflationary expectations mechanism discovered by Friedman (see p. 122). Both Friedman and Mrs Thatcher persuasively seek to redefine and trade-off between inflation and unemployment. At a minimum, the 'Phillips' curve' is misleading once a time dimension is introduced. At the most, moreover, it may be necessary for to eliminate inflation if unemployment is to be cured (see Chapter 5).

Virtually all the arguments that inflation causes inequity or inefficiency are rather *ad hoc*. All implicitly presuppose some institutional framework or other. Sometimes institutional reforms could alleviate the problem, for example, indexation or paying interest on demand deposits. Nevertheless, any political economist – or 'post-Keynesian' – would have to accept the legitimacy of the style of argument. The problem is the empirical evaluation of them.

Those wishing to give priority to the elimination of inflation cannot cite direct evidence to support their hypothesis. Instead they rely on the marked negative relationship between output and inflation, or the rate of change. Sir Geoffrey Howe, when Chancellor, frequently pointed out that inflation and unemployment have risen together consistently: compare the Wilson–Callaghan government (1974–9) with Heath's (1970–4), Wilson's (1964–70) and the Tory years of 1951–64. A host of researchers have produced similar results using more rigorous tests – see especially Kurmendi and Meguire (1985). The negative correlations in these studies are marked but it must be stressed that they are at best suggestive and at worst meaningless since the most orthodox of Keynesian models could generate such results.

7.4 INDEXATION

Indexation means the linking of an amount of money to a general index of prices such as the Retail Price Index (RPI). This means that as money value rises with inflation so the real value remains constant. For example a student might agree to rent a room for £20 per week indexed to the RPI. If prices doubled his rent would rise to £40 per week. In effect he is agreeing to pay an amount which will always buy the same quantity of goods instead of the more conventional, a fixed money amount.

Indexed contracts differ most from money-denominated ones when they are of long duration. Hence the issue has been most discussed in the contract of loans. This is also of practical relevance, given the UK's issue of index-linked debt (see p. 49).

The UK is not the only country to have issued index-linked securities, those on which principal and interest payments rise with a general price index. Brazil, Finland (at one time) and Israel are other well known examples. Even amongst major OECD countries, France issued a large number of bonds in the 1950s linked to various specific price indices (such as railway fares and electricity) as well as the general price level. The UK is, however, unique in doing so as part of a successful anti-inflation policy and with a fully open economy. The UK government is still committed to maximizing sales of index-linked gilts and seeks to raise substantially the proportion of the national debt that is index-linked from its present level of about 10 per cent. Economists are in (very rare) almost total agreement that indexation of bonds is desirable. Friedman's enthusiasm was cited above.

Even economists who are usually Friedman's bitter rivals – such as Tobin – share his enthusiasm for index-linking public sector debt. It is worth, therefore, examining why this is so. An important reason is that it seems to economists the only conceivable just solution. Any change in the price level arbitrarily redistributes income and wealth, usually, from creditor to debtor. The unfairness of this is reinforced by the fact that the biggest debtor is government. It seems wrong that governments should both create inflation and benefit from it. The only means open to creditors to protect themselves is through higher nominal rates. Indeed a relationship between nominal interest rates and inflation, the so-called Fisher effect, has passed from economic theory to conventional wisdom. Nevertheless, as Fisher himself pointed out, the protection is incomplete since nominal rates rarely if ever adjust fully to expected inflation. Any unexpected inflation will, of course, continue to have the unjust effects highlighted by Keynes (1923). Even if interest rates do adjust fully to expected inflation the two underlying problems remain. The first is that inflation creates double uncertainty since both borrower and lender are interested in real magnitudes. Uncertainty about how the actual level will turn out relative to its expected level means that both parties to the contract are uncertain about their real liability or real income. Garfinkel (1989) suggests that the result will be a risk premium which must depress investment. In this sense indexation acts as an insurance policy to both sides. The provision of index-linked securities by the public sector enables the private sector to plan its saving and consumption over time knowing the real cost of present consumption in terms of future consumption. Moreover, the second problem is that high nominal rates and high inflation may lead to a contract that is unsatisfactory to both sides. In part this is because the tax system never discriminates between interest payments necessary to maintain the real value of capital and genuine income. Hence the government is likely to gain at the lender's expense. More basically high nominal rates create a cash-flow problem for the borrower who has to pay the interest in cash even if the real value of his obligation is falling. The latter may not offset the former. If inflation is zero and interest rates 2 per cent a ten-year loan involves a maximum annual payment of £12, even if the loan is paid off by equal instalments; more usually either repayment is delayed until the end of the loan or the interest and capital repaid by equal instalments. If inflation rose to 20 per cent and nominal rates to 15 per cent the lender is clearly worse off: he is losing 5 per cent per year. The real interest rate[6] of −5 per cent may not satisfy the borrower who has to pay £25 (instead of £12) and may not regard a fall in the real value of his debt as compensation for this onerous requirement.

To summarize, indexation offers a means of removing some of the inequity, inefficiency and inconvenience of inflation. There are two counter-arguments. The first is that indexation amounts to a recognition of inflation and so is undesirable. This is a silly argument: by the same token unemployment pay is a recognition of unemployment. To try to reduce the ill-effects of something is more likely to go hand-in-hand with eliminating it than increasing its prevalence. This proposition is reinforced when as in this case indexation, besides reducing the bad consequences of inflation, reduces its benefits to government. The other argument is more plausible. Indexation of loans is, it is argued, desirable but other indexation – especially of wages – is of questionable value. However, indexation of the one may lead to indexation of the other – the argument for Finland abandoning indexation in 1978. Nevertheless the theoretical case for indexation is overwhelming.

The UK authorities may or may not have been interested in the theoretical arguments for indexation, although giving the personal sector the ability to plan for the future was probably an influence. The practical benefits of indexation were, however, probably more influential. The fact was the beneficial effect on government cash flow and debt management of paying only 2 1/2 per cent interest (and writing up the capital value of the debt without needing to sell any securities). Given the refinance problems faced by the US authorities in part because of inflation-driven high nominal rates, the gain is clear. If the government succeeds in conquering inflation, this cash-flow bonus is a permanent gain. In general, if inflation is in the event less than the market's expectation. Indexed debt is attractive to the market when inflationary expectations are rising. This is precisely when the authorities have the greatest need to sell public sector debt to reduce monetary growth but also precisely when non-indexed debt is least attractive. The UK authorities chose to introduce indexed debt in stages between 1975 and 1982.[7] This 'creeping indexation' produced an extra benefit for the authorities. Whenever monetary growth seemed excessive they could increase the offset from debt sales by creeping a bit further – introducing new types of indexed security or permitting new categories of holder to hold existing types of security. Creeping indexation, moreover, was probably one reason why both indexed and non-indexed gilts remained in existence. This surprised many economists, who had perhaps over estimated the appeal of indexed securities. They had assumed that once indexed securities were available then all lenders in all markets would insist on indexation. This was contrary to Brazilian experience but could have happened in the UK. Creeping indexation was probably one reason why it did not. In brief, indexation seems to offer an effective remedy to many of the ills of inflation. However, Leijonhufvud's caveat is relevant. His point is that the arguments for indexation have concerned few economists. It may be that the blinkered vision which has prevented many economists (especially Keynesians) from seeing the evils of inflation has prevented others (especially Friedman) from seeing the inadequacy of indexation.

7.5 CONCLUSION

Inflation is undesirable because of the unjust effects of the random and capricious redistribution it engenders. Indexation can, however, mitigate this. Hence the case against inflation has to be the argument that it reduces output in either the short or long term.

GUIDE TO FURTHER READING

Black (1990).

NOTES

1. The Rooker-Wise amendment means that indexation takes place unless parliament decides otherwise. It has so decided on occasions, the most famous being in 1981 when income tax allowances were not indexed. The significance of the new system is that this was (correctly) represented as a rise in taxation. In the past chancellors often succeeded in disguising a real tax increase as a reduction (if an increase of £300 in an allowance were necessary to maintain its real value an announcement of an increase of £150 is a real reduction and so an increase in taxation. Chancellors often presented this as a generous reduction.)
2. On inflation accounting, see Gowland (1981) which contains a complete bibliography which is still up-to-date; nothing significant has since appeared.
3. Many disputes about economic policy are really debates about ethics. In its simplest form economic analysis is usually about ends whereas ethical debates are often about means. The Adam Smith 'invisible hand' theory arguing that individual greed leads to social good is a classic example of this. Hence the criticisms of capitalism by, for example, the Bishop of Durham. The view about ethical statements in text stems from Christian ethics as restated by Kant. 'Do unto others as you would be done by' seems to impose only a consistency and sincerity test upon ethical statements. Almost any action could be viewed as moral so long as the person claiming that it is moral would so regard it irrespective of the person or group affected. In modern times this view was advanced by Hare whose more recent views can be found in Hare (1989) and Seanor and Fotion (1988).
4. A modern authoritative if semi-popular survey and analysis of the causes of the fall of the Roman Empire does not even include inflation in its index, Grant (1970). The main problem caused by inflation was that it made it harder to raise funds to pay the legions – a defect of the tax system not shared by modern ones. This problem led to Diocletian's attempt to control prices and wages by edict – perhaps the first comprehensive prices and incomes policy.
5. The simplest argument about Weimar is that the lower middle classes both lost from hyperinflation and supported Hitler. Hamilton (1982) has conclusively refuted this. Many of Hitler's supporters were gainers from inflation or unaffected by it.
6. The real interest rate is strictly

$$\frac{1+i}{1+\Delta p} - 1$$

where 1 is the nominal rate and p the rate of inflation. It is usually simplified to i-p.

7. Creeping usually meant either a new type of security or a removal of a restriction on who held an existing one. The first 'creep' was a contractional savings scheme in 1975, the last the removal of restrictions on who held indexed-linked gilts in 1982.

REFERENCES

Black, R.P. (1990), 'In Support of Price Stability', *Economic Review,* Federal Reserve Bank of Richmond, vol. 76, no. 1 (January/February) pp. 3-6.

Cagan, P. (1972), *The Channels of Monetary Effects on Interest Rates*, NBER.

Deaton, A.S. (1977), 'Involuntary saving through unanticipated inflation', *American Economic Review,* vol. 67, pp.889-910.

Desai, M. (1981) *Testing Monetarism,* Frances Pinter, London.

Fforde, J.S. (1983), 'The United Kingdom Setting Monetary Objectives', in Meek (1983).

Foot, M.D.K.W. (1981), 'Monetary Targets: their native and record in the major Economies' in Ariffiller B. and Wood G.E. (eds), *Monetary Targets,* Macmillan, 1981.

Friedman, M. (1969), *The Optimum Quantity of Money and Other Essays,* Aldine, Chicago.

Friedman, M. (1977), *Inflation and Unemployment,* Institute of Economic Affairs, London.

Gaitskell, H.T.N. (1983), 'Four Monetary Heretics' in Cole G.D.H. (ed.), *What Everyone Wants to Know About Money,* Gollanz.

Garfinkel, M.R. (1989), 'What is an "acceptable" rate of inflation?' *Review,* Federal Reserve Bank of St Louis, vol. 71, no. 4 (July/August) pp. 3-15.

Gowland, D.H. (1981), 'Thoughts on Inflation Accounting', mimeo, University of York.

Grant, M. (1970), *The Fall of the Roman Empire,* Annenberg School Press, distributed by Nelson, London.

Gredier, W. (1987), *Secrets of the Temple,* Simon and Schuster, New York.

Hahn, F.H. (1982), *Money and Inflation,* Blackwell.

Hamilton, R.F. (1982), *Who Voted for Hitler?* Princeton University Press, Princeton, New Jersey.

Hare, R.M. *Essays in Ethic Theory,* Oxford University Press, Oxford.

Jansen, D.W. (1989) 'Does Inflation Uncertainty Affect Output Growth?' *Review,* Federal Reserve Bank of St Louis, vol. 71, no. 4 (July/August) pp. 43, 52.

Kaldor, N. (1982), *The Source of Monetarism,* Oxford University Press.

Keynes, J.M. (1923), *A Tract on Monetary Reform* reprinted in the *Collected Writings,* Macmillan for the RES, 1981.

Keynes, J.M. (1930), *The General Theory of Employment, Interest and Money,* Macmillan, also in vol VII of his collected works (Keynes 1971).

Keynes, J.M. (1971), *The Collected Writings of John Maynard Keynes,* Macmillan for the Royal Economic Society.

Kormendi, R.C. and Meguire, P.G. (1985), 'Macroeconomics of Growth: Cross Country and Evidence' *Journal of Monetary Economics,* vol. 16 (Sept) pp. 141-64.

Leijonhufvud, A. (1981), Information and Coordination, Oxford University Press, Oxford.

Mayer, T. (ed.) (1978), *The Structure of Monetarism,* Norton.

Schlesinger, A. (1969), *The Age of Roosevelt,* vol. 2, Houghton Mifflin, Boston.

Seanor, D. and Fotion, N.G. (1988), *Hare and Critics: Essays on Moral Thinking,* Oxford.

Stein, B. with Stein H. (1978), *On the Brink,* Hamlyn, Feltham, Middlesex.

Tylecote, A. (1981), *The Causes of the Present Inflation,* Macmillan.

8. Open-Economy Macroeconomics

B. Hillier

In a world where international trade and capital flows have great practical significance, it is important to extend macroeconomic analysis to deal with the open economy. As a starting point for this analysis, Section 8.1 discusses the definition of the foreign exchange rate. Section 8.2 then presents the basic accounting conventions for recording international transactions. Section 8.3 discusses different exchange rate systems, and Section 8.4 introduces the theoretical treatment of the open economy by modifying the simple Keynesian multiplier model to allow for international trade under a system of fixed exchange rates. The analysis is greatly simplified by assuming that prices are fixed and that there are no capital flows. Section 8.5 examines a similar model under a system of floating exchange rates. Finally Section 8.6 goes beyond the simple model to look at some further topics useful for understanding open-economy macroeconomics. Section 8.6 considers the question of when a current account deficit can be considered a problem, introduces capital flows into the model, examines the role of money and government finance in general, looks at the current account as a constraint on economic growth, and finally illustrates the ideas by examining the problems facing the UK government in late 1988 and 1989.

8.1 EXCHANGE RATES

The most elementary complication introduced by modelling international trade in goods, services, or financial assets involves the fact that the buyers and sellers are used to dealing in terms of different currencies. Consider the case of a French farmer selling apples in England. The farmer wishes to receive French francs whilst his English customers wish to pay with pounds sterling. For such transactions to take place it is necessary to be able to convert one currency into another, either directly or indirectly through the use of some internationally acceptable medium of exchange (such as gold or the US dollar).

The rates at which one currency may be converted into another are known as exchange rates, or, more strictly, nominal exchange rates. The exchange rate between any two currencies, say dollars and sterling, may be expressed in one of two ways: either as the dollar price of a pound sterling or as the pound sterling price of a dollar. If two dollars trade for one pound, nothing of substance hinges upon whether the exchange rate is expressed as two dollars per pound or 50 pence per dollar, but a word of caution is needed. In the UK, it is usual to express exchange rates as the foreign currency price of a unit of the domestic currency, sterling, whilst it is common in other countries to express exchange rates as the domestic currency price of a unit of foreign currency. Hence, under the UK convention a rising exchange rate indicates a rising value of the domestic currency in terms of the foreign currency, but under the alternative convention a rising exchange rate could indicate a falling value of the domestic currency. It is, therefore, necessary to know how the exchange rate has been defined before interpreting statements involving phrases like 'a rising exchange rate'.

The real exchange rate, or terms of trade, is defined as the price, in terms of a common currency, of exports relative to the price of imports. An increase in the real exchange rate, therefore, is an unambiguous statement no matter how the nominal exchange rate is defined: an increase in the real exchange rate means that exports rise in price relative to imports and that fewer domestic goods or services need to be given up in exchange for a given volume of imports than before the increase in the terms of trade, and *vice versa* for a reduction in the terms of trade. Changes in the real exchange rate may be due to a change in the nominal exchange rate or to a change in the price of domestic or foreign goods or services.

8.2   THE BALANCE OF PAYMENTS

The objective of the balance of payments accounts is to record transactions between the residents and government of a country and the rest of the world over a given period of time. An item is entered as a credit when it increases the supply of foreign currency to private residents, businesses or government agencies in the country, and as a debit when it increases the supply of domestic currency to foreigners. Credit items enter the accounts with a plus sign and debit items with a negative sign (see *The Pink Book* CSO, e.g. 1989) The balance of payments accounts are commonly divided into three main components.

1. *The current account*
This records trade in goods, services, investment income and transfers. It is possible to subdivide the current account into categories representing each of these main sub-groups. For example, the trading account, or balance of trade, shows all trade in goods, that is exports and imports of physical merchandise, with export values being entered as credits and import values as debits, i.e. export values enter the accounts with a plus sign and imports with a negative sign. Services include charges for professional services such as banking and insurance,

transport and tourist expenditures. Investment income includes such things as receipt or payment of interest on outstanding loans to or from foreigners, dividend payments, etc. Transfers include private transfers (for example, gifts to or from overseas relatives) and government transfers (for example, aid payments or UK government payments to support the budget of the European Community).

2. *The capital account*

This records all transactions involving the purchase or sale of assets between the domestic economy and the rest of the world, and lending to or borrowing from the rest of the world. When there is an inflow of capital from abroad, this is shown as a credit item because it makes foreign exchange available to domestic residents, even if this is caused by a domestic resident or company borrowing from overseas sources. An outflow of capital is shown as a debit item, since it makes domestic currency available to foreigners. The capital account may also be subdivided, for example into long- and short-term accounts where long-term covers assets with a life-to-maturity exceeding one year.

3. *The official financing account*

This records transactions by the central bank on behalf of the government. It includes changes in official reserves of gold and foreign currencies, government borrowing from abroad and transactions with the International Monetary Fund (IMF). Transactions which produce an increase in the official reserves are shown as debit items since they involve reducing the supply of foreign currency held by domestic residents, and transactions which reduce the official reserves are shown as credit items.[1]

The overall balance of payments includes all outgoings (payments for imported goods and services, purchase of foreign assets, etc.) and all incomings (receipts for export sales, sales of domestic assets to foreigners, etc.), using the double-entry method of bookkeeping, which implies that each transaction involves precisely offsetting debit and credit entries and, hence, that the overall balance of payments must always balance. For example, an import of merchandise will be recorded as a debit on the current account, but the finance for this import purchase must be recorded somewhere else in the accounts – either as proceeds from export sales (a current account credit), as a loan from foreigners (a capital inflow resulting from the sale of a financial asset or IOU to foreigners, recorded as a capital account credit), or as a change in the reserves of foreign currency (due to the government providing importers with foreign exchange and, thereby, diminishing the reserve stock, which shows up as a credit on the official financing account).

While the overall balance of payments accounts must, by definition, always balance, it is not necessary that any of the sub-components balance. Nevertheless, it is common to talk of a deficit or surplus on the overall balance of payments. A 'deficit (surplus) on the overall balance of payments' is used to refer to a deficit (surplus) on the sum of the current and capital accounts requiring a fall (rise) in official reserves or an official international loan to balance the accounts; this convention will be followed below. Note that a 'balance of payments balance' in this sense is consistent with a current account deficit (surplus) matched exactly by a capital account surplus (deficit).

Finally, notice that all transactions in the balance of payments accounts are recorded per period of time and, therefore, represent *flow* variables, although they may involve changes in the *stock* of international reserves held in the country, or of foreign financial assets, or even in the domestic money supply. (A flow variable is one measured per period, and a stock variable is one measured at a point in time; mundane examples are the amount of water flowing into a bath per minute, which is a flow variable, and the amount of water in the bath at some point in time, which is a stock variable.)

8.3 EXCHANGE RATE SYSTEMS

There are several possible ways of organizing the market for foreign exchange. The most important ways are listed below.

8.3.1 Fixed but Adjustable Exchange Rates

This system prevailed in much of the world from 1944 to 1971, following the Bretton Woods conference in 1944. Participants at the conference sought to establish an international monetary system conducive to peaceful international trade. To do this, they agreed on a pattern of exchange rates between the currencies of the member nations and committed themselves to support this pattern. In other words, governments (or central banks) were committed to buying or selling currencies at fixed exchange rates to members of the private sector who wished to make international transactions.[2,3]

Since private sector demands for, and supplies of, currencies do not necessarily always balance, the system implied that central banks were obliged to intervene in the foreign exchange market to sell foreign currencies in exchange for the domestic currency at the fixed exchange rate whenever the supply of the domestic currency on the market exceeded demand for it, and *vice versa*. The amount of such possible intervention for deficit currencies, that is, currencies whose supply exceeds demand on the exchange market, was limited by the amount of reserves of gold and foreign currencies held by the government of the deficit currency, supplemented by the possibility of borrowing from the IMF, which was set up in 1944 to monitor the system.

It was hoped that the system of fixed exchange rates would encourage international trade by removing the risk imposed on importers or exporters by fluctuations in exchange rates, which mean that deals struck in terms of a foreign currency are of uncertain value in terms of the domestic currency and, therefore, involve an extra degree of risk compared to deals struck in terms of the domestic currency. Deals involving imports and exports can be struck in terms of the domestic currency of one of the parties to the deal, but one of the parties must accept some exchange rate risk (although there are ways to insure against this risk on the financial markets it is, even so, an extra cost and complication). Furthermore, it was hoped that the system would avoid the competitive policies of exchange rate manipulation employed during the 1930s to improve domestic employment by making the domestic currency cheap on the exchange market and giving an advantage to domestic exports. Such beggar-thy-neighbour policies were held to be partly responsible for the international depression of the 1930s. In cases of 'fundamental disequilibrium', however, with countries running persistent deficits or surpluses, it was accepted that some adjustment in exchange rates would be necessary, subject to international agreement via the IMF. Hence, the system is often known as the 'adjustable peg' system, since the parities at which currencies were pegged were adjustable.

The system was a compromise between unadjustably fixed exchange rates and freely floating exchange rates (to be discussed below). It suffered from several problems and collapsed in 1971 after persistent deficits by the USA, whose dollar was the key international reserve currency under the system. The problems included the lack of explicit criteria to define 'fundamental disequilibrium', the unwillingness of governments to follow domestic policies necessary to support fixed exchange rates (the constraints on domestic policies implied by fixed exchange rates will be made clear below), and the ease with which the system generated profits for currency speculators. For example, if sterling is currently fixed at $2.40 per £1 and the UK is persistently running deficits, then it is easy to expect a *devaluation* of sterling – that is, a reduction in its value from, say, $2.40 to $2.00 per £1. (A *revaluation* is an increase in the value of a currency.) By selling sterling in exchange for dollars, and then buying sterling after the devaluation of sterling, speculators can increase their sterling holdings. There is little risk involved in this activity, since when sterling is the deficit currency it is not likely to be revalued, so that for the speculators, the worst that can happen is that sterling holds its value and they incur the transaction costs of buying and selling currencies without making any speculative profit or loss. The existence of forward markets may exacerbate the problems caused by such speculative forces. Deals in forward markets involve contracts to trade currencies in the future, say 60 or 90 days, at an exchange rate specified in advance. If devaluation is expected the price of the currency at risk will fall on the forward markets and reinforce the reluctance of speculators to hold it.

The European monetary system or EMS is an adjustable peg system; member currencies are allowed to fluctuate with respect to one another within defined bands and float together against non-member currencies (see Chapter 9 for further details).

8.3.2 Freely Floating or Flexible Exchange Rates

Under freely floating exchange rates, governments do not intervene at all in the exchange market. The exchange rate is free to adjust continuously to achieve an overall balance of payments without the need for official financing transactions. The case for freely floating exchange rates is that domestic fiscal and monetary policies are freed from the constraints implied by support for fixed exchange rates, and that market forces should set the exchange rates at appropriate levels. The case against them is that, left to itself, the exchange market may be highly unstable, and speculative forces may result in highly volatile exchange rates which may hinder international trade by adding an extra element of uncertainty. For example, a UK exporter agreeing a US dollar price, for some deal to be completed in the future, will be uncertain about the sterling value of the deal if he is uncertain about the future value of the sterling – dollar spot exchange rate. He can, of course, hedge against this uncertainty by entering the forward market for currencies, but this is an extra, and possibly costly, complication which may deter him from the export market.

Under floating rates it is usual to talk of *appreciation* and *depreciation* of exchange rates rather than revaluation and devaluation, as under the adjustable peg system.

8.3.3 Managed or Dirty Floating Exchange Rates

Under this system exchange rates are allowed to adjust on a day-to-day basis, but governments intervene from time to time to try to smooth out adjustment. This is the system that has prevailed in many countries since the collapse of the adjustable peg system. Intervention is, however, a difficult operation, since even internationally coordinated central bank actions can prove fruitless in the face of massive private sector capital flows. Such intervention can, however, be successful if it is correctly timed and provides a convincing signal to the markets that the authorities are willing to take action to support a feasible exchange rate or set of exchange rates. For a discussion of UK experience under a dirty floating exchange rate system see Chapter 2.

8.4   THE SIMPLE KEYNESIAN MULTIPLIER MODEL OF A SMALL OPEN ECONOMY UNDER FIXED EXCHANGE RATES

The open-economy macroeconomic model to be examined is the small open-economy version of the Keynesian multiplier model. Although this model is extremely simple, it provides a clear illustration of the effects of open-economy considerations, and provides a useful starting point from which to progress to more complicated ideas.

Imagine the domestic economy to be the UK, and the rest of the world to be one giant economy with which the UK trades. Let the exchange rate, e, measured in dollars per pound sterling, be fixed but adjustable. Assume that domestic output has a fixed price in terms of sterling of £P per unit, and that the output of the rest of the world, which is some good different to the domestic good, has a fixed dollar price of $P* per unit. Assume, for simplicity, that there are no dealings on the capital account. The model under these assumptions is shown in Figure 8.1, where the units on the axes are in pounds sterling.

Figure 8.1   The Keynesian multiplier model of a small open economy under fixed exchange rates (all units in pounds sterling).

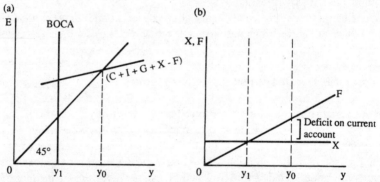

Figure 8.1 (a) shows the well known Keynesian cross diagram extended to allow for exports, X, to be an extra injection or source of demand for domestic output, and imports, F, to be an extra withdrawal, since it is part of spending by domestic residents which does not increase demand for domestic output. The equilibrium condition is, as usual, that the supply of output, y, equal aggregate demand, E, but E now equals $(C + I + G + X - F)$ rather than $(C + I + G)$ as in the closed economy. This condition leads to the level of income y_0 as shown.

Figure 8.1 (b) plots exports and imports against domestic income. The upward-sloping F line (which need not necessarily pass through the origin) indicates that, with foreign and domestic prices and the exchange rate fixed, the demand for imports rises with domestic income. The horizontal X line, on the other hand, shows the demand for exports to be independent of the level of domestic income. Exports are assumed to be dependent on the level of real income in the rest of the world, foreign and domestic prices and the exchange rate, all of which are assumed to be fixed independently from whatever happens in the small domestic economy. The horizontal X line thus embodies the small-economy assumption that the level of real income in the rest of the world is independent of domestic income, because as domestic income, and hence import demand, increase, this has a negligible effect on income in the rest of the world and, hence, no impact on the demand by the rest of the world for the exports of the small domestic economy. Since the X and F lines intersect above y_1, and since to the right of y_1 import demand exceeds export demand, while to the left of y_1 export demand exceeds import demand, then only at y_1 is the current account in balance. To the right of y_1 there is a current account deficit, and to the left a surplus. The vertical line BOCA in Figure 8.1(a) then indicates that a balance on current account occurs only at y_1.

Simple as it is, the model in Figure 8.1 is very useful. First, it shows how exports and imports need to be taken into account in determining the national income equilibrium condition. Second, it shows that there may be a conflict between internal and external policy targets. Imagine that the domestic government wishes to achieve the level of income y_0, which it believes to be consistent with full employment. It can achieve this internal target by adjusting the level of government spending on real goods and services, G, and has done this correctly in Figure 8.1 to achieve y_0. However, with the fixed exchange rate, e, this implies running a persistent deficit on current account, as shown in Figure 8.1 (b). Such a deficit cannot be allowed to continue for ever, for the government would eventually run out of international reserves, and would be unable to support the exchange rate e by borrowing from abroad indefinitely. The government, if it wishes to support the exchange rate e, must sacrifice its policy variable, G, to that end; an independent fiscal policy is not consistent with a rigid fixed exchange rate system. G must be reduced until the C + I + G + X − F line in Figure 8.1 (a) is pulled down to intersect the 45° line above y_1 and balance on current account is achieved. This discussion illustrates a result due to Tinbergen (1952) that, in order to achieve *n* targets or goals, a government usually needs at least *n* policy instruments, although satisfying this condition will not always guarantee success.

The policy of adjusting G up or down is known as an 'expenditure-changing policy', since it drives expenditure up or down as it is varied. Reliance on expenditure-changing policy alone when attempting to achieve both internal and external targets will not allow both targets to be achieved simultaneously. Instead, reliance on the one policy would generate what might be called a stop–go cycle, in which output is pushed up and down between y_0 and y_1 as first the policy is adjusted to achieve internal balance, then external balance, then internal balance, and so on. Such a simple picture may quite well represent UK experience in the 1950s and early 1960s, when the balance of payments alternated with domestic output and employment levels as the prime target of policy. The exchange rate was fixed and prices were relatively stable during this episode of UK economic history, so the simple model may not be too unrealistic, although in practice monetary policy as well as fiscal policy was used to affect the level of aggregate demand in the UK economy.

To achieve both internal and external targets simultaneously, it is necessary to use an additional policy tool, and, importantly, to use a tool which causes expenditure switching, that is, one which for any level of domestic income affects the gap between imports and exports. Such policies might include direct controls on imports, tariffs on imports, subsidies to exports and so on. In principle, an increase in the rate of income tax may work to lower the level of expenditure in the domestic economy and, thereby, lower the demand for imports, with an increase in government expenditure concentrated on domestic production in order to boost the level of aggregate demand back-up to a level high enough to achieve the internal target. Such a policy mix might be very difficult to bring about, however, and might imply an unacceptably high level of government expenditure. Therefore, tax policy is best viewed as a supplement to government expenditure policy in this type of context, both policies being part of fiscal policy. Let us, instead, consider an adjustment in the exchange rate as the extra policy tool needed to enable the simultaneous achievement of both internal and external targets.

Adjustments to the exchange rate work by affecting the real exchange rate or terms of trade, TT, defined as the price, in terms of a common currency, of exports relative to the price of imports. Using sterling as the common currency, and defining e to be the dollar price of sterling, yields TT equal to P, the sterling price of exports, divided by P^*/e, the sterling price of imports; that is, TT equals Pe/P^*. Exactly the same value for TT would be obtained if the dollar were used as the common currency, although the formula would look a little different. With P and P^* given, a devaluation of sterling will lower the terms of trade and make imports relatively more expensive (in sterling terms) on the UK market than before the devaluation, and exports relatively cheaper (in dollar terms) on the overseas market. The effect of a devaluation, therefore, will be to shift the X line upwards and the F line downwards in a figure such as Figure 8.1 (b), assuming that demand for imports falls as they become dearer, while that for exports increases as they become cheaper.[4,5]

The government can now achieve its internal and external targets simultaneously, but it must carefully combine its expenditure-switching and expenditure-changing policies if it is to do so. The arguments may be illustrated using Figure 8.2 for the case of a devaluation (a similar analysis may easily be applied for the case of a revaluation). Assume that the government's internal target is to achieve an income level of y_0, and that it initially does so, at the exchange rate e, with a level of government spending of G. Thus, in Figure 8.2(a) the initial $C + I + G + X - F$ line is given by $(C + I + G + X - F)$ (e) and achieves y_0. However, with an exchange rate of e, exports and imports are given in Figure 8.2(b) by X(e) and F(e). A balance on current account would, thus, be achieved at y_1 and so the BOCA line is drawn vertically above y_1 in Figure 8.2 (a). The government, therefore, is achieving its internal target of y_0, but at the expense of a deficit on current account.

To achieve both internal and external targets simultaneously, the government must adjust the exchange rate, but, less obviously, it must also adjust its fiscal policy as will be shown. First of all the government must obtain agreement with the nation's trading partners for a devaluation of the currency by just enough, given knowledge of the relevant price and income elasticities, to move the intersection of the X and F lines to above y_0. In Figure 8.2 (a) this is shown to be achieved by a devaluation of the exchange rate to e', giving the lines X(e') and F(e'). This devaluation improves the international competitiveness of the nation's producers; that is, it lowers the terms of trade and lowers the relative price of the domestic output on the international market, so that exports increase and

Figure 8.2 Simultaneous use of devaluation and fiscal policies to achieve internal and external balance

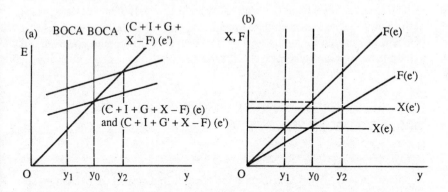

imports fall for any level of domestic income. The effect of this, however, is to cause the $C + I + G + X - F$ line to move upwards to $(C + I + G + X - F)$ (e'), in turn causing income to rise to Y_2 and a deficit still to occur on current account. It is necessary, therefore, to adjust fiscal policy at the same time as the exchange rate is adjusted if y_0 and a balance on current account are to be achieved together. In the present case the $C + I + G + X - F$ line must be pulled back down to intersect with the 45° line in Figure 8.2(a): this can be done, for an exchange rate of e', by reducing the level of government expenditure from G to G' as shown.[6]

Thus, simultaneous achievement of the internal and external targets would require a careful coordination of devaluation and a restrictive fiscal policy. In practice the restrictive fiscal policy would probably be justified by the monetary authorities arguing that, for the devaluation to succeed, it was necessary to ensure that the goods be made available for export and not for home consumption, and also that it was necessary to prevent the devaluation from generating domestic inflation, which would offset the boost to the competitiveness of domestic producers given by the devaluation if it were allowed to occur.

Finally it should be noted that the actual adjustment of exports and imports to a devaluation is complicated by the fact that the response of supply and demand to the relative price change brought about by devaluation is slow. Thus, initially exports rise very little in response to their new lower price, whilst imports hardly fall even though they have become more expensive. This can mean that the balance on current account initially moves into a larger deficit position after a devaluation, and only improves once the relative price changes begin to cause demands to respond. A graph of the current account deficit or surplus plotted over time would, in such a case, look like a letter J, and so this dynamic response to devaluation is often known as the J-curve effect. A successful combination of fiscal policy and devaluation would, therefore, require not only accurate knowledge of the parameters of the economy, but also strong nerves in the face of the initial current account deterioration.

The next section extends the analysis by dealing with flexible exchange rates in the simple Keynesian multiplier model. Once this task has been completed it is useful to consider the limitations or weaknesses of the simple model, and to extend the discussion accordingly in Section 8.6.

8.5 THE SIMPLE KEYNESIAN MODEL OF A SMALL OPEN ECONOMY UNDER FLOATING EXCHANGE RATES

Consider the same model as in the previous section, but now let the exchange rate e be freely floating. In this case the exchange rate will be determined by the forces of supply and demand on the foreign exchange market. Assuming that the foreign exchange market works perfectly, the government need no longer worry about achieving a balance on current account. If at some exchange rate the demand for sterling on the foreign exchange market differs from the supply, then the exchange rate, that is the price of sterling, should automatically adjust until supply and demand are brought into equality with one another. The supply of sterling on the foreign exchange market is offered in exchange for foreign currency by UK residents wishing to buy imports, and the demand for sterling is by foreigners offering foreign currency in exchange for sterling with which to buy UK exports, so that equality of the supply and demand for sterling implies that the current account is in balance with the demand for exports equal to the demand for imports.

The above argument may be illustrated quite simply using Figure 8.3. Figure 8.3(a) shows two $C + I + G + X - F$ lines, both drawn for the common levels of government expenditure, G_0 and investment, I_0, but for different exchange rates, e_0 and e_1. At the exchange rate e_0 the equilibrium level of income would be y_0. Figure 8.3(b) shows two pairs of X and F lines, one pair for the exchange rate e_0, and one for e_1. It is easy to see that for the exchange rate e_0 and income level y_0, the value of imports would exceed the value of exports, F_0 being greater than X_0 (both in sterling values). Thus, with government expenditure set at level G_0, equilibrium in (a) would not be consistent with a balance on current account in (b) if the exchange rate were e_0. Under a fixed exchange rate system this would, in the short run, imply that the central bank would be running down reserves (or borrowing from abroad) in order to provide the funds to pay for the excess value of imports over exports and, in the long run, that action must be taken to eliminate the deficit. However, under perfectly floating exchange rates, the central bank would not intervene to provide the funds to finance such a deficit, which would not prevail even in the short run. Instead, the exchange rate would adjust away

Figure 8.3   The Keynesian multiplier model of a small open economy under flexible exchange rates

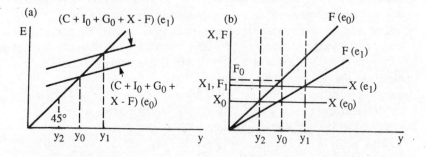

from e_0 until the values of export and import demands were brought into equality with one another. In the case of a deficit the exchange rate would fall. Let the new lower exchange rate consistent with a balance on the current account for the government expenditure level of G_0 be e_1. The depreciation to e_1 causes the X and F lines to move to $X(e_1)$ and $F(e_1)$ respectively in (b) and the increase in exports and fall in imports for any income level causes the $C + I + G + X - F$ line to move upwards to $(C + I_0 + G_0 + X - F)$ (e_1) in (a). (The slope of the $C + I + G + X - F$ line in (a) would also change but this is not shown.) The new equilibrium income level in (a) is y_1, which is shown to be consistent with a balance on current account in (b).

Thus Figure 8.3 shows that with a level of government expenditure of G_0, the equilibrium level of income will be y_1 and the exchange rate consistent with a balance on current account at this level of income will be e_1. If the exchange rate were at any other level, such as e_0, with corresponding output level y_0, the forces of supply and demand would cause the exchange rate to adjust, in this case downwards, towards balance of payments equilibrium at e_1. Furthermore, this exchange rate adjustment would cause domestic output to adjust upwards towards y_1 as the aggregate demand for domestic output responded to the exchange rate adjustment. The appendix to this chapter shows how the figure may be extended to show the foreign exchange market explicitly. The resulting analysis is, however, more difficult than that in the text and may be omitted if the reader wishes.

It is possible to show that if the government wished to achieve a level of domestic income in excess of y_1 it could do so by increasing G, but it would have to accept that this would bring about a devaluation of the domestic currency: the increase in G would cause income to rise and, hence, the current account to worsen (as import demand rises with income); therefore a reduction in the exchange rate would be needed to restore balance to the current account. An implication of this analysis is that under floating exchange rates the government need not concern itself with achieving a current account balance. It can set expenditure at any level it wishes, and let the exchange rate adjust to bring about a balance on current account. However if it wishes to target a level for the exchange rate, then, just as under a fixed exchange rate system, it would have to adjust the level of government expenditure to that end. Imagine the government wished to achieve the exchange rate e_0, then it would have to adjust the level of government expenditure until the level of domestic income generated import demand equal in value to export demand at e_0. The required level of income is shown to be y_2 in Figure 8.3(b); achieving it would require reducing government expenditure to lower the $C + I + G + X - F$ line for the exchange rate e_0 until it intersected the 45° line above y_2 in Figure 8.3(a).

In the absence of an exchange rate target, the freedom to let the exchange rate adjust to bring about a balance on the current account means that the government can achieve an internal target level of income by adjusting government expenditure without having to worry about the balance on current account or seek agreement to adjust the exchange rate as under a fixed exchange rate system. This does not, however, mean that it can totally neglect the external sector of the economy, since the choice of the appropriate level of government expenditure to achieve an income level target must take into account the effects of changes in government expenditure on the exchange rate, and the repercussions of the resultant effects on exports and imports on the level of aggregate demand for domestic output. Indeed such effects enhance the power of fiscal policy since, from an initial position of current account balance, an expansionary fiscal policy would cause a depreciation which would boost the competitiveness of domestic products on both home and overseas markets, whilst a contractionary fiscal policy would cause an appreciation and so damage competitiveness. Nevertheless, it would be easier under flexible exchange rates to adjust government expenditure by trial and error to achieve a given income target, whilst letting the exchange rate adjust to maintain current account balance, instead of having to repeatedly seek agreement for devaluation (or revaluation) as under fixed-but-adjustable exchange rates.

Such benefits of the floating exchange rate system must be weighed against any damage done to international trade by the extra uncertainty created by fluctuating exchange rates. Also depreciation of the exchange rate may create inflationary pressures in the domestic economy, since it pushes up the price of imports. Therefore, the freedom to let the exchange rate adjust on the foreign exchange market is not gained without accepting a potential cost. Indeed it is possible to argue that a fixed exchange rate system provided a benevolent constraint on governments, concern over the balance of payments preventing them from following over expansionary aggregate demand policies and, hence, preventing them from generating inflation (see Laidler, 1978 and 1986). Experience with floating exchange rates has involved considerable volatility of exchange rates, and has disappointed some of the proponents of the floating rate system. However the world has experienced several important shocks since the system was introduced, most notably the oil price shocks in the 1970s, and governments have, at times, pursued widely divergent policies in response to them. In such circumstances, no pattern of exchange rates could have been expected to hold steady, so a fixed-but-adjustable exchange rate system may have fared little better: frequent exchange rate adjustments would have been required since governments seemed unwilling to sacrifice domestic policies to support stable exchange rates. In a stable world without large shocks and with stable government policies the flexible exchange rate system may have fared much better. With such stability the benefits of a fixed-but-adjustable exchange rate system would seem much less, and without it such a system might have collapsed in any case.

Thus, the simple Keynesian model of the small open economy is a useful introduction to the macroeconomics of the open economy, and can help in understanding the links between the exchange rate system, government policies and macroeconomic variables in the real world. It is, however, a very simplified model. The following section, therefore, discusses the major limitations of the model, indicates how it can be extended and considers the resulting implications for policy.

8.6 BEYOND THE SIMPLE MODEL

Useful as it is, the simple model developed above does have important weaknesses. This section, therefore, introduces a number of ideas which extend the discussion beyond the simple model.

Perhaps the most obvious extension is to consider capital flows, since in the real world they are very important. Once the capital account is recognized, it is no longer necessary for the current account to balance for the overall balance of payments to balance. There may be little, if anything, wrong with current account imbalances matched by offsetting capital account flows. For example, a developing nation borrowing on capital account to finance current account deficits may well be doing exactly the right thing if the imports are being used to develop natural resources and, eventually, generate the finance to pay off the loans within an agreed timescale. In such a case the borrower and the lender may both benefit from the extension of credit. Current account deficits are, therefore, not necessarily a problem – they may be looked upon in a similar way to an individual running up an overdraft at the bank, that is as borrowing which may be helpful so long as it does not become too big a burden to pay off one's debt in the future. Indeed, just like an individual might be happy to run up an infinite overdraft were it not for the fact that some day he would be expected to pay it off, then a nation might be happy to run a current account deficit forever – which after all means that it is receiving more from overseas in the form of imports than it is paying for by its exports. However, it will at the same time be running up debts on the capital account or spending its reserves of foreign currency.

Thus a current account deficit is only a problem when it implies that the deficit nation is getting into debt at a greater rate than is desirable given that the debt must be serviced in the future. On the other hand, a current account surplus is not necessarily desirable since it implies that the surplus nation is swopping its current output of goods and services for assets, which may be looked upon as similar to saving by an individual. Obviously in some circumstances saving is desirable, but it is possible to save too much and spend too little, especially if the saving is in foreign currency denominated assets which might fall in value if the foreign currency depreciates. In other words, an imbalance on the current account may only be deemed to be a problem if it is different from the optimal, or most desirable, imbalance given a nation's planned allocation of consumption and investment expenditure over time; an imbalance cannot be deemed necessarily to be a problem. The reader should note that it is not possible to define a current account deficit to be a problem when it is used to finance consumption but all right when it is used to finance investment. Whether it is a problem or not depends on whether it is helping the nation to reallocate expenditure patterns in a better manner than in the absence of the deficit.

Capital flows may be introduced into the model initially, and very simply, by assuming that capital flows into the domestic economy from overseas if the domestic interest rate is higher than that in the rest of the world, and *vice versa*. The logic behind modelling the capital account in this way is, quite simply, that investors transfer their funds from one country to another in response to the relative yields their investments will produce.[7,8] The workings of the capital account under this assumption may be illustrated using Figure 8.4.

The vertical axis of Figure 8.4 shows the domestic interest rate, and the horizontal axis shows the net capital account position. Two capital account lines are drawn. The upward sloping line represents a situation of imperfect capital mobility. It shows that if the interest rate on assets invested in the domestic economy, r, is equal to r^*, the interest rate in the rest of the world (which is assumed to be given exogenously), then capital neither flows into nor out of the domestic economy. If the domestic interest rate differs from that in the rest of the world then capital flows in or out, depending on whether r exceeds or falls below r^*.

The greater the response of capital flows to a given interest differential, the nearer to the horizontal becomes the capital account line. In the extreme case of perfect capital mobility, the capital account line becomes horizontal at the interest rate r^*. In this case investors treat domestic and foreign assets as perfect substitutes for one another, so that any difference between the domestic and foreign interest rates would induce such enormous capital flows that the difference would be immediately eliminated.[9] For example, if the interest rate in the domestic economy rose above that in the rest of the world there would be such an inflow of capital that the domestic interest rate would immediately be returned to the same level as in the rest of the world, as the domestic money supply rose in response to the capital inflow and caused the domestic interest rate to fall.

In the real world capital is, indeed, highly mobile, especially between the developed market economies. The extreme case of perfect capital mobility, therefore, may provide a reasonable approximation to reality. The reader may wonder then why it is that in the real world interest rates so obviously differ from one economy to another. The answer is that in a world of flexible exchange rates which frequently change, it becomes necessary to recognize that expectations of exchange rate changes are as important as interest differentials in driving the capital account. The reason for this is that an investor deciding where to allocate his funds to achieve the best return must consider not only the interest payments he will receive on those funds, but also any capital gains or losses brought about by changes in the interest rate or the exchange rate. Investors, therefore, have an

Figure 8.4   The capital account

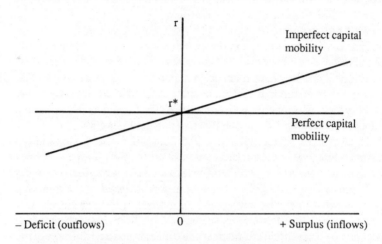

incentive to form expectations about interest rate or exchange rate changes in an attempt to maximise total returns on their funds.

Imagine that the financial assets which give rise to capital account flows are of the fixed nominal value, variable interest rate type (like interest-earning bank deposits), and that they are denominated in terms of one currency, either domestic or foreign. In this case there will be no capital gains or losses associated with interest rate changes, but there may still be capital gains or losses due to exchange rate changes. In terms of the domestic currency, the return on an asset denominated in the domestic currency is simply the interest yield, but the return on an asset denominated in the foreign currency is the interest yield plus a capital gain or loss due to any exchange rate change. For instance, if the interest rate on foreign currency denominated assets were 5 per cent per annum, and domestic currency depreciated by 5 per cent over the year, then the total yield of the asset in terms of the domestic currency would be 10 per cent, that is a 5 per cent interest yield plus, in terms of the domestic currency, a 5 per cent capital gain.

The importance of adding capital flows to the model stems from the fact that they make it possible to achieve an overall balance of payments balance without having a balance on current account; it becomes possible to support a given exchange rate without having to accept whatever level of domestic income is consistent with a balance on current account for that exchange rate. Instead a current account deficit (or surplus) may now be financed out of an equal capital account surplus (or deficit); all that is needed is that the domestic interest rate be adjusted to ensure the appropriate level of capital inflows (or outflows) is achieved. Adjusting the interest rate is a matter for monetary policy, which should be considered as an extra weapon in the government's policy armoury.

Armed with the two policies of expenditure and monetary policy, the government should be able to achieve its internal and external targets simultaneously, providing, of course, that it carefully coordinates its policies. The need for coordination of policies occurs because as the interest rate is varied to support the overall balance of payments it affects aggregate demand in the domestic economy, which, therefore, necessitates an adjustment of government expenditure to maintain aggregate demand at the desired level. The interest rate affects aggregate demand by making credit more or less expensive and, thereby, affecting demand for consumption and investment.

Once the role of money in the economy is acknowledged it becomes possible to argue that the rate of growth of the domestic money supply is of crucial importance for the exchange rate and the balance of payments. An expansion in the domestic money supply which boosts the spending power of domestic residents will boost their demand for imports. Under fixed exchange rates this will adversely affect the current account and under flexible exchange rates it will put pressure on the exchange rate to depreciate, whilst in both cases it will probably cause the capital account to show a smaller surplus or larger deficit as the domestic interest rate falls. Furthermore, once the role of expectations of exchange rate changes is recognized, it can be argued that merely the expectation of a policy change can cause speculators to reallocate their funds in advance of the policy change to take advantage of how they expect the exchange rate to move. Of course the actions of the speculators, in buying currencies they expect to appreciate and selling those they expect to depreciate, themselves help to bring about the changes the speculators expect even before the expected policies are enacted, which makes it very difficult to observe straightforward empirical relationships between policies and economic variables.

Another important argument often put forward is that, in the long run, balance of payments imbalances are self-correcting and need no specific government action to remedy them. This may be argued since under fixed exchange rates an overall deficit, say, will cause a loss of money from domestic residents to foreigners, which will cause domestic residents to cut back their spending and as they spend less the balance of payments will improve until eventually the process removes the imbalance. Under floating rates this process will be replaced by changes in the exchange rate which will continue until a position of overall balance is achieved.

There are, however, a number of problems with this argument. First of all, the resulting equilibrium level of income need not be satisfactory, which is most easily seen for the fixed exchange rate case since then the process of achieving equilibrium depends on income and, hence, imports falling to remove an overall balance of payments deficit. Second, it neglects the role of government finance in determining asset flows. For example, if the government is running a deficit on its budget, with expenditure exceeding tax receipts, and if this deficit is financed by creating money (or borrowing from the central bank), then the continued flow of money from the government into private hands will offset the outflow of money via the overall balance of payments deficit. Hence private sector behaviour will not adjust and the balance of payments problem will remain as long as the government has an imbalance on its budget. It seems, therefore, that balance of payments problems require specific action to be taken to remove them and that they cannot be left to cure themselves.

An important condition for long-run equilibrium on the balance of payments is that the government budget be in a position of balance with tax receipts just covering expenditure. Any other position would mean that the government must be adding to the money supply or borrowing by selling government bonds if its budget is in deficit, or else reducing the money supply or buying back government debt if its budget is in surplus, and in either case these asset changes will affect private behaviour and cause it to change, in turn causing the balance of payments or exchange rate to change.

Furthermore, although overall balance of payments balance in the short run may consist of a current account imbalance and an offsetting capital account imbalance, long-run equilibrium requires that the capital and current accounts both be individually in balance. The need for this latter condition is often forgotten, but it is quite easy to understand once one remembers that dividend and interest payments from foreigners are included in the current account. Consider, for example, a country running a current account deficit and financing this by borrowing on capital account, all the while it is doing this it is getting deeper into debt and, other things being constant, causing the current account to worsen as the interest payments on the overseas debt grow. Of course there may well be reasons why the current account may improve over time, for example if the current account deficits have been used to build up the nation's productive sector, but the point remains that in long-run equilibrium the country must not be getting deeper into debt. Nevertheless, this latter point means that the focus upon the current account in the simple model used in earlier sections was not really too misleading, since current account balance is necessary in the long run anyway.

The point made in the previous paragraph is very similar to one made by Thirlwall that 'in the long run a country cannot grow faster than the rate of growth of output consistent with balance-of-payments equilibrium on current account' (1986, p.251). Thirlwall also emphasizes that if the demand for imports grows faster than the demand for exports over time then there will be persistent pressure on the exchange rate to depreciate, since depreciation will only offer a temporary cure unless something can be done to make the demand for exports grow more quickly or the demand for imports grow more slowly.

Last but not least it must be noted that the simple models used above assumed a fixed price level in the domestic economy, but in the real world the price level is variable and controlling its rate of change over time, the inflation rate, is an important goal of policy makers. This is important to note because actions taken to control inflation may have implications for the balance of payments and the exchange rate, and *vice versa*, whilst changes in the exchange rate affect the price of imports and so directly affect the overall price level in the domestic economy.

The interaction of the arguments presented in this and previous sections may be illustrated by considering the problem facing the UK Government in late 1988 and early 1989. The UK Government at that time was running a substantial surplus on its own budget and, therefore, receiving advice from some quarters to cut taxes or increase expenditure. But the current account of the balance of payments was in substantial deficit at the same time and causing much concern, although some people said the deficit was being created partly by imports of capital machinery which would help to rebuild UK industry and so would be temporary – once the machinery was in place it would increase exports and reduce imports. Even so, in an attempt to dampen aggregate demand and reduce the demand for imports, the UK interest rate was forced up to a very high level, compared to the interest rates in the rest of the world, in order to prevent the exchange rate from rapidly depreciating, and fiscal policy was not slackened for fear that tax cuts or expenditure hikes would add to the balance of payments problems. Furthermore inflation was going ahead faster than for several years and was another reason for following a tight policy. Even though rising interest rates added to inflation by increasing the cost of borrowing (and in particular mortgage repayments which feature in the cost-of-living price index), it was felt better to have high interest rates than to let sterling depreciate too quickly and thereby boost inflation.[10] Some economists, however, felt that trying to support the exchange rate was a foolish policy; instead they argued that the exchange rate should be left to the foreign exchange market and a tight monetary policy followed to control domestic demand and inflation. Other criticisms of the high interest rate policy were that it discouraged investment and harmed growth prospects, acted as a rather inequitable tax which hit only those in debt, and by pushing up mortgage payments and the cost-of-living-index created inflationary wage pressures. Domestic industry, therefore, could be faced with high interest rates making borrowing expensive, low demand at home, a high exchange rate making their goods uncompetitive on the international market, and unions pushing for high wage increases. The policy, therefore, risks creating a recession if pushed too far. In response to these criticisms, some critics proposed a similar policy, but based around higher taxes rather than high interest rates to reduce private sector expenditure.

The dilemma facing the authorities stemmed partly from the fact that whatever they did to reduce the government budget surplus tended to worsen the balance of payments position, and *vice versa*, and that on the one hand they risked inflation, which is often followed by high unemployment as a cost of reducing inflation, whilst on the other hand they risked immediate recession if their policies were too tight. It would seem that the best that may be hoped for in such a situation would be a steady depreciation of the currency and a steady rate of inflation. The reader may, perhaps, know how this episode of economic history developed and if the government resolved its dilemma without a major depreciation of sterling, high inflation and/or high unemployment.

For a more detailed discussion of the ideas presented in this chapter see Hillier (forthcoming, 1991).

NOTES

1. Since 1986 the official statistics for the UK no longer explicitly present the official financing category on the grounds that 'over recent years, ... , the monetary authorities' use of reserves for balance of payments related purposes has been much reduced and the official financing category has lost much of its significance' (*The Pink Book*, CSO, 1989). This change in reporting procedure may not, however, be a good one, since the authorities may, and do, intervene in the foreign exchange market. Fortunately, the transactions previously included in the official financing category remain identifiable in the accounts (e.g. the change in official reserves now presented in Table 1.4, *The Pink Book*, represents a large part of official financing). The current official presentation is into two main categories: the current account and the transactions in assets and liabilities account, which includes items previously shown in the official financing category and the capital account. For a fuller discussion of the problems of presenting the balance of payments statistics see Johnson (1988).
2. This does not imply that governments placed no restrictions in the way of international transactions; in fact they often felt a need to do so, for example by limiting how much foreign currency a holidaymaker could buy before going abroad on holiday, and how much domestic currency he could take with him.
3. Obviously, in a world of many currencies the agreed parities had to be mutually compatible, for example the rates between sterling and the dollar, say, and the dollar and the franc must be compatible with the rate between sterling and the franc. In simple numbers, if $2 bought £1 and $1 bought 1 franc then 2 francs must buy £1 – any other franc-sterling rate would imply that people could 'make money' simply by buying and selling currencies to and from central banks. For example, consider how to make money if $1 bought £1, $1 bought 1 franc, and 2 francs bought £1. For very small movements away from the agreed parities arbitrage transactions were not profitable, given dealing costs, hence exchange rates were, in practice, allowed to vary by 1 per cent on either side of the agreed values or parities.
4. Strictly, since £P is given, the demand for exports, measured in pounds sterling, must increase as long as the quantity sold rises. However, the sterling demand for imports could rise when sterling is devalued, since the sterling price of imports rises and, depending on the price elasticity, this could more than offset the reduction in quantity of imports demanded. Thus, it can be argued that the current account balance will improve (that is, will reduce a deficit or increase a surplus) for any income level only if the price elasticities of demand for imports and exports are sufficiently large. It is assumed in the text that the condition for this to be the case is satisfied.
5. Notice that since we are dealing with a two-currency world we have to consider only one exchange rate. In the real world, with many currencies, it is possible for a currency to rise in value in terms of some currencies whilst falling in value in terms of others (especially under floating exchange rates). It is, therefore, common to discuss the effective or trade-weighted exchange rate. This takes into account the importance in trade, for the country concerned, of the different currencies for which its currency may be converted, to produce a kind of average expression of the relative value of its currency. Similarly, it is possible to set up a measure of the effective or trade-weighted terms of trade. It is sometimes argued that the terms of trade

should be expressed in terms of export prices versus import prices, but in practice it is usually derived using broader price indices (which are formed using the prices of goods which are not traded internationally as well as the prices of internationally traded goods).

6. Actually the new line $(C + I + G + X - F)$ (e′) would have a different slope than the old line $(C + I + G + X - F)$ (e), but, to avoid cluttering the figure, this is not shown.

7. It ought to be clear that 'investments' here refers to financial assets and not real, physical investment, I, although in fact, of course, some of these financial flows will be used to purchase direct or indirect claims on real capital or land.

8. It should be noted that the response of capital flows to a given interest differential may vary over time. Consider, for example, the response of capital flows to an increase in the domestic interest rate from r* to a new level above that in the rest of the world. There may be an initial surge of capital inflows as a result of this, as investors reallocate their portfolios and move capital into the domestic economy. Once this initial reallocation has been carried out, however, the inflow of funds may be considerably reduced, so that maintaining a high rate of inflows may require further increases in the interest rate, possibly to unsustainably high levels.

9. The reason for the terminology of perfect versus imperfect capital mobility is that perfect capital mobility exists when foreign and domestic assets are perfect substitutes, and imperfect capital mobility when they are imperfect substitutes.

10. It might be noted that within the EC only Ireland and the UK include mortgage interest payments directly in the cost-of-living index; other sizeable nations to do so include Australia, Canada, and New Zealand. Clearly care must be taken with international comparisons of inflation or, indeed, of most important economic variables.

11. Since income rises (from y_0 to y_1 in Figure 8.5(d)) as the exchange rate depreciates, this will tend to moderate the reduction in import demand as a result of their price rise. Furthermore, since imports rise in price in sterling terms as the exchange rate falls, a demand for fewer imports could involve an increase in expenditure on them, and that expenditure is the supply of sterling to the foreign exchange market.

   It may be noted that, given a downward sloping demand for sterling curve, the exchange rate will move towards its equilibrium value, from any disequilibrium value, providing the exchange rate falls (rises) when there is excess supply of (demand for) sterling, and the supply curve is upward sloping or more steeply downward sloping than the demand curve. Alternatively, under an adjustable peg system such conditions would guarantee that a devaluation of the currency would lead to a smaller deficit or larger surplus on the current account, and *vice versa* for a revaluation.

12. Notice that the supply of sterling curve may be interpreted as the demand for dollars curve, since sterling is only supplied to the foreign exchange market by those who wish to obtain dollars in order to buy imports (in the real world these actions are, of course, usually carried out indirectly by banks and importers and the consumers of imports do not actually go to the foreign exchange market themselves). Similarly, the demand for sterling curve may be interpreted as the supply of dollars curve. Also notice that although the supply and demand curve in Figure 8.5(b) may be interpreted in a similar way to standard microeconomic supply and demand figures, the underlying derivation of the supply curve is rather different from that in the standard microeconomic case. Specifically, the supply curve shows how the supply of sterling varies with its price (the exchange rate) after taking into account changes in income associated with changes in the exchange rate, whereas the supply curves drawn in standard microeconomic textbooks usually assume income to be given.

REFERENCES

CSO (1989), *United Kingdom Balance of Payments* (also known as *The Pink Book)*, HMSO, London.

Hillier, B. (1991), *The Macroeconomic Debate: Models of the Closed and Open Economies*, Basil Blackwell, Oxford.

Johnson, C. (1988) *Measuring the Economy*, Macmillan, London.

Laidler, D. (1978) 'How to Maintain Stability – A Monetarist View', *The Banker*, April, pp.38–40.

Laidler, D. (1986), 'International Monetary Economics in Theory and Practice' in Sargent J. (ed.), *Postwar Macroeconomic Developments*, University of Toronto Press.

Thirlwall, A.P. (1986), *Balance of Payments Theory and the United Kingdom Experience*, (3rd edition), Macmillan, Basingstoke.

Tinbergen, J. (1952), *On the Theory of Economic Policy*, North-Holland, Amsterdam.

APPENDIX: THE KEYNESIAN MODEL OF THE SMALL OPEN ECONOMY AND THE FOREIGN EXCHANGE MARKET

Consider, first, the model under floating exchange rates as in Section 8.5 above and use Figure 8.5. Figure 8.5(a) and (d) are identical to Figure 8.3(a) and (b); Figure 8.5(b) and (c) introduce the foreign exchange market. Figure 8.5(c) shows exports, X, and imports, F, measured on the vertical axis and the foreign exchange market supply, S, and demand, D, for the domestic currency, sterling, on the horizontal axis. The demand for sterling on the foreign exchange market is derived from the demands of the rest of the world for UK exports. With an exchange rate of e_0, export demand is for X_0 worth of exports (measured in

Figure 8.5 The Keynesian multiplier model of the small open economy and the foreign exchange market

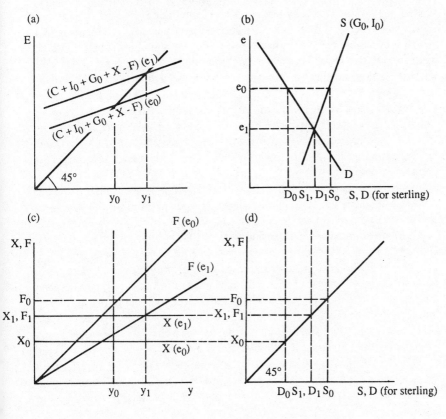

sterling), as shown in Figure 8.5(d). Hence at e_0 the demand for sterling on the foreign exchange market, D_0, equals X_0. With common scales on the vertical and horizontal axes of Figure 8.5(c), the 45° line may be used to convert X_0 into D_0 by reading X_0 across from Figure 8.5(d) to (c). The value for D_0 may then be transferred upwards into Figure 8.5(b), which shows the demand for sterling against the corresponding exchange rate, D_0 against e_0 in this case. This yields one point on the demand curve for sterling; another such point may be found by carrying out a similar exercise for the exchange rate e_1. Joining the locus of all such points would yield the D curve in Figure 8.5(b), which slopes downwards as shown under the assumption that, other things being constant, the demand for exports would rise as their price on the foreign market fell (remember that their price in terms of domestic currency is fixed).

The supply of the domestic currency, sterling, to the foreign exchange market is derived from the demand for imports by the domestic economy, the UK in this case. With an exchange rate of e_0, and government and investment spending of G_0 and I_0 respectively, import demand is for F_0 worth of imports (measured in sterling), as shown in Figure 8.5(d). This value may be converted into the supply of sterling, S_0, equal to F_0, by reading across from Figure 8.5(c) to (d) and using the 45° line. The value for S_0 may then be transferred upwards into Figure 8.5(b), which shows the supply of sterling against the corresponding exchange rate, S_0 against e_0 in this case. This yields one point on the supply curve of sterling, another such point may be found by carrying out a similar exercise for the exchange rate e_1. Joining the locus of all such points would yield the S curve in Figure 8.5(b). The S curve is drawn such that the supply of the domestic currency to the foreign exchange market falls as the domestic currency depreciates and imports become relatively expensive on the domestic market. This is not necessarily the case, but will depend upon the price and income elasticities of the demand for imports.[11,12]

Since the demand for imports at any exchange rate depends on the level of domestic income, and this in turn depends upon the exogenous levels of investment and government expenditure, the position of the S line depends on the levels of government expenditure and investment too, which is indicated by the G_0, I_0 terms in the brackets alongside the S line in the figure. For example, an increase in the level of government expenditure would cause an increase in domestic income at any exchange rate, and hence an increase in import demand and an increase in the supply of sterling on the foreign exchange market. The S line would, therefore, move rightwards if G were increased, so that an increase in G would reduce the market-clearing value of the exchange rate on the foreign exchange market as stated in the text. The reader may verify this by working through the effects of an increase in G on the figure, starting with the effects on the C + I + G + X − F lines for e_0 and e_1. Similarly, the interested reader could work out the effects on the equilibrium level of domestic income of changes in the level of real income in the rest of the world, or of changes in the domestic or foreign price levels by working through the effects of such changes on the lines in the figure.

Notice that the figure may also be used for analysis under the assumption of fixed exchange rates. For instance, if the fixed exchange rate is e_0 and the level of government expenditure is G_0, the level of domestic income will be y_0 and there will be a current account deficit of $(F_0 - X_0)$, or equivalently of $(S_0 - D_0)$. This excess supply of sterling to the foreign exchange market will require the central bank, the Bank of England in this case, to purchase sterling to the value of $(S_0 - D_0)$ to support the exchange rate e_0. In exchange for this sterling, the Bank of England would have to provide dollars and, hence, its reserves of foreign currency would fall (unless it restored them by borrowing from abroad). If the government wishes to persist with its expenditure level of G_0 then it must seek agreement, under the adjustable peg system, to devalue the currency to e_1, which would not only improve the current account position, but also cause income to increase to y_1.

9. The European Monetary System

T. Hitiris

So much barbarism, however, still remains in the transactions of most civilized nations, that almost all independent countries choose to assert their nationality by having, to their own inconvenience and their neighbours', a peculiar currency of their own (John Stuart Mill, Principles of Political Economy)

9.1 INTERNATIONAL MONEY MARKETS AND THE EC

When the Treaty of Rome was signed on 25 March 1957 by the original six members of the European Community (EC, EEC) the international monetary system in operation was that of fixed, periodically adjustable exchange rates, the Bretton Woods system. The fixed exchange rates system implied a worldwide integrated market. Hence, the Treaty did not make any specific reference to the need for monetary integration among the EC countries except for general provisions, such as that the Community will pursue its objectives by 'progressively approximating the economic policies of the Member States' (Article 2). However, in the late 1960s and the early 1970s increasing pressures on the dollar arising from the global financial and strategic commitments of the USA, and general exogenous shocks and disturbances in world markets, such as oil embargoes, induced policy makers to adopt floating exchange rates in an attempt to insulate domestic policy from external constraints. By reducing international interdependence, floating exchange rates induce the development of national rather than international markets and price systems and thus they operate against international market integration.

Meanwhile, the EC had already embarked on common objectives which were to be pursued by coordination of national policies at the level of the member states and by common policies at the level of the Community. The most important of the latter was the common agricultural policy (CAP) which was (and to a large extent still is) the only inter-state integrated policy of common prices, thus establishing a single Community market for agricultural products. However, the ongoing exchange rates turbulence of the international markets had repercussions on the EC member states, some of which were forced to alter their priorities by temporarily curtailing their commitments to inter-state co-operation within the EC; and by resorting to the use of policies selected on purely

192

domestic economic considerations, such as monetary policy for price stabilization and exchange rate policies for balance of payments objectives. Thus, while the international economy was moving towards a system of floating exchanges, divergences from policy coordination in the EC confirmed that the foundations of the common market, that is: free trade in goods, services and factors of production; competition on equal terms; and common policies for common objectives, could not be sustained without the support of a fixed exchange rate system among the Community partners. Hence, in December 1969 the EC heads of state proclaimed at the Hague Summit that the intention of the Community was to proceed gradually towards economic and monetary union (EMU). Thus, monetary integration was officially declared to be a Community target.

Although all the members of the EC agreed in principle that EMU should be implemented gradually, differences emerged as to whether the economic precedes or follows the monetary component of the union. The 'economist' group of countries (Germany, the Netherlands) argued that harmonization of economic policies and convergence of economic performance should come first and then stable exchange rates would normally follow, or at any rate be more easily achieved. The 'monetarist' group of countries (France, Belgium, Luxembourg) argued instead that, by adhering to narrow exchange rate fluctuations, the participating countries would compel themselves to aim at greater convergence of economic policy and performance; therefore, monetary integration should precede the convergence of economic policies.

This problem was considered by the Werner Committee which published its deliberations in 1970. The Werner Report, which was implicitly based on the assumption of continuous existence of the international fixed exchange rate system, recommended the establishment of EMU in stages by 1980. This would involve irrevocably fixed exchange rates, perfect convertibility of members' currencies, liberalization of capital markets, creation of a common currency and centralization of monetary and credit policy exercised by a Community central bank. The EC Council meeting of March 1971 accepted the substance of the Werner Report's recommendations and attempted to reconcile the different views regarding issues which were judged to impinge on national sovereignty. Thus, it was decided that the first stage of monetary integration should include the narrowing of exchange rate fluctuation margins, coordination of monetary policies, harmonization of national economic policies and establishment of an institution, the European Exchange Stabilization Fund, to provide credit facilities to the members for policies in support of monetary stability.

However, the worsening situation of the international money markets precipitated the need for immediate action. Hence in 1971 the EC countries took the first positive steps towards monetary integration by establishing, within the existing fixed exchange rate system, the 'European band' or the 'snake'. This was a variant of the adjustable peg exchange rate system, combining adherence to the international agreements with partial implementation of the Werner Plan. At the centre of the 'band' remained the US dollar with margins of permissible fluctuations set at ± 2.25 per cent for each of the participating currencies (except the Italian lira which was allowed ± 6 per cent margins), giving a maximum of intra-EEC exchange rates fluctuation between any pair of currencies of 4.5 per cent. The agreement provided that the system would be run and supervised by the European Monetary Cooperation Fund and that the margins of fluctuations would be adhered to by coordinated monetary policy and concerted action of the members' central banks. However, as a last resort, the participating countries were allowed to withdraw from the system, temporarily or permanently, if this was at any time deemed necessary.

The narrowing of exchange rate fluctuations was rapidly achieved. In addition to the six countries of the EC, the UK, Ireland and Denmark also joined the 'band' in anticipation of their imminent entry (1972) to the Community. Two other countries, Sweden and Norway, joined the system while Switzerland and Austria became associate members. However, when just a few weeks after joining, sterling came under speculative pressure, the UK and soon after Ireland abandoned the 'snake'. Within days Denmark followed suit, although it rejoined later on. Thus the first attempt towards coordination and progress towards European monetary integration was undermined right from the beginning.

Subsequently, under increasing US balance of payments deficits causing loss of confidence and flight from the dollar, the international fixed exchange rate system finally collapsed in March 1973 and nothing was put in its place. During 1973–74 the oil crisis also affected international trade and production of both developed and less developed economies. Many countries then adopted floating rates, openly intervening in the exchange rate market which thus became subservient to domestic policy targets and national economic priorities without consideration to their international economic repercussions. This caused wide and frequent fluctuations of market exchange rates and extensive divergence of national economic policies leading to diverse national inflation rates. The EC member states continued to make decisions according to national criteria, disregarding their commitment to monetary unification, while at the same time the currencies in the 'European band' came repeatedly under destabilizing speculative pressure. For some of the participating countries continuation in the system proved to be unworkable. The Italian lira was withdrawn in 1973, and the Swedish krona and Norwegian krone in 1977. France left the system in January 1974, rejoined it in July 1975, and left it again in August 1977. From April 1972 to March 1979, committed participants left and rejoined the system 18 times in all and the 'fixed' parities in the 'European band' were adjusted 31 times.

The altered economic conditions and the abandonment of the dollar-based fixed exchange rate system showed clearly that progress towards economic and monetary union in the EC, along the lines and the timetable advocated by the

Werner Report, was not feasible. Nevertheless, dissatisfaction with the floating exchange rate system; the ensuing uncertainties about exchange rate movements; the danger of increasing problems over the operation of existing common policies; and halting progress towards integration convinced the EC authorities that for both political and economic reasons they should institute their own system of fixed exchange rates as a first step towards monetary integration. Consequently, a new agreement was reached at the Council meetings in Bremen (July 1978) and Brussels (December 1978) and the new scheme for monetary cooperation, now called the European Monetary System (EMS), was launched on 13 March 1979. The European Council declared that objective of the EMS was 'closer monetary cooperation leading to a zone of monetary stability in Europe', 'as a fundamental component of more comprehensive strategy aimed at lasting growth with stability, a progressive return to full employment, the harmonisation of living standards and the lessening of regional disparities in the Community'.

For the new system, the margins of exchange rates fluctuations around the central rates were set at ± 2.25 per cent, except for Italy which was given 6 per cent margins. The UK and Ireland were also offered the wider band of fluctuations (6 per cent); but the UK decided to stay outside the exchange rate mechanism (ERM) of the system, while Ireland opted for the 2.25 per cent margins. Of the new members of the Community, Spain (member since 1986) joined the system in June 1989 at the ± 6 per cent margin, while Greece (member since 1981) and Portugal (member since 1986) decided to remain temporarily outside the ERM.

It must be emphasized that the EMS agreement had economic and political origins and objectives. The system would not have been instituted without the political commitment to the idea of a united Europe held by France and Germany and their desire to regain momentum to this end. A common monetary system, through its effects on real variables in the markets of interdependent economies and as a technical initiative in the monetary field for realization of the general objectives of integration, goes beyond monetary and exchange rates arrangements. The EMS was an attempt to give a fresh impetus to political and economic integration after the 1971–78 stagnation, and to establish a limited area of stability in the turbulence that followed the demise of the international fixed exchange rates system. However, the long-run viability of the EMS continues to depend on the will of the member states to progress towards economic and monetary union. If the political will is strong enough to promote convergence of national policies and economic performance, then exchange rate stability will ensue and monetary integration will become a reality.

9.2   THE EUROPEAN MONETARY SYSTEM

9.2.1   Mechanism.

The institutional arrangements of the EMS include three activities:

1.   The Exchange Rate Mechanism (ERM);
2.   Credit facilities to help defend these pegged rates; and
3.   Establishment of a European Monetary Cooperation Fund (EMCF) which
     would ultimately be replaced by a European Monetary Fund (EMF).

These three activities of the EMS are described briefly in the following:

1.   The Exchange Rate Mechanism (ERM)
The EMS is based on an exchange rate mechanism of fixed, though adjustable,
exchange rates. All members of the EMS may join the ERM. This obliges them
to maintain their exchange rates within certain bands.

In general there are two types of exchange rate pegging arrangements: the
parity grid, which ties every currency to every other in a system of mutually
agreed and consistent rates, and the *basket*, which ties every currency to a common currency unit. The EMS is based on a hybrid system of a parity grid with
features of the basket. The central rates of the parity grid are defined in terms of
the *European currency unit* (ECU) which is a basket-type common currency unit
made up of specific amounts of member states' currencies. The composition of
the basket and the weights of each currency in it are determined collectively by
precise criteria regarding the relative economic strength of each member country
in the Community, such as the member countries' shares in EC Gross National
Product and intra-EC trade. They are re-examined every five years or on request,
if the weight of any component currency has changed by more than 25 per cent.
The composition of the ECU and the weights of each currency at the time of
writing are shown in Table 9.1. The basket contains currencies of all member
states, including the associate members of the EMS (Greece, Portugal and the
UK) which do not participate in the exchange rate mechanism (ERM), although
they take part in discussions on the functions and development of the system.

The ECU is assigned four functions; it serves as:

a.   the denominator (numéraire) for the exchange rate mechanism;
b.   the basis for a divergence indicator;
c.   the denominator for operations in both the intervention and credit mecha-
     nisms;
d.   the means of settlement between monetary authorities of the European
     Community.

Table 9.1   *The ECU basket: weights, currency units and central rates[1]*

National currency		Weight	Units	Central rate for 1 ECU[2]
Belgian/Lux franc	BFR/LFR	0.0790	3.343	42.1679
Danish krone	DKR	0.0245	0.1976	7.79845
Deutschmark	DM	0.3010	0.6242	2.04446
Dutch guilder	HFL	0.0940	0.2198	2.30358
French franc	FF	0.1900	1.332	6.85684
Greek drachma	DR	0.0080	1.44	187.934*
Italian lira	LIT	0.1015	151.8	1529.70
Irish pound	IRL	0.0110	0.008552	0.763159
Portuguese escudo	ESC	0.0080	1.393	177.743*
Spanish peseta	PTA	0.0530	6.885	132.889
UK pound	UKL	0.1300	0.08784	0.72815*

1. From 20 September 1989.
2. From 5 January 1990
* notional rate.

Accordingly, the system provides that a central rate expressed in ECUs is fixed for each currency (as in Table 9.1). These central rates are used to establish a grid of implicit bilateral exchange rates around which permissive fluctuation margins of ± 2.25 per cent are set.

The ECU is also used as the indicator of divergence. This indicator is a kind of early-warning system based on the spread observed between a currency's market rate in ECUs and its central rate. It flashes when a currency crosses its 'thresholds of divergence' which are fixed at 75 per cent of the maximum spread of divergence allowed for each currency (calculated by 0.75 x 2.25 x 1 *minus* the weight of the currency in the ECU basket). Therefore, the larger the weight of a currency, the narrower is its 'threshold of divergence'. When a currency activates the early-warning system by crossing its thresholds of divergence, there is a 'presumption' that the country concerned will take remedial policy action (changes in interest rates, other changes in domestic economic policy) and, if necessary, unlimited intervention in the foreign exchange market (sales or purchases of currency by the central bank) to keep it within the permitted band of fluctuation. However, when a currency reaches its trigger point against another member's currency, it is expected that both countries will intervene to restore parity. As a last resort, if market pressures become too great and the policies required to maintain exchange rates within the bands become unsustainable, adjustments of a more general nature are implemented by *rea-*

lignment, that is by mutually agreed devaluations/revaluations of the central rates. Realignments are also necessary when the trade balances and/or differences in inflation rates between the partners show the parities to be broadly out of line. Hence the EMS is not a system of irrevocably fixed, but of managed exchange rates subject to periodic changes by collective decision and a common procedure.

2. Credit Facilities

As a denominator of operations the ECU is the currency used for intervention by the monetary authorities of the member states, that is for buying or selling foreign exchange with the aim of influencing their national currency's market exchange rate.Credit facilities for these operations are provided by the EMS through the European Monetary Cooperation Fund (EMCF) and are expressed in ECUs. To facilitate compulsory intervention, ERM participants created a 'very short-term financial facility' consisting of a reciprocal cash facility among their central banks. In addition, all EC members can also use the following credit facilities:

a. The *Short-term monetary support* which is a quasi-automatic facility that provides short-term (up to 75 days, but renewable for three months) finance for temporary balance of payments deficits. Under the facility each member is assigned a creditor quota that determines the extent of support it is expected to provide and a debtor quota that specifies the amount of assistance it can obtain. The original agreement provided that the ECU can be used for settlement of 50 per cent of the debts arising from short-term financing; but since 1985 this restriction no longer applies if the central bank accepting ECUs is itself a net debtor in ECUs;

b. *A Medium-term financial support* (9 months) consisting of mutual credit among central banks for up to 14 billion ECUs; and

c. *Long-term mutual financial assistance* (5 years) up to 11 billion ECUs.

3. The European Monetary Cooperation Fund (EMCF)

This fund is the central monetary institution of the Community. Its membership consists of the countries in the ERM of the EMS and the UK. The board of the EMCF consists of the Governors of all the Community's central banks. The EMCF is essentially a book-keeping operation. It issues ECU to central banks in exchange for deposits by them of 20 per cent of their gold and dollar reserves in the form of three-month revolving swaps. Consequently, the ECUs issued are entirely matched by a counterpart deposit of gold and dollar reserves. A swap is the combination of a spot purchase (or sale) of a currency and a forward sale (or purchase) of the same currency at a fixed rate. The gold and dollar reserves do not actually change hands and the central banks continue to manage and earn interest on their dollar deposits. A drawback of this system is that the amount of

ECUs created is determined by external factors (the value of dollars and gold) largely beyond the Community's control. Since 1985, central banks requiring intramarginal (that is before the divergence thresholds have been reached) intervention funds can acquire dollars or Community currencies against their net creditor positions in ECUs with the EMCF, and repay in ECUs. It has also been decided that the official ECU may be held as reserve currency by non-EC countries.

In an attempt to strengthen the system, the European Council decided in 1985 to enshrine it in the EEC Treaty by a new Article 102A. This made the EMS and the ECU part of the Treaty which established the European Community and instruments for the progressive realization of economic and monetary union (EMS). The latter was reaffirmed at the Luxembourg Conference in February 1986 when the member states added in the Preamble of the revised Treaties (Single European Act) that economic and monetary union is a long-term objective of integration in the Community and that the EMS is a stage towards achieving that goal. A first step towards this target was taken by the Committee of EC Central Bank Governors at Basle-Nyborg (1987) which decided to extend the duration of medium-term financial assistance for balance of payments difficulties or for capital market liberalization; increase the short-run availability of funds for intramarginal interventions, extend the payback period to 3.5 months with right of renewal for another three months; and expand the official use of the ECU. However, many problems still remain unresolved, such as, first, that not all members of the EC are full members of the EMS; and second, that the EMS, being focused on rather short-term exchange stability, does not seem to be subject to a built-in evolutionary process which would transform it into the EMU. The EMS system of pegged exchange rates at agreed values is maintained by the separate national central banks of the member states by coordinating domestic monetary policy appropriately. This system is successful for as long as the national central banks shape their policies solely with an external target objective, that of keeping the exchange rates of their currencies at the agreed level. However, if at any time pressures to use monetary policy for domestic purposes become irresistible, the exchange rate will become unstable. This may lead to periodic crises which, if they are major, may even cause the eventual collapse of the pegged exchange rate system. This is exactly what happened to the 'snake', the previous European exchange rate system. Consequently, a truly unified European currency requires the replacement of all the national central banks by the central bank of the European Community. Wider acceptance of the need for a common currency within the single European market may provide the necessary impetus for closer economic and political integration leading to the European economic and monetary union (EMU).

The everyday running of the EMS is currently assigned to the EMCF in consultation with member states' committees, such as the Monetary Committee and the Committee of EC Central Bank Governors. Final decisions are taken by the Council of Economic and Finance Ministers (ECOFIN). The EMS agreement provided that the EMCF would be replaced by the European Monetary Fund (EMF) which, vested with institutional autonomy, would be developed as the central bank of the Community, administering a common monetary sector and holding the members' deposits on a permanent basis.

9.2.2   Performance

When the EMS was introduced many observers found a variety of defects in it and predicted its imminent collapse. This was based, among other reasons, on the arguments that: nominal exchange rate rigidity will amplify the real exchange rate movements and increase the demands for protection as a result of costs and prices in different member countries getting 'out of line'; the asymmetry in the burden of adjustment would force weak currencies to abandon the fixed exchange rates arrangement; the availability of credit facilities would encourage diverging countries to postpone adjustment and this in turn could cause massive destabilizing speculation. However, the EMS surprised many by surviving a number of crises, and is still going strong.

For an assessment of the EMS we must examine whether the objectives set by the EC at the time of launching the system have been approached. Convergence of economic and financial policy among the members and establishment of a zone of monetary 'internal and external stability' are the two immediate objectives, while a third objective, that of creating economic and monetary union in Europe, is the most important but also the most remote one. 'Internal and external stability' seems to have meant a reduction in the overall inflation level and in the differentials between member countries with a stabler/less-volatile exchange rate. Therefore, the progress towards achieving these objectives can be studied by examining the effects of the EMS on two related issues: exchange rate stability and convergence of economic policy and performance.

1. *Exchange rate stability*

The performance of the EMS has been evaluated by comparing the volatility of exchange rates between member states since 1979 with that experienced before the establishment of the system, and with that of currencies of non-participating states. Reported statistical findings confirm that, despite the unstable international monetary environment, relative stability of the currencies participating in the ERM of the EMS has been achieved: there is strong evidence of reduced intra-ERM exchange volatility post-March 1979, and signs of increased volatility in dollar and (to a slightly lesser extent) sterling rates (Artis and Taylor, 1988). Moreover, the stability of the ERM exchange rates does not seem to have been reached at the cost of higher volatility of short-term interest rates, which in fact shows some evidence of reduction after 1979. These conclusions hold for both *nominal* exchange rates, which are the formal objective of the 'zone of monetary stability', and *real* exchange rates, regardless of the measure of variability (IMF 1983, Artis 1987). In general, the EMS 'has made a positive contribution to exchange rate stability' (EC, 1984) by successfully anchoring nominal exchange rates without causing intra-trade disturbances and misalignments in real exchange rates.

2. *Convergence*

This includes both the convergence of economic policy (money supply growth) and performance (inflation rates) among the members of the Community as well as the coordination of members' policies *vis-à-vis* third countries.

At the time of launching the EMS many observers argued that the system's fixed exchange rates would undermine the participating countries' ability to pursue domestic monetary targets in their anti-inflationary policies. Actually, the EMS has no direct mechanism for a common policy in pursuit of low inflation. Anti-inflationary policy is an outcome of the requirement that countries participating in the EMS are committed to operate coordinated and converging monetary policy. The evidence suggests that during the EMS years monetary growth has been significantly lower than during the period of floating rates and that 'the EMS has not laid the ground for a looser monetary policy but rather provided a framework in which anti-inflationary policies could be pursued more effectively' (IMF, 1986). In fact average inflation in the ERM countries has fallen steadily from a peak of 11.6 per cent in 1980 to 2.3 per cent in 1986 (Russo and Tullio, 1988). Although price stability cannot be wholly attributed to the existence of the EMS, inflation in the member countries has been sharply reduced and convergence of inflation rates among the EMS members has occurred. Undoubtedly, the credibility of anti-inflation policy of the system increased by virtue of the close links between the monetary policies of France and Germany. In conclusion, the experience of the first decade of the system at least suggests that neither the pessimistic predictions about its inflationary nature have been borne out nor can it be argued that participation in the EMS has actually reduced the ability of countries to pursue domestic anti-inflationary policies.

The EMS has also helped to decrease the frequency of simultaneous movements between the EC currencies and the dollar, thus asserting the independence and identity of European monetary policy. This has been achieved mostly by the relatively strong performance of the Deutschmark in the world financial markets and the weight it carries in the EMS; hence by the implicit acceptance of German monetary leadership within the EMS and coordination of other members' monetary policy with that of Germany (Giavazzi and Pagano, 1986).

Another question concerns the operation of the EMS mechanism, in particular whether the divergence indicator has worked in practice as a reliable early-warning signal of potential strains in the system. It is true that the hopes placed in the ECU as a divergence indicator have only been partially fulfilled and that as critics have pointed out, under certain circumstances two currencies could reach their intervention limits against one another well before the alarm starts flashing. However, in practice the authorities recognized that there is no unique standard against which the deviations of all currencies can be measured and therefore did not rely exclusively on the divergence indicator for initiating policy changes. Nevertheless, some observers argue that the divergence indicator provisions of the EMS agreement have contributed positively to the stability of the system and the convergence of members' monetary policy by forcing 'monetary discipline', that is by inducing the participants to undertake action in time on their own initiative and at their own discretion (Melitz, 1988).

In conclusion, clearly the EMS has not yet achieved completely its objectives, but it has led to a significant degree of policy approximation and closer cooperation between the central banks of the members. However, this policy approximation has been almost exclusively concentrated in the field of direct monetary policy with as yet very little coordination in other policies, such as public deficit management which has a direct influence on monetary developments. Hence, the exchange rates in the EMS have tended to diverge, and this is one of the reasons for the frequency of realignments of the central rates (eleven since 1979 and in some cases by a wide margin). Nevertheless, timely and mutually agreed realignments have offered the opportunity for a thorough examination of the operation of the system and provided it with the flexibility which made it adapt to changing economic conditions both domestic and international.

The EMS provisions did not require capital market liberalization, which are an integral part of an economic and monetary union. In fact, some of the ERM states (France and Italy) retained exchange and capital controls throughout the first ten EMS years. Actually, some observers believe that the relative stability of the EMS can be attributed partly to the protection afforded by these controls rather than by the convergence of economic policies (Artis, 1988). According to this argument, these controls narrowed the margin of domestic interest rate fluctuations and caused the need for constant monitoring of performance, with frequent intervention in the form of realignments which kept the system on the right path. The counter-argument is that, in general, there is no evidence that exchange controls are effective in the longer run. Moreover, extensive liberalization took place in Italy and Denmark in 1988 and in Ireland in 1989 with no apparent difficulties to the countries concerned or the EMS.

Progress towards the EMU requires action for the liberalization of capital markets. The Single European Act (1985), which envisages the creation by 1992 of a large internal market comprising all the Community countries, has led to the formulation of the Delors plan which foresees two stages for advancing monetary integration. In the first stage, the aim is to achieve effective liberalization of capital transactions most directly necessary for the proper functioning of the internal market. This came into effect on 1 March 1987 and concerns an unconditional liberalization of capital movements most directly affecting the cross-border exchange of goods and non-financial services. In the second stage liberalization will be extended to all financial and monetary transactions. Following this, in June 1988, on a proposal from the Commission, the Council adopted a directive on the abolition of all remaining capital controls and complete liberalization of capital movements by mid-1990. Four member states (Greece, Ireland, Portugal and Spain) were allowed the use of a derogation to maintain certain restrictions until 1992. The agreement is a precondition for the liberalization of financial services within the single Community market by 1992 and the setting up of a common regulatory structure for financial institutions. It is expected that similar liberalization measures will be adopted concerning capital movements occurring between EC and non-EC countries. Provided monetary policy in the EC remains a 'matter for common concern' and convergence in economic policy and performance continues unabated, 'the EMS should be able to function smoothly even after the liberalisation or abolition of capital controls'(Gros and Thygesen, 1988).

The ECU is used officially by the Community and all its institutions. However, a development which had not been envisaged at the time of the introduction of the EMS is the growth of markets in private ECUs, that is ECU-denominated financial instruments outside the context of the EMS. Although this was not much in evidence during the first years of the EMS, it took off in 1981 thus making the ECU, which is not yet legal tender, one of the five important currencies (the other four are the dollar, sterling, yen and DM), dealt in on the foreign exchange markets of the world. The comparatively high intra-EMS exchange rate stability and the fact that the ECU bond market is unique in that it lacks a clear-cut domestic counterpart, might explain why investors have turned to the ECU as a hedging against exchange rate risks. A practical step towards the greater use of the ECU in financial markets was taken in the summer of 1988, when the UK government offered to tender Treasury bills denominated and payable in ECUs. This commitment of the UK authorities is expected to promote the ECU and widen its use by more investors and governments.

Another important step towards monetary integration was taken at the Hanover Summit (June 1988), when the European Council set a special committee under the chairmanship of J. Delors, President of the European Commission, 'to study and propose concrete stages leading towards Economic and Monetary Union'. The Delors Report (published in April 1989) linked completion of the single market to a single currency, coordination of all macroeconomic policies and 'binding rules for budgetary policies'. Centralization of fiscal policy is considered essential because, if exchange rates between members are fixed and interest rates are the same in every member country, a fiscal expansion in one country would lead to a rise in prices in other countries and, under certain conditions, in the Community as a whole.

The Report proposed three stages of transition towards EMU. During the first stage, all member states would participate in the ERM, as full members of the EMS, and would endeavour to improve their economic policy coordination and convergence. In the second stage, the member states would set guidelines for common economic objectives and precise rules on national budgetary deficits, and would also consider the setting up of a European system of central banks (ESCB) as an autonomous Community institution consisting of the national central banks of the member states ranged around a common central institution. Through the federal structure of the ESCB central banks would move gradually from national to common monetary policy and narrower fluctuation margins in exchange rates. The final stage would begin with the introduction of irrevocably fixed exchange rates, common management by the ESCB of the pooled official reserves of the member states, and binding guidelines on the exercise of monetary and budgetary policies. The formality of a central bank and the introduction of a single currency would then follow. The Report admits that monetary union will involve a transfer of power to the Community at the cost of national sovereignty, but argues that the gain will be greater economic opportunities for all the member countries. In any case the experience gained from operating the EMS shows that, as the economies of the member states become progressively more interdependent, sovereignty over monetary matters is something which can only be exercised fully at the level of the Community.

The Delors Report was considered by the European Council at the Madrid Summit in June 1989. The leaders of the twelve member states agreed that the first stage for establishing the EMU should start on 1 July 1990. This will be followed by an intergovernmental conference (IGC) by the end of 1990 to consider the EC Treaty changes needed to set up a federal banking system along lines suggested by the Delors Committee. The Community finance ministers also approved a set of regulations, the Second Banking Directive, to govern banking in the unified European markets after 1992. However, no explicit commitment was taken to proceed to the subsequent two stages and no terminal date was set for completion of the EMU. The agreement was hailed by many observers as launching the EC definitely on the 'irreversible process' leading to a single European currency and to full EMU.

9.3 THE UK AND THE EMS

As a member of the EC, the UK is automatically an associate member of the EMS. But successive UK governments have declined to make the country a full member of the EMS by locking sterling into the ERM, contending that 'the time is not ripe' because sterling is either overvalued or undervalued or even that, unlike the ERM currencies, sterling is a 'petro-currency' subject to the gyrations of oil prices. Sterling, however, no longer behaves like a petro-currency. At a more elevated level, what the UK – EC debate seems to be about is whether the UK government can pursue effectively anti-inflationary policy by subordinating domestic monetary policy to the requirements of exchange rate policy within the EMS.

The UK governments since 1979 have declared that the permanent reduction in the rate of inflation is their prime objective. According to the monetarist dogma which they have embraced, control of the rate of inflation requires control of money supply growth. This is feasible only under flexible exchange rates which permit currency values to be determined in the foreign exchange market and allow each country to pursue an independent monetary policy and to choose its own level of inflation. The price one has to pay for this freedom of choice includes high instability of financial markets, that is of exchange rates and interest rates.

This argument would have been a convincing reason for remaining outside the ERM, if the UK economy had had a better record of reducing inflation than the ERM countries whose exchange rates are pegged in the EMS. However, the evidence shows that participation in the ERM has not in practice proved inconsistent with a price stability target and adherence to domestic monetary targets. The average growth rates of monetary aggregates in the ERM countries have fallen and their correlation increased; inflation rates have slowed down and inflation differentials narrowed; and nominal as well as real interest rates have shown a marked increase in correlation (Padoa-Schioppa, 1985). Moreover, the average rate of inflation of the ERM members is lower than that of the UK: 3.4 per cent against 7.9 per cent in the UK in 1988–89, the highest among the main industrialized countries. Similarly, wage increases in the UK are running at an annual rate of 9.3 per cent – nearly three times higher than the rate in France and Germany. In addition to these problems, the fluctuations in interest rates and exchange rates experienced by the UK have been particularly severe. For example, sterling over-appreciated in 1980–81 to $2.45, reducing the UK's competitiveness, and plummeted to $1.04 in 1985, threatening the resurgence in domestic inflation. The UK government's objections to these arguments are that the EMS discipline has worked for the ERM countries only because their capital markets are still protected by explicit (France, Italy) or implicit (Germany) controls on international capital flows, while the UK's capital market is completely liberalized. Accordingly, the UK is crucially different from the other EMS members and therefore a higher underlying rate of inflation would not be contained by the EMS exchange rate discipline.

However, the differences in relative monetary performance between the UK and the EMS member states can be explained by a different set of arguments.

First, one of the basic objectives of the EMS and the countries participating in it is to curb inflation; this objective has on the whole been met by the sharp reduction of inflation rates in the ERM countries. Second, the EMS is not a system of rigidly fixed exchange rates. Full membership of the system provides the members with sufficient exchange rate flexibility (around the agreed central rates) to exercise adequate control over their money supply. Third, in an economic union and, in general, in an integrated world market the independence of national monetary policy is severely curtailed; therefore the basic monetarist propositions are subject to qualifications. In an interdependent world with substantial spillover effects of policy from one country to another the demand and supply of money transgress national frontiers. Therefore it cannot any more be assumed that the demand for money is stable or that the increase in money supply is determined by the domestic supply of money. In the integrated world markets, the demand for money takes the form of a diversified portfolio of different currencies which together with the world money supply growth determine the rate of inflation. Hence, the proposition that inflation will be reduced if the ratio of domestic money to a stable domestic demand for money is reduced, is a necessary but not a sufficient condition. What is required is international monetary cooperation which has not as yet been re-established. The EMS aims at, and has already made some progress towards international monetary cooperation by actually establishing a 'zone of [relative] monetary stability in Europe'.

Although the UK government has refused to put sterling in the ERM, in 1987 and early 1988 the pound followed the movements of the DM so closely that it became a *de facto* full member of the EMS. The assumption made at that time was that a policy of shadowing the DM rather than joining the EMS provided an anchor against domestic inflation combined with flexibility in monetary and fiscal policy. The link between sterling and the DM was maintained by increasing interest rates when the pound was falling, and decreasing them when the pound was rising. However, the combination of a strong pound and low interest rates obviously has different effects on domestic demand from those of a weak pound and high interest rates. In 1985 the monetary controls on the economy were somewhat weakened and deregulation of the financial markets led to a credit boom that encouraged expansion of demand. Further increases in demand were also induced by successive cuts in income tax rates. However, supply was in no shape to respond and when in early 1988 sterling kept appreciating against the DM while domestic credit and money supply kept rising fast, the alternatives left to the UK authorities were either to maintain currency stability by reducing interest rates, which might increase the rate of inflation, or to contain the rise in inflation by increasing interest rates and allowing sterling to rise further. Confirming that its first priority was to fight inflation, the UK government chose the second alternative by uncapping the pound from the DM and increasing interest rates by ten successive steps during 1988 which pushed the pound up. Such a diversion of monetary policy from exchange rate to domestic price targets would not have been possible under full membership in the EMS.

When the links with the DM were broken, the UK's monetary policy was left anchorless. The adopted policy can in the short run reduce the rate of inflation. However, its effects on the foreign trade sector are detrimental: UK imports rose at twice the pace of exports and the balance of payments deficit reached record levels for reasons both of excess demand and inadequate domestic supply. Whether sterling can remain strong under these conditions is ultimately a matter to be decided by the financial markets' attitude to the UK government's conduct of economic policy and by the relative performance of other economies and currencies. If in the longer run the effect of the strong pound and high interest rates will be to reduce investment and to push up wages and prices, the international competitiveness of the UK economy will decline.

Critics of the government's policies argued that, arising from international interdependence which is particularly strong and rising between the EC members, UK 'sovereignty' over domestic monetary policy is small and declining, and cannot be very successful. For example, when in September 1989 Germany raised its interest rate, the UK followed suit thus proving that, despite the UK government's insistence that money matters are a vital part of a nation's sovereign rights, there is no monetary independence in interdependent economies. This does not necessarily mean, although it frequently is argued, that the situation would have been radically different and much better than it had been, if the UK had formally joined the EMS. The EMS should not be seen as a universal panacea: if there are structural problems in the UK economy causing instability and inflation, they must be sorted out before the country becomes a full member of the EMS. In general, participation in the EMS must be seen as an integral part of the process of economic integration which may or may not confer short-term benefits.

Although the UK government eloquently protects its sovereignty on monetary matters, it accepted officially the Delors Report at the Madrid Summit and agreed to join the exchange rate mechanism of the EMS if certain conditions were met. The conditions were that:

1. The UK should have made substantial progress in reducing inflation.
2. The European internal market should be completed.
3. EC competition policies should be strengthened by the abolition of state subsidies and protectionist measures.
4. All the EC countries should liberalize all capital movements and financial services.

Given the timetable for abolition of exchange controls in Portugal and Greece, the latter condition may mean that the UK will attempt to keep sterling out of the EMS at least until the mid-1990s. Many opponents of the EMU in the UK believe and hope that the EMS will have collapsed before that date. However, since the Confederation of British Industry (CBI) and the City have come out in favour of immediate entry in the ERM, the real possibility is that the UK will become a full member of the EMS before 1992. Alternatively, the then members of the EMS will push ahead with the process leading to eventual merger of their monetary policies, irrespective of whether the UK will participate or not. Although the UK can still veto treaty changes, it cannot stop others setting up new monetary institutions outside the formal framework of the European Community. Therefore, the sooner the UK joins the EMS, the greater will be its ability to influence the line of developments from the inside. If the UK continues its opposition to EMU, this would probably be the first step towards the *de facto* creation of a two-speed Europe, in which the enthusiasts make faster progress towards integration, while the rest are left behind. Obviously, the members of the second tier cannot expect to have much influence in the development of the economic union. Sterling's entry in the EMS would accelerate monetary integration by resolving the ambiguities in the UK's policies towards the single market and EMU. It would also provide the EMS with greater monetary cohesion which in turn would make it gain more influence over financial markets for a wider agreement on international monetary cooperation.

GUIDE TO FURTHER READING

The central ECU rates for each member state's currency and the daily market rates of the ECU are published in the *Official Journal of the European Communities;* they also appear daily in the *Financial Times*. For an extensive bibliography on the EMS see: Deville, Volker, *The European Monetary System and the ECU. Bibliography*. Florence, European University Institute, 1986 (EUI working paper 206). More references on monetary and other EC matters are in: Lodge, Juliet, *The European Community. Bibliographical Excursions,* Frances Pinter, London, 1983. For a general introduction to EC policies see Hitiris (1988).

REFERENCES

Artis, M.J. (1987), 'The European Monetary System: An Evaluation', *Journal of Policy Modelling*, vol. 9, pp. 175-198.
Artis, M.J. (1988), 'The EMS in the Face of New Challenges', in P. Arestis, (ed.) *Contemporary Issues in Money and Banking, Macmillan, London*.

Artis, M.J. and Taylor, M.P. (1988), 'Exchange Rates, Interest Rates, Capital Controls and the European Monetary System: Assessing the Track Record', in Giavazzi *et al*, (1988).

EC, Commission of the European Community (1984), *Five Years of Monetary Co-operation in Europe*, COM(84) 125 Final, Brussels.

European Community (1987), *The ECU* (second edition), European Documentation, Office of the Official Publications of the European Communities, Luxembourg.

Giavazzi, F., Micossi, S. and Miller, M. (eds) (1988), *The European Monetary System*, Cambridge University Press, Cambridge.

Giavazzi, F. and Pagano, M. (1986), 'The Advantage of Tying One's Hand: EMS Discipline and Central Bank Credibility', *Centre for Economic Policy Research Discussion Paper No. 135*, London.

Gros, D. and Thygesen, N. (1988), *The EMS: Achievements, Current Issues and Directions for the Future*, Centre for European Studies Paper no. 35, CEPS, Brussels.

Hitiris, T. (1988), *European Community Economics*, Harvester–Wheatsheaf, Hemel Hempstead.

International Monetary Fund (1983), *The European Monetary System: The Experience 1979–82*, Occasional Paper no. 19, Washington, D.C.

International Monetary Fund (1986), *The European Monetary System, Recent Developments*, International Monetary Fund, Occasional Paper no. 48, Washington, D.C.

Melitz, J. (1988), 'Monetary Discipline and Cooperation in the European Monetary System: A Synthesis', in Giavazzi *et al*, (1988).

Padoa-Schioppa, T. (1985), *Money, Economic Policy and Europe*, European Perspectives, EC Commission, Brussels.

Russo, M. and Tullio, G. (1988), 'Monetary Policy Coordination Within the European Monetary System: Is There a Rule?', in Giavazzi *et al*, (1988).

10   Consumption, Borrowing and Saving

D.H. Gowland

10.1 INTRODUCTION

Macroeconomic policy makers face many problems in the real world which do not exist in the well behaved world of textbook models ('A' level Keynesian, IS-LM and the rest) as well as many which do. Amongst these the explanation and prediction of consumer's expenditure has been the most important in the UK since 1970.The Keynesian definition is that

Saving = income – consumers' expenditure

In many cases, consumers finance expenditure, especially on durables, by borrowing. Borrowing is therefore negative saving in that it increases spending compared to income. Hence to explain consumption is also to explain borrowing and saving. Indeed a Keynesian analysis of borrowing is simply an analysis of dissaving. The consumer credit boom in the later 1980s, discussed in detail in section 10.4, has posed problems for policy makers both in predicting the strength of the boom and then in controlling it after its disastrous effect on inflation and balance of payments impinged on Mr. Lawson in 1988. This is but the latest of a series of similar problems which have faced Chancellors; the unexpected rise in savings in the mid-1970s and again around 1980 being the most discussed of these. Table 10.1 shows the fluctuations in the savings ratio (or average propensity to save) since 1950, both being defined as saving divided by (disposable) income. Its instability has been reinforced by measurement problems and frequent revisions of data.[1] The problem of predicting consumers' expenditure is likely to continue to be difficult because of the marked change in the pattern of income and wealth in the UK since 1970, discussed in Section 10.4.

These policy issues reflect the theoretical debate about what determines consumers' expenditure. Keynesian models assume that it is determined by current disposable income whereas other schools of thought disagree. The issue of consumers'expenditure is critical to the Keynesian economic system in general and the concept of the multiplier in particular. The multiplier is the short-hand phrase to describe the magnification of an initial shock to the economy[2]. The role of Keynesian demand management is in large part to offset such

Table 10.1   Consumers' expenditure and saving

1. Savings ratio (APS) 1950–88

1950	1.0	1960	7.1	1970	8.9	1980	14.2
1951	1.1	1961	8.6	1971	8.5	1981	13.1
1952	3.0	1962	7.4	1972	10.5	1982	12.2
1953	3.4	1963	7.5	1973	11.7	1983	10.7
1954	2.6	1964	8.0	1974	11.4	1984	11.2
1955	3.5	1965	8.8	1975	12.3	1985	9.7
1956	5.2	1966	9.1	1976	12.0	1986	7.5
1957	4.7	1967	8.5	1977	10.4	1987	5.6
1958	4.0	1968	7.9	1978	11.8	1988	4.6
1959	4.8	1969	8.1	1979	13.0		

2. Consumers' income expenditure 1980–88

	Income	Expenditure	Savings ratio
1980	160 297	137 470	14.2
1981	176 132	153 027	13.1
1982	190 938	167 599	12.2
1983	205 096	183 068	10.7
1984	220 711	195 912	11.2
1985	238 804	215 535	9.7
1986	246 260	227 757	7.5
1987	254 342	240 100	5.6
1988	266 479	255 624	4.6

magnification. The multiplier depends on a high and constant marginal propensity to consume (MPC) out of current disposable income. MPC is that fraction of extra income that is consumed (see p. 215). The formula for the Keynesian multiplier (KM) which shows the change in income for a given change in injections is:

$$KM = \frac{1}{\text{marginal propensity to withdraw} - \text{marginal propensity to inject}}$$

The second term is often omitted, though of relevance in the multiplier-accelerator model where the accelerator coefficient is the marginal propensity to invest and hence to inject. In fact estimate values of the multiplier are usually low – between 0.9 and 1.3 – see Table 10.2, and were of similar magnitude in the 1930s; see the survey by Collins in Hillard (1988).

Table 10.2   Value of the multiplier: government expenditure: model simulations

	London Business School	National Institute	Treasury	Bank of England
Basic after 1 year	0.84	1.06	0.95	0.92
Basic after 4 years	0.98	0.95	1.13	0.91
(ie interest rate held constant)				
Money-financed				
Basic after 1 year	0.96	1.29	0.96	Not
Basic after 4 years	1.53	1.26	1.01	calculable

Source: K.F. Wallis *et al* (ed) (1988)

It seems at first sight that this Keynesian system violates both economic theory and common sense, since it denies the assumption that consumers maximize welfare. It is easiest to see this by using the principle of diminishing marginal utility, the most fundamental proposition of micro-choice theory. Diminishing marginal utility means that the pleasure derived from, for example, the eighth unit exceeds the pleasure from the ninth. This means that it is desirable to smooth out patterns of consumption. For example, to drink eight pints one night and eight the next is preferable to nine and seven because the pleasure from the ninth foregone is less than from the eighth gained.

The anti-Keynesian extends this concept to total spending. Consumers should borrow or save to maintain an even flow of consumption faced with a fluctuating income. Irrespective of the income in a particular year their expenditure would not vary. Hence their marginal propensity to consume will be equal to zero as shown in Table 10.3. When there is a change in income there is no change in consumption, hence the MPC is zero. (This presentation ignores rates of interest, uncertainty and so on to illustrate the key point.) Compared to

Table 10.3   Constant spending and fluctuating income

Income	Spend	Borrow(–) Save	ΔY	ΔC	MPC
100	100	0			
200	100	100	100	0	0
60	100	–40	–140	0	0
40	100	–60	–20	0	0
100	100	0	+60	0	0

a 'Keynesian' who consumed all his income in the period of receipt this consumer has foregone 100 of consumption in period 2 so as to increase consumption in periods 3 and 4. The principle of diminishing marginal utility says he has thereby increased his welfare since the benefit of the consumption foregone (units 101–200) is less than that gained (61–100 and 41–100). Almost all economists would expect such smoothing in the face of short-term shocks such as illness. Moreover most would expect such smoothing to cover seasonal variations – a York café owner will smooth his summer profits over the entire year just as a student does with vacation earnings. The controversy between Keynesians and anti-Keynesians arises over longer periods. Do consumers smooth from year to year or even quinquennium to quinquennium?

The chief defence of the Keynesian position came from Clower (1965) and Leijonhufvud (1968). They sought to justify the Keynesian consumption function as part of the appraisal of Keynes[3]. In particular they argued that the optimization procedure only determined what an individual would like to do, that is in Clowers terminology *notional* demand. His actual spending, *effective* demand, might be very different. Institutional arrangements and limits to borrowing might make actual, or realized, income a binding constraint on spending. Clower makes realized income constraints the centrepiece of his neo-Keynesian models. Leijonhufvud (1968) went further. He argued that 'the multiplier was an illiquidity phenomenon', that the downward spiral of contraction in income caused by an initial shock was caused by the forced reduction in consumption by the initially unemployed. If they had been able to borrow in unlimited amounts against future income, or sell labour forward, then there would be no slumps. A market in human capital is illegal and it is very easy to see why no one would lend to the unemployed in the necessary amount. Virtually every form of market failure is present in this market.

The difference between the Keynesian and the classical analysis can be highlighted in this context by using the example of a 30-year-old building worker who earns £250 per week and spends it all. One week his wages fall to £50 because of bad weather. The classical story is that he borrows £199.85 and spends £249.85 in the relevant week. He repays the loan at the rate of 15p per week for the remainder of his working life. Hence his consumption in all subsequent periods is £249.85. In other words he has smoothed the shock of one week's bad weather over his working life. His MPC is virtually zero; faced with a fall of £200 in his income his spending has fallen by 15p so his MPC is 0.0075. In consequence the shock is not magnified. The Keynesian story is very different: he cannot borrow so his expenditure falls to £50, that is his MPC is equal to 1. In consequence there is a magnification of the shock – perhaps the local pub has to lay off a barperson and so on. Two interesting features follow from the Clower-Leijonhufvud analysis: the efficiency case for unemployment pay and the corridor theory. The policy consequences of this point are to highlight the role of credit availability in determining behaviour (see p 232).

Of all the features that have wrecked the simple Keynesian model of consumption, the most important and controversial is inflation. In the 1960s and 1970s, many economic 'popularizers' argued that a rise in the rate of inflation would make people less willing to save, as 'it would not be worthwhile'. Accordingly, they believed that if inflation rose there would be a fall in the savings ratio, that is to say saving as a percentage of personal disposable (that is after tax) income. More rigorous economic theorists disagreed and argued that an increase in inflation would almost certainly lead to an increase in the savings ratio, although strictly the result was ambiguous. Events in the UK have shown the theorists to be right, a reassuring result! The relationship between inflation and the savings ratio in the UK is a strongly positive one. Of especial interest is the 50 per cent rise in the savings rate from 9 to 14 per cent in the early 1970s while inflation trebled. The sharp rise in inflation in 1979–80 also produced a very sharp rise in saving, the ratio exceeding 20 per cent in one quarter. The fall in saving in the latter half of the 1980s was also a partial consequence of the fall in inflation (see p. 232).

This positive relationship between inflation and saving is one of the brute facts facing economic policy makers in the 1980s.[4] Indeed it is one of the linchpins of Mrs Thatcher's economic strategy. One of her main propositions is that inflation causes unemployment and that a reduction in inflation is both necessary and sufficient for a reduction in unemployment. One reason for this belief is the expectational argument discussed on p. 118 above. Another stems from the relationship between saving and inflation: a variant of the paradox of thrift discussed below. In the context of most elementary economic textbooks this chapter is an argument for a change of emphasis. It is conventional to consider the relationship between income and saving and consumption and then consider other factors that may influence consumption. It used to be argued that these are interesting but unimportant. However, the evidence of the 1970s and 1980s suggests that they are in fact critical. Section 10.2 outlines the development of the theory of consumption and saving. In Section 10.3 these other factors – wealth, liquidity, real interest rates – are analysed in the context of the role of inflation on saving. Section 10.4 extends the analysis to the later 1980s when saving seemed to collapse.

10.2 THE THEORY OF CONSUMPTION AND SAVING

The modern theory of consumption was pioneered by Keynes in the *General Theory* (1936). His basic argument was that consumption depended only on current income and a number of unchanging psychological attitudes.[5] Changes in consumption and saving would occur only when income changed. Moreover any change would be predictable, the stability of the relationship being embodied in the concept of the marginal propensity to consume. This Keynesian or absolute income hypothesis is embodied in the familiar:

$C = a + bY$ (or $C = 10 + 0.9Y$ for those who prefer arithmetic examples)

where a is a constant and b is equal to the marginal propensity to consume, that fraction of extra income spent, in this case

$MPC = b \; APC = \dfrac{a}{Y} + b$

(in the arithmetic example $MPC = 0.9$ and $APC = \dfrac{10}{Y} + 0.9$)

Thus APC is greater than MPC. It is worth emphasizing that the consumption function is expressed in this way in order to incorporate Keynes's fundamental psychological law that the average propensity to consume is greater than the marginal. The inclusion of a constant term ensures this, since $a + b/y$ is necessarily greater than b.

The relationship is only supposed to be valid over relevant ranges of income and cannot sensibly be extrapolated back to zero income. The constant is not included as the minimum level of consumption, that is it cannot be interpreted as an estimate of what consumption would be if income were equal to zero. Instead of Keynes's hypothesis it could be that $APC = MPC$ in which case the function would be

$C = bY \; (C = 0.9Y)$

When APC and MPC are both equal to b (0.9) *or* it could be that $MPC > APC$, in which case the function would be

$C = -a + bY \; (C = -10 + 0.9Y)$

when APC equals $b - a/y$, and so is necessarily less than MPC, which is equal to b. Alternatively, as Keynes (1936) p.XX mused, the MPC falls as income rises, in which case

$C = a + bY - 2gY^2$

and

$MPC = b - 2gY$

By definition

$$C + S = Y$$

so

$$MPC + MPS = 1$$

and

$$APS + APC = 1$$

Thus it is possible to transform any statement about consumption into one about saving and *vice versa*. Returning to

$$C = a + bY$$

where MPC = b and APC = a/y + b, then

MPS = 1 − b because MPC + MPS = 1 so MPS = 1 − MPC
$APS = 1 - \dfrac{a}{y} - b$ because APS + APC = 1 so APS = 1 − MPC

Alternatively, as S = Y − C, the consumption function could be rewritten as a savings function:

$$
\begin{aligned}
S \; &= Y - C \\
&= Y - (a + bY) \\
&= a + (1 - b)\, Y.
\end{aligned}
$$

The implications of some of these transformations can sound puzzling or paradoxical. For example, it is easy to argue that higher wealth should increase spending for example through a rise in the value of a house or shares owned by the individual. However, the corollary that it reduces the saving ratio is hard for some students to grasp. Yet this follows from the definition of saving as income less expenditure; more expenditure means less saving for a given income. Presumably the confusion arises from the difference between changing a single variable (wealth) and analysing its consequences on the one hand and an intuitive belief that if wealth changes other things are likely to change as well. However analysis of a wealth effect is the former not the latter. Moreover in both the examples cited above there is a change in wealth but not in income.

The first challenge to the Keynesian consumption function came from Duesenberry (1949). He suggested an alternative relationship between consumption and income and called it the *relative income hypothesis*. His work was inspired by an examination of the American national income data produced by Kuznets. In particular, he observed that in cross-sectional studies the average propensity to consume declined and the savings ratio rose with income, that is the rich saved a higher fraction of their income than the poor. Hence cross-sectioned data were in accord with Keynes's theory. On the other hand, the aggregate savings ratio was constant over time.[6] If the average propensity to save, and to consume, are constant when income varies then, by definition, the average and marginal propensities to consume are equal – that is contrary to Keynes's hypothesis. To reconcile these apparently conflicting data, Duesenberry suggested that a person's consumption depends on other people's consumption and on his past consumption. The relatively poor consumed a higher percentage of their income than did the richer classes in an attempt to 'keep up with the Joneses'. However, if everyone became richer, everyone's saving ratio (APS) would remain unchanged. As further evidence, Duesenberry cited the higher savings at each level of income by black Americans. In the 1940s blacks and whites were almost totally segregated in the USA, especially in the southern states, so they could be treated as separate communities. Duesenberry thought that the higher level of saving reflected the fact that black consumption was not influenced by the richer whites whereas white consumption at an equivalent income was. The implications of Duesenberry's analysis were:

1. The more equally distributed income was, the higher savings would be, in marked contrast to the Keynesian theory which implied the opposite (where a transfer of income from rich to poor increases the spending of the poor by more than it reduces that of the rich).
2. Any attempt to redistribute income in any direction would reduce saving because the losers would not reduce spending by as much as the gainers would increase theirs.
3. In a downturn savings ratios would fall thus acting to stabilize the economy.

The next significant contribution to the consumption function was made by Friedman (1957). He distinguished sharply between consumers' expenditure and consumption whereas earlier writers had blurred the distinction. The principal difference arises with consumer durables. A durable appears as part of consumers' expenditure only when it is purchased, but it yields a flow of services which are consumed over a period of years. If a television is purchased in 1990 for £300 and lasts ten years, consumers' expenditure is £300 in 1990 and 0 thereafter. On the other hand, consumption may be 300 hours per year (of declining quality) which might be valued at £100 in 1990, £90 in 1991 and so on.

Friedman sought to explain consumption, not consumers' expenditure. He argued that consumption should depend only on wealth and the liquidity of wealth. Wealth should include human wealth, that is to say the net present value of (expected) future income. Friedman stressed that consumption depends on all one's resources, not just on current income. However, wealth in the form of money will be spent more readily and easily than wealth in the form of land and both more than wealth in the form of future income. Friedman's next step was to consider how human wealth might be estimated. He suggested that 'permanent income' might be the best methods of measuring human wealth, hence the term *permanent income hypothesis* for his theory. Permanent income is the income a person expects to go on receiving rather than any transitory or windfall element. Imagine a worker whose income rises from £240 to £260 per week as a result of a pay settlement. As an additional clause of the settlement he receives a lump sum of £1000. His permanent income has risen from £240 to £260 while the lump sum is transitory income. Keynesian theory treats the two as identical. For Friedman the MPC from permanent income is close to unity. For transitory income, the MPC is equal to zero. Hence the short-run observed aggregate MPC will be much less than the APC since some changes in income will be transitory. In the example above income is £240, £1260 and £260 in successive weeks whereas spending is £240, £260, £260 – a measured MPC of either 0.02 (20/1020) or 0 (0/–1000).

Moreover even permanent changes may not be viewed as permanent in the short run; an individual who has just seen his income rise may not know if this is temporary or permanent, so he will not increase his consumption by as much as he will when he knows the increase is permanent. This would explain the paradox noted by Duesenberry. Cross section data would measure the short-run MPC and time series data the long-run one.

The principal practical merit of the permanent income hypothesis is not that it explains the behaviour of most consumers better than a Keynesian consumption function, since for most consumers expected, present and past income are closely related. It is that it is significantly better at explaining the behaviour of the small minority who are both hardest to predict and most crucial to any successful prediction of consumers' expenditure. This is the small minority who do most of the discretionary saving in contrast to contractual saving such as pension contributions, life assurance, and the like. Of income recipients, 5 per cent, not the richest 5 per cent, are responsible for more than half of the changes in discretionary saving. This group includes many of the self-employed and others with fluctuating incomes. Undoubtedly these groups do maintain long-term consumption patterns and have a very low short-run marginal propensity to consume.

Friedman's theory has implications for fiscal policy which are radically different from Keynes's. These policy issues reflect the theoretical debate about what determines consumers' expenditure. Keynesian models assume that it is determined by current disposable income whereas other schools of thought disagree. The lower MPC in itself reduces the value of the multiplier and so the scope of fiscal policy. More importantly, many fiscal actions will not boost permanent income and will leave consumption unchanged. For example, a tax rebate is normally welcomed by Keynesians as a quick acting boost to the economy. As a transitory windfall in Friedman's analysis, it has little effect on the size of permanent income and in itself is useless as an expansionary device (that is unless it increases the money supply). Nevertheless, the difference between Friedman and Keynes is not as great as it seems even in this respect because Friedman sought to explain consumption, not consumers' expenditure as Keynes did. If transitory income is spent on consumer durables both theories may be right. Expenditure on durables has an element of 'saving' about it in that in transfers consumption from present to future: a television bought in 1990 provides consumer service in 1991 and 1992. Thus it is not inconsistent with Friedman's analysis to expect transitory income to be spent on durables. Consumers' expenditure could increase substantially when income changes while consumption changed little. In other words consumers may have an uneven expenditure path, as Keynes argued, but a smooth consumption path as Friedman argued.

The next development in the consumption function literature was an elaboration of Friedman's model that produced a more rigorous, if less plausible, model. This was the *life cycle hypothesis* of Ando and Modigliani (1963). They postulated that an individual, or household, would determine its optimal lifetime consumption path in the light of all its available resources, including the receipts of income at different periods. Borrowing and lending, dissaving and saving, would then be used to adjust the income path to match the desired consumption path. In any period in which income exceeded optimal consumption, the excess would be invested and in any period in which planned expenditure exceeded income the deficit would be borrowed. Interest would be received or paid on these funds and this would affect the amount available for consumption in other years. In consequence the real rate of interest became a principle determinant of the consumption opportunities facing consumers, in other words their budget line (see p. 226). The life cycle hypothesis, in other words, analyse the consumption-saving decision as a classic microeconomic theoretic choice problem involving the choice between consumption at different periods. This was analysed using the tools developed to analyse choice between different goods in the same period. Many other writers have followed this approach. These models of optimization have grown ever more complex (see, for example, Mussa, 1977 or Blanchard and Fisher 1989). The models are most plausible for the salaried middle classes with predictable changes in income, but even here the models are not operational. Instead their role is to point out a number of aspects of the savings decision not explicitly captured in the other analyses.

The first of these factors is the role of age. Ando and Modigliani suggested that most individuals were likely to receive a steadily rising income, say from 20 to 60, followed by a sharp drop on retirement. On the other hand, they would have to incur heavy expenditure when setting up a home (and perhaps having children) early in life. Thus expenditure would be heaviest between perhaps 20 and 40. No one would wish to see a sharp drop in living standards on retirement. Therefore, the analysis hypothesized that individuals would be net borrowers in the first phase of their working lives. Then they would be heavy net savers, say from age 40 to 60, both to pay off the debts incurred earlier and to build up assets to dissave and so finance consumption during retirement. Similar life cycle models had earlier been applied to poverty, see Maynard (in Gowland, 1979), but neither rigorously nor to saving decisions. One implication of this was that the age structure of the population could affect saving, a factor of importance in the 1980s. Another was that a large part of observed differences in wealth holdings might be a result of age differences.[7] The notion that inequality in wealth exists because the middle-aged are rich and the young poor is more attractive to some than others. A lively debate ensued to see how much wealth inequality is in fact attributable to this factor. On the whole it seems that, to quote Atkinson (1975), 'the distribution of wealth cannot be attributed simply to age differences' (p.142), a conclusion endorsed by Flemming and Little (1974).

Another implication of the life cycle model is that the growth of real incomes is likely to be a major determinant of saving.[8] The argument is that net saving is equal to saving by the young less dissaving by the old. With growth, the young receive higher incomes than the old did when they were young, so net saving is higher as a percentage of income than in a static society. Another consequence of the Ando–Modigliani model concerned the role of fiscal policy. No *anticipated* change in income affected planned consumption at all. Hence the role of fiscal policy had to be either direct or to arise through causing unexpected changes in income. Even an unanticipated change in income will lead to a very small change in consumption as it will be smoothed over all future years. Hence the MPC in this model is virtually zero. The role of Ando and Modigliani is to establish a model in which all resources are relevant to consumption decisions, not just income: the world of the 1980s?

Econometric studies had helped to produce a consensus (which proved misleading) in the late 1960s. Variables other than income did not seem to be a significant influence on expenditure in the short term in the UK, in part because the crucial variables were almost constant.[9] Permanent income had to be measured by past income. Any model that explained consumers' expenditure by current and past income was consistent with Friedman's model, at least while wealth and liquidity were constant. The results could equally well be explained as an absolute income model with lagged values. The econometric models relying on such a consumption function proved inadequate in the UK in the 1970s as saving and inflation developed a symbolic relationship. In fact such models were mis-specified: in plain language they had failed to identify important determinants of consumers' expenditure: see the Wallis quotation in note 4.

10.3 SAVING AND INFLATION

The 'other factors' which may influence consumption–saving decision are analysed in this section. In view of its policy relevance the section is oriented towards their interaction with inflation. It became clear in the 1970s that in the UK saving and inflation were strongly and positively related. The various possible reasons for this are analysed in this section. More than one may be right but it is crucial which matter and which do not. This is because they concentrate on different aspects of inflation, some on the price level and some on the rate of inflation, some on anticipated inflation, some on unexpected inflation, some on the level of inflation, others on changes in the rate. Not only are these differences important analytically, but they are also crucial to the effect of falling inflation, or a stable price level, on saving. Some of the theories predict results very different from others and so have very different implications both for the interpretation of the 1980s and the necessity to treat inflation as 'public enemy number one'.

The argument is a variant of the paradox of thrift: *a change in the propensity to save affects income not the level of savings*. This is illustrated in the following simple example:

$$S = 0.1Y \quad I = 10$$

$$Y = 100 \quad (\text{and } S = 10)$$

If saving propensities double such that APS = MPS = 0.2 and $S = 0.2Y$ then the new equilibrium level of income is 50 (and S still equal to 10). In other words the greater desire to save has reduced income whilst leaving saving unchanged. By extension inflation creates unemployment through this mechanism – more inflation, more saving, less income and output and so more unemployment.

10.3.1   Wealth Effects

It is generally accepted that the wealthier a person is the more he will spend at each level of income, whether one uses Keynes's or Friedman's model. Hence the wealthier a person is, the less he will save at each level of income. In other words, there is a downward shift of the entire consumption function. Thus a reduction in wealth holdings with income constant would cause a fall in consumption and a rise in observed saving. Hence the savings ratio (APS) will rise when the value of wealth falls. A fall in the value of wealth is precisely what inflation causes. Much of the personal sector's wealth is in money-dominated forms, especially bank deposits, gilt-edged securities and national savings (for building society deposits, see Section 10.3.2 and for housing and equities, see

Section 10.4). A rise in the price level reduces the real value of these assets. This wealth is less and so consumers' expenditure lower and saving higher (this is an extension of what is sometimes called the real balance effect or Pigou effect). The effect of inflation on the real value of money-denominated assets is dramatic – the fall was 50 per cent in 1974–75. Thus even a small wealth effect, as a proportion of wealth, multiplied by an enormous change in wealth would lead to a large absolute change in consumers' expenditure and a dramatic effect on saving, as Townend pointed out (1976). This wealth effect was publicized in the UK by Forsyth of Morgan Grenfell (1975). He argued for a special form of the hypothesis with an optimal liquid assets to income ratio (about 87 per cent on his definition). Consumers would alter consumption dramatically to re-attain equilibrium if the actual value of their holdings deviated from the optimal level. In this form the theory is akin to a version of the quantity theory with a very wide definition of money. In summary, wealth is agreed to be a major determinant of consumers' spending and consequently of saving. Changes in the price level have a dramatic effect on the real value of personal sector wealth.

10.3.2 Liquidity

It is generally agreed that, if wealth and income are held constant, the more liquid a person's wealth the higher his spending will be. The theme is as central to the modern Keynesianism of either the Tobin or the Clower variety as it is to monetarism, whose emphasis is on the money–non-money distinction. This proposition is that the higher liquidity is (wealth and income being constant), the lower the level of savings and thus the APS or savings ratio. In general there is a negative relationship between saving and liquidity.

There is an equally clear relationship between inflation and liquidity. A high level of prices in itself does not change the total net value of assets, but it redistributes wealth by reducing the value of both assets and liabilities in money terms. Sometimes, as demonstrated in Section 10.3.1 this reduces personal sector wealth, when the counterpart liability which is reduced is a public, corporate or overseas one – for instance, the case of government bonds. Sometimes, it redistributes wealth within the personal sector. The most obvious example of this is building society mortgagees who gain at the expense of depositors and shareholders. Redistribution will have some effect in itself but more importantly liquidity is reduced by the simultaneous destruction of both asset and liability. This can be seen in the following example. Imagine a representative individual with a mortgage of £10 000 and building society deposits of £10 000. If inflation were to destroy both then his net worth is unaltered but his stock of liquid assets falls. By definition, his liquidity is less. Intuitively this is easy to justify. Imagine that the individual decides he would like to buy a new car. In the first state he can do so easily – he simply takes the money from his building society account. In the second state he no longer has this option: he may be able to borrow but he may not or may not choose to. Thus, his spending will fall and in consequence there will be a rise in his saving, the residual between income and spending. Many individuals are in this position: a third of mortgagees have building society deposits greater than their mortgages. More generally, this example combines the negative effect on some agents with a positive one on others. At an aggregate level, personal sector liquidity falls with inflation, that is the higher price level, so there is a reduction in spending and measured saving increases.

10.3.3 Other Effects

As argued above, inflation effected a large *redistribution of wealth* in the UK in the 1970s. Leijonhufvud (1968) argued that one of the main faults in conventional economic analysis is that it ignores such effects. He is right inasmuch as such a sizeable redistribution could have large effects. However, conventional analyses explains the 1970s and 1980s satisfactorily without reference to distributional effects and, moreover, it is difficult to see how a redistribution could have led to more saving.

Just as inflation redistribution wealth in a capricious and unjust fashion so does it *redistribute income*. To some extent, this is systematic, for example, away from fixed-income groups and the old. To a large extent it is purely arbitrary depending on such whims of fate as one's place in the wage round. The redistribution effected in the 1970s was very large but, again, there seems no evidence that it led to more saving. Indeed, at the level of casual empiricism, the most obvious gainers came from traditional low-saving groups, such as miners, and the losers from higher-saving strata. Thus while redistribution of wealth and income *could* have led to an increase (or fall) in the savings ratio, there is no evidence that it did. This is important for the 1980s where redistribution was also massive, for example from public to private sector employees.

It might be argued that there is a logical flaw in the argument in Sections 10.3.1–10.3.3 in that in all of them it was implicitly assumed that the change in the price level is unexpected. Instead if it were anticipated, then wealth holders should have received compensation in the form of higher *nominal interest* payments, the so-called Fisher effect. This counter-argument is not convincing but even it it were the effect is to strengthen the underlying theses. It does not seem that much of the surge in inflation in 1974–75 and 1979–80 was anticipated, certainly not more than a few months in advance. Even in so far as it was expected, nominal interest rates did and do not adjust sufficiently to compensate for inflation for a variety of reasons. Moreover, recipients of interest payments may not distinguish appropriately between income and compensation. Nevertheless, it is the case that some part of interest payments in an inflationary age are disguised repayments of capital. If inflation were to rise, the amount of compensation would normally rise although by a smaller amount. This compensation would not be regarded as income by a rational individual but is treated as such in the national accounts (and by the Inland Revenue). Thus it might be reasonable to save the whole of this increase in compensation for inflation. In this case the observed savings ratio and APS both necessarily rise. This is part of a general argument that income is not adequately measured by official statistics and so measured saving is largely meaningless.

The *effect of inflation on cash flows* through nominal interest rates was the basis of an interesting theory put forward by the OECD. Their argument was that inflation leads to a lower level of borrowing and so a lower level of spending. The savings ratio is both a residual and a net variable (net of dissaving). Thus the spending-inflation relationship was presented as an argument that higher (expected) inflation leads to more saving. Their thesis seemed to be applicable to those continental countries that experienced a similar positive relationship between saving and inflation in the mid-1970s but not to the UK. The argument starts with the truism that a high nominal rate of interest acts as a form of compulsory repayment. To borrow at 10 per cent interest when inflation is 25 per cent is to borrow at a real rate of –15 per cent. However, it is not the same as borrowing at an interest rate of –15 per cent when inflation is zero even though the real interest rate is identical. Instead it is the same as borrowing at –15 per cent together with an obligation to repay 10 per cent of the loan each year (you pay £10 and the real value of the debt falls 25 per cent). The OECD argument is that this compulsory repayment causes cash-flow problems which deter borrowing. This would be so unless it were both possible and acceptable to borrow to pay interest. This OECD theory is probably more applicable to corporate than individual borrowers in the UK.[10]

However, a wider version of this cash-flow problem may have some relevance. This concerns mortgagees who in 1972–73 and 1978–80 and 1988–89 saw substantial rises in (nominal) mortgage rates. At the time with accelerating inflation and soaring house prices, mortgagees' real wealth was rising very rapidly (although higher mortgage rates soon choked-off the rise in house prices). Nevertheless few mortgagees rejoiced at the consequences of a replay of Barberism even in a minor key. Instead of focusing on the increase in wealth they, not unreasonably, felt the cash-flow constraint. If mortgagees' spending fell, observed saving would rise unless depositors increased theirs (in fact, as argued above, they cut theirs). This may have been a minor factor in the rise in saving. Certainly macroeconomic policy in 1989 seems to have placed considerable reliance on this though with little apparent effect. Until 1984, an increase in interest rates increased personal sector income since the sector was a net creditor in variable-rate assets, that is holdings of building society deposits, bank deposits etc, exceeded mortgages, overdrafts etc. After 1984, the personal sector was a net debtor and so the possible impacts of interest rate changes on spending increased.

By the end of 1987 this net debt amounted to £46 billion and by the end of 1989 to £100 billion.

The arguments presented in sections 10.3.1 and 10.3.2, concerning wealth and liquidity, involved changes in the level of prices. The next argument concerning redistribution and expected inflation involved both the level of prices and inflation, usually assumed to be anticipated. In this section and the next attention is paid to both the level of inflation and its acceleration. It is explicitly assumed that inflation cannot be predicted accurately.

The first of these arguments seems to have originated with Juster and Wachtel (1972). This is that one of the main motives for saving is *uncertainty*, especially uncertainty about future real income and future real commitments. The more uncertain the future is, the higher the level of saving. Both of these propositions are undeniable unless some unusual assumption such as risk-lovingness is assumed. Juster and Wachtel argued that both higher inflation and accelerating inflation made it harder to estimate its future level. In other words the future level of inflation is more uncertain. Hence also uncertain are the future level of real income and the expected real cost of unknown contingencies (such as medical bills or roof repairs). Thus people will save more because inflation is higher or accelerating. An even simpler argument is that more inflation means more uncertainty in general (Keynes and Friedman have both endorsed this view) and so more saving. Clearly other variables, for example unemployment, could have had similar effects but seem not to have done.

Another reason why higher and/or accelerating inflation may lead to an increase in saving was advanced by Deaton (1977). This argument involves a version of *money illusion*. The argument is that individuals mistake a change in absolute prices (that is inflation) for a change in relative prices. To take an example, an individual goes shopping to supermarket A and finds baked beans are more expensive than he had expected because of unanticipated inflation. Therefore he decides to buy them at supermarket B later in the week or to buy fresh vegetables when he passes the greengrocer's instead. On arrival in supermarket B he finds the price of baked beans is also at the higher level. He may then buy his baked beans but may also find some other good to be more expensive, and again delays his purchase. Some purchases are continually delayed (not always the same one, of course) so spending is always below the expected level so observed saving is higher.

This hypothesis is obviously more relevant to some purchases than others. It is probably more applicable to one-off purchases (search goods) than repeated ones (experience goods). Nevertheless it seems, to me at least, implausible that it could be a significant explanation of a *large, prolonged* increase in saving as experienced in the 1970s and 1980s since:

1. As both Keynes and Friedman argued, inflation may lead to relative price changes being mistaken for absolute ones (our hypothetical shopper notices that tomatoes are more expensive than expected in supermarket A but assumes, wrongly, that they will have gone up everywhere else and buys some anyway).
2. One might expect search activity to increase for goods (in practice durables) expensive enough to justify prolonged search rather than see purchases deferred.

In brief Deaton's theory is important in stressing the role of accelerating inflation, and of the distinction between expected and unanticipated inflation. His model is probably important on occasions as a very short-run phenomenon but as Townend (1976) put it, '(the nature of this hypothesis) makes robust econometric results extremely hard to obtain' (p.72).

10.3.4 The Popularizers Refuted Income and Substitution Effects

Finally, in this section, the popularizers' argument is analysed and its inadequacies explained. The argument is that people will save less because it is not as worthwhile to save. In other words inflation reduces the real rate of interest and so reduces the incentive to save. This can be restated by saying that the opportunity cost of present in terms of future consumption has fallen so present consumption will rise. In other words, the issue is a problem of choice (between present and future consumption) when relative prices change. Accordingly the problems can be set up and analysed within the conventional microeconomic framework.

This analysis is presented in Figure 10.1 and Table 10.4. It illustrates the case of an individual who receives income in one period but spends it in two. This is chosen in part for simplification since the analysis can easily be extended to incorporate receiving income in both periods, borrowing, and more than two periods. (The appendix shows the diagrams for some relevant cases.[11]) However, it can be argued that most saving is for retirement and so this is the most interesting case where period 1 is one's working life and period 2 the period of retirement. The axes show consumption in the first period (C_t) and in the second period (C_{t+1}). To explain the individual's choice it is first necessary to draw the budget line; this shows the boundary of his consumption opportunities. The most he can consume in the first period is his income (Y_t), shown as OA. The most he can consume in period 2 is his income, plus the interest he receives less the effect of inflation on its purchasing power. Strictly this is:

Maximum $C_{t-1} = Y_t\{(1 + i)/(1 - p)\} = Y_t(1 + r)$

Figure 10.1   The saving decision

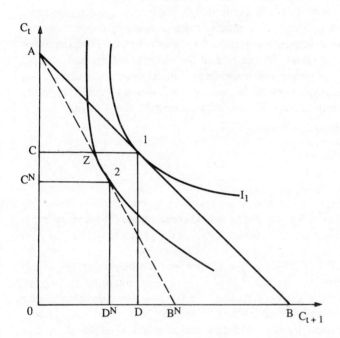

Table 10.4   The impact of inflation on saving

Original level of inflation					
Income	Y_t	:		OA	
Consumption	C_t	:		OC	
Saving	S_t	=	Y_t	$-$	C_t
		=	OA	$-$	OC
		=	AC		
New level of inflation					
Income	Y_t	:		OA	
Consumption	C^n_t	=		OA^n	
Saving	S^n_t	=	Y_t	$-$	C^n_t
		=	OA	$-$	OC^n
		=	AC^n		
Change in saving		=	S_t	$-$	S^n_t
		=	AC	$-$	AC^n
		=	CCn		

where i is the nominal rate of interest, r the rate of inflation and r the real rate of interest. In practice the real rate is often simplified to $r = i - p$.

This maximum is drawn as OB and the budget line is the line joining these two maxima, A and B. Its slope is the relative price of future in terms of present consumption (and is a straight line because the individual cannot influence either inflation or interest rates). The individual then selects his optimal level of consumption in each period: this is shown as 1 and is where the budget line is tangential to indifference curve 1. He consumes OC in period 1 and OD in period 2. More significantly as $OA = Y_t$ and $OC = C_t$, then AC is his saving.

$$S_t = Y_t - C_t$$
$$= OA - OC$$
$$= AC$$

The effect of changes in inflation, or interest rates, on consumption and saving can now be calculated. So long as OA is held constant, the change in saving is also the change in the savings ratio (or APS). (If not the calculation of the APS is simple.)

In particular, it is possible to see what happens when either (expected) inflation or interest rates change, that is when the real rate of interest varies. Hence it is possible to analyse rigorously the thesis that people cease to save 'when it isn't worthwhile', in other words when a higher expected level of prices increases the opportunity cost of future consumption in terms of present consumption. This is represented as a pivot of the budget line from AB to AB^n. Maximum present consumption OA is unchanged but maximum future consumption (AB^n) is reduced. The individual's new optimal position is where an indifference curve is tangential to the new budget line. In Figure 10.1, the example makes the standard assumption of unitary income elasticity, homothetic tastes, and consequently indifference curves are parallel. The equilibrium is represented by point 2 where the dotted indifference curve 2 is tangential to the new budget line. Present consumption is OC^n and future consumption OD^n. The new level of saving (S^n_t) is:

$$Y_t - C^n_t = OA - OC^n = AC^n \text{ (see Table 10.4)}$$

Saving is higher despite the higher price of future consumption. In fact the 'income effect' has outweighed 'the substitution effect', as can be demonstrated by the usual method of drawing a budget line parallel to AB^n tangential to indifference curve 1. The reader may have seen the same diagram used to illustrate the ambiguous effect of income tax changes on work effort (for example Brown, 1980). As in that case, the effect is ambiguous, as either the substitution or the income effect may be larger. To use Figure 10.1, if the relevant indifference curve is tangential to AB^N along AZ, the substitution effect is larger and saving falls. If the tangency is at Z, the two effects exactly balance and the savings ratio is unchanged. If the tangency is between Z and B^N saving and inflation are positively related.

This ambiguity is useful in explaining the divergence between UK and US behaviour, see Harnett (1988):

> The investigation of the wealth position of US consumers suggests that they reacted to inflation by increasing their levels of debt, by running down their stock of financial assets and consuming more...Such behaviour is in stark contrast to the UK where consumers held back from consuming to maintain their financial assets relative to income.

Harnett suggests that the greater ease of consumer borrowing in the USA prior to 1982 explains the difference. It could also explain changes in UK behaviour over time. Dicks (1988) claims that in the UK a rise in interest rates now reduces spending and increases saving. This is in marked contrast to earlier work and could also reflect the change in the personal sector's net financial creditor position, see Table 10.4.

10.3.5 Real Saving

The final puzzle concerns the implicit assumption made throughout this analysis. It has been assumed that the private sector saves only in money-denominated assets. This is true, except for durables, especially housing.

Hence two questions are left unanswered by the analysis presented above. The first is why do savers invest so heavily in money-denominated assets rather than in real assets? The other is how are the conclusions reached above affected by the investment in real assets which does take place, especially houses and consumer durables (see Taylor and Threadgold, 1980)?

There are a number of overlapping reasons why savers hold monetary assets on such a large scale:

1. There are few alternatives – even the assets touted as hedges against inflation have not proved very effective in this role, especially equities. The one exception is property.
2. Management and transaction costs on real assets are high. Whether one examines auctioneer's fees or dealers' margins, the cost of investing in antiques or art are very large. Commodities such as copper are cheaper but storage costs are enormous. Property is the most attractive real investment but when not owner-occupied, there are substantial problems of management ranging from rent control to defaulting tenants.

3. Real assets are available only in, for most individuals, very large units. It is difficult to think of a real asset for which an investment of less than £10 000 is possible, or, at least, where the risks are not extremely high.
4. Because real investments are often risky: some paintings, stamps and coins have risen in value and more than kept pace with inflation since 1960 but many individual paintings etc. have fallen in value.
5. Real investments are illiquid, almost by definition.
6. The generality of money, the lack of commitment to any particular real asset or spending plan, remains immensely attractive despite inflation.

In brief, investment in real assets is not really a practicable proposition for most savers. One reason why inflation is so unfair is that only the wealthy can insure against it. This is one of the many arguments for indexation (see p. 163) at last conceded in the 1982 Budget.

In fact, the only real assets which have proved attractive to most savers are those that yield services directly to the holder, namely consumer durables and housing. The analysis presented above only explained consumption and it is necessary to expand the model to include assets which yield services over many periods. The above analysis is maintained intact as an explanation of consumption. However, a second stage is added – what assets does the individual hold and what does he choose to consume? Durables and houses whose return is fixed in real terms become more attractive relative to other assets when inflation rises (unless nominal rates rise to compensate the lenders). Hence, more wealth will be held as durables and housing and less as other assets. This is reinforced by resale considerations, especially in the case of housing. This is matched by a switch in relative prices, for example television services become cheaper relative to attending cinemas. For example, £300 could be invested in a building society and the interest used to purchase a number of cinema seats every year or to buy a colour television. Inflation will reduce the seats purchased at the cinema but leave the real television services unchanged. Indeed, one can generalise: services from durables will be consumed less because of the income effect (total consumption is reduced) and more because of the substitution effect (they are cheaper). This is most marked in housing where services are often available at a negative price if one allows for the resale opportunity.

It is possible to leave this rather abstract analysis and present some conclusions about the effect of inflation:

1. Consumption will almost certainly fall when inflation rises.
2. Consumption on non-durables will fall as a percentage of consumption.
3. From 1 and 2, expenditure on non-durables will fall as a percentage of PDI (personal disposable income).

4. Expenditure on durable goods, as a percentage of PDI, could either rise or fall (in the UK it largely remained unchanged).
5. Saving is likely to rise as a percentage of income but need not do so.
6. Expenditure on housing, not part of consumers' expenditure, will rise. The enormous level of expenditure on housing investment in the UK is almost certainly as attributable to inflation as to the tax system.

10.4   THE 1980s

It is no longer true that short-period changes in consumption largely depend on changes in the rate at which income (measured in wage units) is being earned and not on changes in the propensity to consume out of a given income (Keynes, 1936). Both theorists and policy makers have to note the other influences on consumption. Further, it seems to be the case that in the UK there is strong support for the view that a reduction in inflation is necessary (if not sufficient) for sustained expansion because otherwise saving would rise to wipe out the impact of government spending. Inflation may not have caused unemployment but it may well be that there is no possibility of reducing unemployment by accepting a higher rate of inflation.

The collapse in the savings ratio (APS) can now be examined against this background. The savings ratio fell from over 14 per cent in 1980 to less than 5 per cent in 1988. Indeed it may have been negative in the final quarter of 1988. The decline in inflation from its peak in 1980 can explain most of the fall in inflation until 1985 but thereafter additional factors must be analysed. *Inflation* remained an important determinant of saving but it is no longer plausible for it to be the sole explanatory factor. *Wealth effects* are probably still the most important reasons for consumption decisions but in the 1980s changes in personal sector wealth were largely caused by change in *house prices* and to a lesser extent share prices. Table 10.5 (p. 232) shows that net personal sector wealth doubled in the period 1982–7 despite the rise in borrowing. Indeed between 1982 and 1987 wealth net of borrowing rose by 60 per cent and the wealth income ratio rose from 3.3 to 4.7. It may be that it is better to analyse consumption decisions using stock data on wealth and its composition rather than flow data on income. If one only had access to wealth data it might seem that one needed to explain why spending was so low, not why saving had fallen. This would in effect be an argument that the more abstract theoretical models of Friedman and Ando Modigliani are now more relevant than the simple Keynesian consumption function. Further weight is given to this by consideration of *inheritances* and pension fund arrangements. The size of inheritances has grown enormously, backed by rising owner occupation and house prices. In 1970 property inheritances amounted to £703m; in 1987 to £6.8 billion. These inheritances are normally received when people are in their 50s, when they are also likely to

Table 10.5   Personal sector balance sheet (year end)

£ billion	1982	1985	1986	1987
ASSETS				
Dwellings	349.9	527.3	617.9	730.8
Financial Assets	222.3	315.0	371.5	427.7
Insurance, Pension				
Equity	156.2	271.6	329.2	369.9
Other	24.9	37.2	41.6	44.9
Total Assets	753.3	1,151.1	1,360.2	1,573.3
LIABILITIES				
Mortgage Dept.	76.4	127.6	154.0	183.5
Bank lending	25.1	39.9	44.2	52.7
Credit Companies	3.1	5.0	6.0	6.7
Other	22.0	31.8	35.5	39.8
Total Liabilities	126.6	204.3	239.7	282.7
NET WEALTH	626.7	946.8	1,120.5	1,290.6

Source: Central Statistical Office

receive lump-sum pension fund payments. It may be that these and the expectation of them explain a large part of the decline in saving in the 1980s. Expenditure may be financed from these sources. More often individuals are happy to run up debts knowing that these can be payed off from such sources – *remaindering* in legal parlance. As a friend put it 'I've no need to save; my savings are my parents' house'. This is a version of the life-cycle model but one where endowments are received late in the cycle.

Demography may have a part to pay in explaining behaviour in the 1980s: the increased rate of household formulation largely caused by the changed age structure of the population, including many more young people. Again, the life-cycle model offers more insights into the problem than a Keynesian approach.

A much touted explanation is the *changing pattern of income,* see Table 10.6. Wage income has declined as a percentage of total income but not by so much and it is difficult to see why by itself this amounts for any change in saving. Indeed Keynesians would have expected the change towards self-employment and the more general regressive changes in income distribution to *increase* saving. A similarly implausible explanation is that the personal sector regarded corporate saving as a substitute for its own saving; a rather implausible application of the Miller–Modigliani theorem. The argument is that if shareholders

Table 10.5 UK income (per cent)

	1976	1986
Self-employed	9.1	9.4
State transfers	10.6	13.3
Investment income	5.7	6.8
Wages	66.4	58.5

observe more (or less) saving by the companies in which they own shares they will regard this as their saving because they own the company. Ignoring all else corporate saving also fell in 1987–8 so the impact should have been the reverse.

The final and crucial factor to be analysed is *credit availability*. There is no doubt that credit has a large part to play in explaining the decline in saving. It may have been largely permissive. For example 'remaindering' or liquidizing capital gains on housing[12] both require borrowing. Hence a neo-classical economist would stress credit availability as a necessary factor for some forms of wealth effect and a useful but not essential one for others. An individual observing his wealth in one form rising could liquidate his remaining assets but would probably prefer to borrow rather than finish up with such an unbalanced portfolio. The Keynesian would accept such arguments but would stress the role of credit availability as an independent factor. Financial deregulation made it much easier for many more people to borrow much more. They were previously constrained *à la* Clower–Leijonhufvud. Hence they borrowed. QED. The pessimistic aspect of this is an argument that financial innovation necessarily cuts saving;[13] not a very good augury for future growth.

To end as the chapter began, the prediction of the APC/APS is a major problem for macroeconomic policy. Its elucidation requires emphasis on inflation, wealth, credit and the 'other' factors of the elementary textbook, not on Keynesian absolute income models.

GUIDE TO FURTHER READING

The best and most up-to-date reading is the topic in Dean (1989), available free by writing to the OECD in Paris; otherwise it is very difficult to suggest suitable further reading that is not extremely technical. The consumption function literature is set out well in most macroeconomics text-books, such as Levacic and Rebman (1982). The savings–inflation connection is discussed in Dorrance (1980).

NOTES

1. Consumers' expenditure and saving data have been massively revised in recent years in the UK, see for example Johnson (1988). Almost all empirical analysis, econometric or informal, has found that a major conclusion disappeared when data were revised. See Wallis (1987) especially the quotation included in note 4 below.
2. For the dynamic and static multiplier see Gowland (1989) and Beckerman (1968).
3. Leijonhufvud's and Clower's arguments are reproduced in Surrey (1976), but Leijonhufvud (1968) is one of the classics, see also Chapter 5 and Chapter 6.
4. The best summary of the inflation–saving relationship is Wallis (1987):
   The high inflation [in the 1970s] drew attention to the misspecification [omission of inflation effects on saving], and inflation effects were found to be significant during the earlier period: they could have prevented the forecasting failures, if only they had been looked for. Subsequent data revisions have reduced the dramatic changes in the savings ratio that were observed in contemporary data in the 1970s. Inflation sometimes has a direct effect on consumption and sometimes an indirect one via real financial assets or real wealth.
5. See Keynes (1936), Chapters 8 and 9, including the famous list of motives for saving: precaution, foresight, calculation, improvement, independence, enterprise, pride and avarice.
6. A cross-section study analyses the behaviour of a number of people at a single point in time – as with a Gallup Poll. The sample is then divided into categories (in this case by income) and their (savings) behaviour compared.
7. See Atkinson (1975) which summarizes both his 1971 research paper and the debate.
8. A variant of the life-cycle model is Samuelson's (1968) loan–consumption model (see Dixit, 1976, pp. 116–122). This was used to demonstrate the superiority of non-market to market as the means of providing for expenditure when the beneficiary receives no income. In particular, Samuelson argued that the family is a more efficient means of providing for one's expenditure during childhood than either a hypothetical market in which children borrow against future income or slavery. Similarly, a state-financed system of pensions is more efficient than market provision. Extensions to Samuelson's model are now central to all advance macroeconomics. Blanchard and Fisher (1989) analyse them: Ramsy rule saving (chapter 2) and 'overlapping generations' models (chapter 3). They describe them as the two great work houses of advanced macroeconomics.
9. See Gowland (1989) p.51 ff. esp. p.54.
10. See Gowland (1979), chapter 4, 'UK Financial Institutions: Have they Failed the Nation?', for a fuller presentation of this argument in the context of corporate borrowing.
11. It is also assumed that the individual is certain about the rate of inflation, for a relaxation of this, see Hey (1979).
12. For an early discussion of this see Gowland (1978).
13. Gowland (1989).

REFERENCES

Ando, A. and Modigliani, F. (1963), 'The "Life Cycle" Hypothesis of Saving' *American Economic Review,* vol. 55 (June).

Atkinson, A.B. (1975), *The Economics of Inequality,* Oxford University Press, Oxford.

Beckerman, W. (1968 and 4 subsequent editions), *An Introduction to National Income Analysis,* Weidenfeld and Nicholson, London.

Blanchard, O.J. and Fischer, S. (1989), *Lectures on Macroeconomics,* MIT Press, Cambridge, Mass.

Brown, C.V. (1980), *Taxation and the Incentive to Work,* Oxford University Press, Oxford.

Clower, R.W. (1965), 'The Keynesian Counter-revolution: A theoretical Reappraisal' in

Hahn and Brechling (1969), also reprinted in Clower (1969).

Clower, R.W. (ed) (1969), *Monetary Theory,* Penguin Modern Economic Readings, Penguin, Harmondsworth (includes his 1965 paper).

Deaton, A.S. (1977), 'Involuntary Saving Through Unanticipated Inflation' *American Economic Review,* vol. 67, pp. 889-910.

Dean, A. et al (1989), *Savings Trends and Behaviour* in OECD Countries, OECD Working Paper No. 67.

Dicks, M.J. (1989), 'The Interest Elasticity of Consumers' Expenditure' *Bank of England* Discussion Paper No 33 (Technical Series) (Sept.)

Dixit, A.K. (1976), *The Theory of Equilibrium Growth,* Oxford University Press, Oxford.

Dorrance, G. (1980), 'Saving in the 1970s', *Lloyds Bank Review* No. 138 (October), p 12.

Duesenberry, J.S. (1949), *Income, Saving and the Theory of Consumer Behaviour,* Harvard Economic Study, 87 reprinted by Oxford University Press, 1967.

Fleming, J.S. and Little, I.M.D. (1974), *Why We Need a Wealth Tax,* Methuen, London.

Friedman, M. (1957), *A Theory of the Consumption Function,* Princeton University Press, Princeton, N J for NBER.

Gowland, D.H. (1978), *Monetary Policy & Credit Control,* Croom Helm, London.

Gowland, D.H. (1979), *Modern Economic Analysis,* Butterworths, Sevenoaks.

Gowland, D.H. (1989), *Whatever Happened to Demand Management?* RJA (Books), Bedford.

Hahn, F. and Brechling, F.P.R. (ed) (1965), *The Theory of Interest Rates,* Macmillan, London.

Harnett, J.R. (1988), 'An Error Correction Model of US Consumption Expenditure', *Bank of England Discussion Paper* No. 34 (October).

Hey, J.D. (1979), *Uncertainty in Microeconomics,* Martin Robertson, Oxford.

Hillard, J. (ed) (1988), *J M Keynes in Retrospect,* Edward Elgar, Aldershot.

Keynes, J.M. (1936), *The General Theory of Employment, Interest and Money,* Macmillan, also in Vol VII of his *Collected Works.* (Keynes, 1971).

Keynes, J.M. (1971), *The Collected Writings of John Maynard Keynes,* Macmillan for the Royal Economic Society.

Johnson, C. (1988), *Measuring the Economy,* Macmillan, London.

Juster, F.T. and Wachter, J.T. (1972), 'A Note on Inflation and the Saving Rate' *Brookings Papers on Economic Activity,* vol 3, pp. 765-8.

Leijonhufvud, A. (1968), *On Keynesian Economics and the Economics of Keynes,* Oxford University Press, New York.

Levacic, R. and Rebmann, A. (1982), *Macroeconomics,* Macmillan (2nd edition).

Morgan Grenfell (1975), 'A New Analysis of the Savings Ratio' *Morgan Grenfell Economic Review,* (Sept.)

Mussa, M. (1977), *A Study in Macroeconomics,* North Holland.

Samuelson, P.A. (1968), 'An exact consumption loan model of interest with or without the social contrivance of money' *Journal of Political Economy,* vol. 66, no. 6, pp. 467-82.

Surrey, M.J.C. (1976), *Macroeconomic Themes,* Oxford University Press, Oxford.

Taylor, C.T. and Threadgold, A.R. (1980), *Real National Saving and Its Sectoral Composition,* Bank of England Discussion Paper no. 6 (October).

Townend, J.C. (1976), 'The Personal Savings Ratio' *Bank of England Quarterly Bulletin,* vol. 16, no. 1 (March), pp 53-73.

Wallis, K.F. et al (1987), *Recent Developments in Macroeconomic Modelling,* E.S.R.C. Macroeconomic Modelling Bureau, Warwick.

Wallis, K.F. et al (1988), *Models of the UK Economy* (4th Review), Oxford University Press, Oxford.

APPENDIX: SOME EXTENSIONS

Figure 10.A.1   Income in both periods (y_t, y_{t-1}) and borrowing

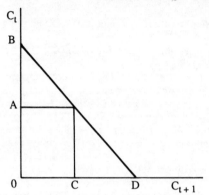

OA = Y_t
AB = Y_{t+1} $(1-r)$ that is what you can borrow, spend in period t and
             repay out of period $(t-1)$ income.
OC = Y_{t+1}
CD = Y_t $(1-r)$
if $C_t > OA$; borrow etc.

Figure 10.A.2   Borrowing at a higher rate of interest than lending

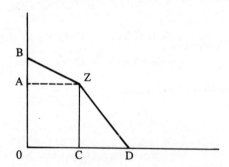

As above but AB smaller because agent is borrowing at a higher rate of interest than that at which he lends so budget line is BZD.

Figure 10.A.3   A borrowing limit

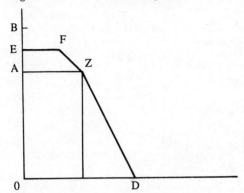

As before but maximum borrowing is AE

Figure 10.A.4   Pension contribution: no borrowing

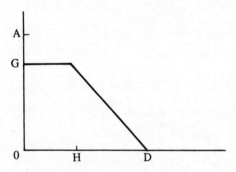

As basic case but the individual is forced to save AG
AG $(1+r)$ = OH

Index